Table of Contents

Introduction

As the state of information technology has advanced, the number of vulnerabilities and regulatory concerns have exponentially increased. Fortunately, the tools, methodologies, and core technologies available to enhance our security posture have also increased. The current iteration of the technology life cycle has positioned containers front and center; backed by a myriad of underlying open source (and commercial) projects and products.

The rapid adoption and blazingly fast upstream development of open source projects can sometimes prevent necessary and newly introduced security protections from being applied right out of the box. *Red Hat OpenShift Container Platform* (OCP) addresses these and other concerns by expanding upon Red Hat's open source heritage to tackle security concerns as a forethought instead of as an afterthought.

This book describes how security is addressed at core layers of the OpenShift 4 technology stack, and how compliance and regulatory concerns can be mitigated. Whether investigating how to deploy a cluster, or fine-tuning security for an existing cluster, it is important to first understand the high level components that make up the OpenShift Container Platform.

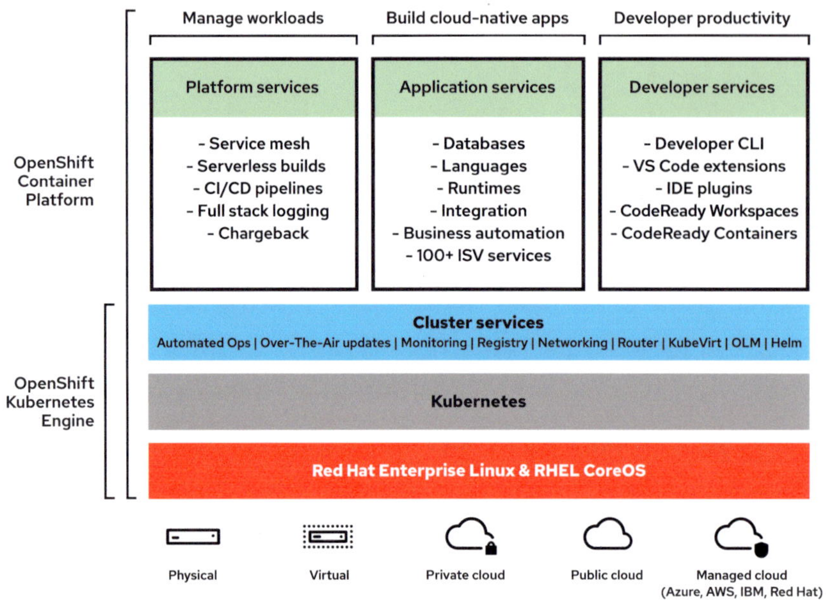

Figure i.i: OpenShift stack diagram

OpenShift Container Platform

Starting from the lowest layer, OpenShift can be deployed on a variety of infrastructure which includes bare-metal servers, virtualized environments, private, public, managed, and hybrid cloud environments. Red Hat Enterprise Linux (RHEL) and RHEL CoreOS are the underlying operating systems upon which OpenShift is run. Kubernetes provides the basic container orchestration and cluster services providing advanced automation management features.

Building on the Kubernetes engine, OpenShift adds platform services that manage and deliver containers with the cluster. Application services let users pull in databases and other services to use with their applications. Developer services help developers create and manage the life cycle of application containers.

OpenShift Kubernetes Engine

The Kubernetes container orchestration engine is at the core of OpenShift. Additional cluster services are run on top of Kubernetes, including :

- **Automated Operations** : Operators provide the facilities needed to enable automated operations within OpenShift. They are a critical addition for the set-up and on-going maintenance of both critical infrastructure and applications in OpenShift. Operators, such as the Machine Config Operator (MCO), manage direct configuration and updates to nodes, while the Cluster Version Operator (CVO) manages multiple operators in the OpenShift infrastructure.

- **Over-the-air-updates** : Updates to both RHCOS nodes and the OpenShift cluster itself are applied by over-the-air-updates. The updates are packaged in containers and can be set up to apply automatically from selected channels and releases.

- **Monitoring** : A preconfigured monitoring stack, based on the Prometheus project, is included in OpenShift Container Platform 4 clusters. This uses Grafana analytics dashboards to visualize and analyze metrics.

- **Registry** : Each OpenShift cluster comes packaged with a built-in registry which can be used to push images from, and pull images to, the OpenShift cluster. Red Hat also offers a separate Red Hat Quay registry product, for more advanced and scalable registry solutions.

- **Networking** : Networking services include the ability to set network policies and manage ingress and egress communications for the cluster.

- **Router** : OpenShift includes the HAProxy router, which can be optimized and configured to scale as needed.

- **KubeVirt** : OpenShift container-native virtualization (currently in Technology Preview), offers the means of running virtual machines alongside containers on an OpenShift cluster. That feature is built on Kubernetes KubeVirt technology.
- **OLM** : The Operator Lifecycle Manager (OLM) provides the framework for OpenShift cluster users to find and use operators. With OLM, users can install, upgrade and assign role-based access control to available operators.
- **Helm** : Helm is a command-line tool that was created to simplify how applications and services are deployed on a Kubernetes cluster. Support for Helm 3 is in Technology Preview for OpenShift 4.3.

Ultimately, OpenShift enables three core capabilities to the enterprise, each of which is supported by its own stack of related technologies. These are :

Platform Services

Containers encapsulate critical business workloads. The management of these workloads must be fully automated with appropriate levels of traceability. These needs are accomplished via the OpenShift platform services technology stack, including Service Mesh (based on Istio), Serverless, CI/CD pipelines, full stack logging, and chargeback.

Application Services

Cloud-native applications allow the enterprise to deploy their workloads to multiple cloud-based platforms with minimal refactoring. OpenShift supports the development of these applications by supporting multiple databases, programming languages / run times, enterprise integration, business automation, and 100+ Independent software vendor (ISV) services.

Developer Services

Fast turnaround times are a requirement when it comes to creating and maintaining enterprise applications. OpenShift developer services enhance productivity by providing developer command line interfaces (CLI), visual studio code (VS Code) extensions, integrated development environment (IDE) plug-ins, and cloud-native IDEs in the forms of Code Ready Workspaces. Code Ready Containers (CRC) also allow developers to spin-up local OpenShift environments they can use for experimentation.

Audience

The audience for this book is not expected to have expert-level knowledge of core OpenShift concepts. However, basic knowledge of Linux, Containers, and Kubernetes from a user or administrative perspective will certainly be useful, especially when reading through some of the technical implementation described in the chapters.

This book was created to help those in cloud infrastructure and security engineering roles address the many security challenges facing them. Cloud security is complex, and Red Hat understands that users need more than just guidance in technical system configurations. The authors have identified approaches that aid in the triaging of security trade-offs and risk, policy enforcement, reporting, and the validation of system configuration.

The cloud infrastructure and security engineering roles are central to establishing and preserving security postures. It is the book's intent to support these roles by providing the proper mixture of conceptual, organizational, and technical guidance, thereby increasing the security vigilance and effectiveness of those with such responsibilities.

For the cloud security auditor, whether in an internal role or as a third-party assessment organization, this book intends to provide the technical guidance needed to verify, validate, and enforce security controls. For technology professionals charged with security policy management, this book should offer insight into related organizational policy, functional testing, and data stewardship tasks while augmenting knowledge in these areas.

While the book speaks to OpenShift from a holistic infrastructure perspective, it does cover areas that application developers and reliability engineers may find valuable. With the ever evolving trends in container-based microservices, baking security into the continuous integration and delivery pipelines is a fundamental requirement. Build and runtime security features are discussed, and advantages of a secure container baseline image are covered as well.

What's in the Book?

The content of this book is organized into the following chapters :

Chapter 1 : Risk Management and Regulatory Readiness

The chapter on risk management and regulatory readiness provides an overview of the business and legal drivers behind a successful security posture. Approaching security from a continuous process perspective is not only required, but extremely effective in establishing an approach that ensures full coverage of threat vectors.

The content focuses heavily on the NIST model of managing risk but exposes the international nature of compliance as well.

Chapter 2 : Red Hat Enterprise Linux CoreOS Security

Red Hat Enterprise Linux CoreOS (RHCOS) is the preferred operating system to power each node of the OpenShift cluster. RHEL worker nodes are also available. How RHCOS is configured has major implications on the security of the containers and infrastructure components running on those systems. Because RHCOS nodes are meant to run with minimal changes, it is important that any security-related enhancements to those nodes be done carefully.

This chapter on RHCOS provides a technical overview of RHCOS security features. As the foundational layer of the OpenShift Container Platform, RHCOS has been designed to efficiently work within the context of controlled immutability, while seamlessly exposing strong security features available for consumption higher in the stack. The RHCOS life cycle, and by extension the control plane life cycle, is also covered in this chapter.

Chapter 3 : Container Security

Every Linux container running on an OpenShift platform is protected by powerful RHEL security features built into the nodes in OpenShift. These features protect containers from one another and protect the underlying operating systems from the containers. In OpenShift 4, containers are ultimately managed on each node by the CRI-O container engine.

This chapter describes how OpenShift container security comes preconfigured out of the box. This includes how container namespaces (such as process tables, network interfaces, and file systems) are separated from the host, and how host access can be allowed or blocked in relation to system calls and capabilities. Likewise, it explains how SELinux keeps containers from accessing any resources from the OS or from other containers that are not explicitly allowed by SELinux policy.

Chapter 4 : Kubernetes Security

As the orchestration layer in an OpenShift cluster, Kubernetes security implementation spans security considerations across OpenShift. At the Kubernetes level, OpenShift security professionals need to be concerned about managing the safety and updating of certificates. They also must be concerned with access to underlying components, such as the API server and OpenShift master data in etcd.

Understanding the components that make up the Kubernetes orchestration platform, and how the security of those components is protected and managed, is the focus of this chapter. This chapter includes techniques which can be incorporated to meet security needs, such as moving components to separate infrastructure nodes or reconfiguring monitoring at the Kubernetes level.

Chapter 5 : Identity and Access Management

Every OpenShift cluster maintains user accounts at different levels of the cluster. There are user accounts on each node, as well as system and regular user accounts at the cluster level. Managing the access each user has to features on the OpenShift cluster and being able to authenticate the identity of each user, are critical to properly securing an OpenShift cluster.

This chapter describes the unique identities that are assigned at each level of an OpenShift 4 cluster by default and the different types of users which can be configured. It also describes how to use, and protect, the kubeadmin account and kubeconfig credentials. As to authentication, the chapter describes how OpenShift interfaces with the Kubernetes Authentication Layer to establish OpenShift's authentication of its users with different identity providers.

Chapter 6 : Networking Security

OpenShift builds on Kubernetes networking by enhancing internal and external networking security with operators, plug-ins, and many advanced network security features. OpenShift plug-ins extend Kubernetes CNI communications by simplifying connections to different underlying network types. The OpenShift Cluster Network Operator manages basic networking configuration and upgrades, while other OpenShift Operators help to secure specific network-related features, such as DNS and ingress.

Use the Networking Security chapter to learn how OpenShift simplifies network management. See how advanced networking features such as Multus enable creation of multiple network interfaces to a pod to separate sensitive and non-sensitive data. Understand how OpenShift Service Mesh assists oversight of all the components of a microservice-based application through the addition of sidecars to monitor communications.

Chapter 7 : Auditing

A solid auditing framework does more than just log activities – it also raises alerts when those activities pose a threat to infrastructure, applications, or data. For many organizations, auditing is required to meet security policies. In OpenShift 4, auditing is enabled by default and provides extraordinary flexibility for configuring management and access to auditing data.

At its core, OpenShift 4 auditing was designed using a cloud-native approach to provide both centralization and resiliency. This chapter describes how OpenShift auditing works, as well as how to configure it for a variety of Role-Based Access Control (RBAC) roles and security demands.

Chapter 8 : Encryption, Secret Management, and Data Protection

Data in transit and data at rest can be secured throughout the OpenShift cluster. Kubernetes secrets provide the means of storing passwords, OAuth tokens, ssh keys, and other sensitive security elements. Encryption protects those secrets as well as the data, to both keep content safe and to be in line with required regulatory and compliance frameworks.

In this chapter, learn how encryption is implemented and how certificates are managed and used in OpenShift. For encryption between applications, Transport Layer Security (TLS) provides the foundation for protecting data in flight. Authentications rely on certificates, such as X.509, for both validating and protecting internal and external communications. For many organizations, understanding how cryptographic standards, such as Federal Information Processing Standards (FIPS) apply to their compliance requirements, is critical.

Chapter 9 : Securing CI/CD

Securing containerized applications begins well before their deployment to OpenShift. This chapter outlines the choice of components of the Continuous Integration and Continuous Delivery (CI/CD) pipeline that feeds into an OpenShift cluster. Those components need to be hardened and should come from a trusted supply chain.

As a foundation for images, Red Hat Universal Base Images (UBI) (which are continuously tested, health-checked, and able to be freely redistributed) allow combination of the container images with real Red Hat Enterprise Linux RPM packages. By using automation software, such as Jenkins, container images can be built and tested before deploying. With image scanning features such as OpenSCAP or Clair, vulnerabilities in containers can be looked for and any issues discovered can be acted on before any damage is done.

1. Risk Management and Regulatory Readiness

As a global company, Red Hat is intimately involved on multiple levels with the security of enterprise systems. Red Hat's global experience has also allowed the discernment of a consistent pattern in the areas of risk management, threat modeling, and compliance (regulatory readiness). Customers are typically required to adhere to an industry, national, or internal corporate governance framework when it comes to information systems security.

For example, both the United States and French governments have identified critical infrastructure sectors with assets, systems, and networks vital to the general, economic, public health, or safety of the country. In these cases, sovereignty and industry designation dictate which risk management frameworks the cloud environment will have to adhere to. Awareness of this compliance pattern allows us to increase the security posture of OpenShift and other products, so that the process of deployment is made easier from a technical compliance perspective.

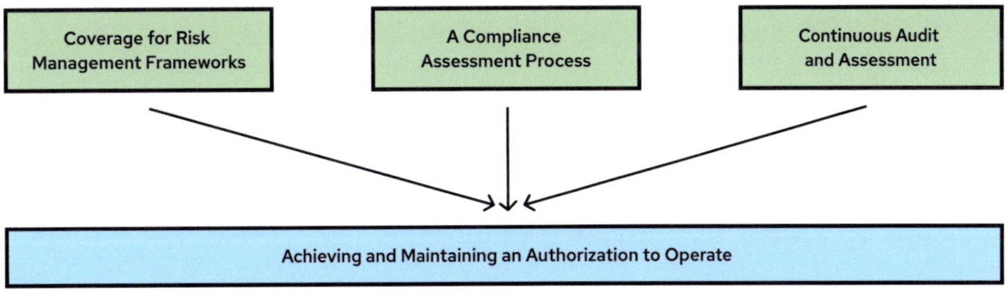

Figure 1.1: Global Compliance Model

In addition to the cloud platforms software we provide, this book should be considered a supportive artifact that accelerates system documentation efforts. These efforts on the part of cloud implementers are formed into policy statements, procedural guidance, and actionable risk management information. OpenShift implementers engaged in Information Security risk management generally operate under or adapt an authoritative risk management framework. Generally, risk management frameworks are overseen by third-party organizations with a vested interest in the consequences of the operations under management. For example :

- The Joint Authorization Board (JAB) of the Federal Risk and Authorization Management Program (FedRAMP) evaluates third-party assessment organization (3PAO) assessments of cloud providers

- FedRAMP itself evaluates the 3PAOs and creates policy guidance so that cloud operators can create and operate a compliant and verifiable Information Security Program

- In a slightly modified model, the National Cybersecurity Agency of France (ANSSI) performs security assessments and provides authorizations to *Operators of Essential Services (OES)*. Cloud platforms managed by these operators are known as *Essential Information Systems (EIS)* and carry the designations as supportive or responsible for the critical functioning of the French economy or society.

One of the goals of this book is to enable security practitioners to achieve the critical milestone of receiving their own *authority to operate* (ATO) or equivalent, regardless of the framework that applies.

Well-evolved and comprehensive organizational Information Security Programs generally require adaptive work, related risk management, and acceptance. The goal is to take a product such as OpenShift from its default security posture, expand controls to meet security objectives, and allow the product to deliver service. No cloud product automatically and completely meets the demands of any Information Security Program since many of the activities of the program are based on the organization's own reporting and vigilance capability.

At the very least, security practitioners and evaluators want to know what control elements to engage vigilance toward. Even when given the many advanced security features and workflow designed into OpenShift, there is more work to do on site. Since security is a process and is always evolving, Red Hat is continuously evaluating OpenShift's security posture against the compliance frameworks. This is the value of the Red Hat subscription.

This chapter focuses on risk management and regulatory readiness as applied to OpenShift at a high level. Most of the chapter will feel official and factual in tone, however, it is important for the information security professional to understand Red Hat's strategy around risk management through the use of NIST's Risk Management Framework and other regulatory legal and certification requirements.

Risk Management Frameworks

While this section highlights the NIST Risk Management Framework (RMF), it is also possible to address general requirements found in other frameworks such as Control Objectives for Information and Related Technologies (COBIT) and the Information Systems Security Association (ISSA). There tends to be a large overlap between other available risk management frameworks, and as a result many follow what NIST has established.

NIST Risk Management Framework (NIST RMF)

The National Institute of Standards and Technology (NIST) Risk Management Framework is designed to help manage organizational risk. The security controls specified by the framework serve as a target to be remediated by the security capabilities of OpenShift as a platform. The NIST RMF provides a broad scope for assessing risk and subsequently configuring infrastructure to meet the requirements specified in the framework.

The NIST RMF provides an approach that continuously manages and evaluates the security posture life cycle of the system. This risk-based approach resolves the constraints presented by the global compliance pattern introduced in the beginning of this chapter. The approach allows the security practitioner to select and specify controls based on sovereign laws, technical effectiveness, and business constraints.

The diagram in figure 1.2 shows the cyclical nature of security and risk management activities within the NIST RMF.

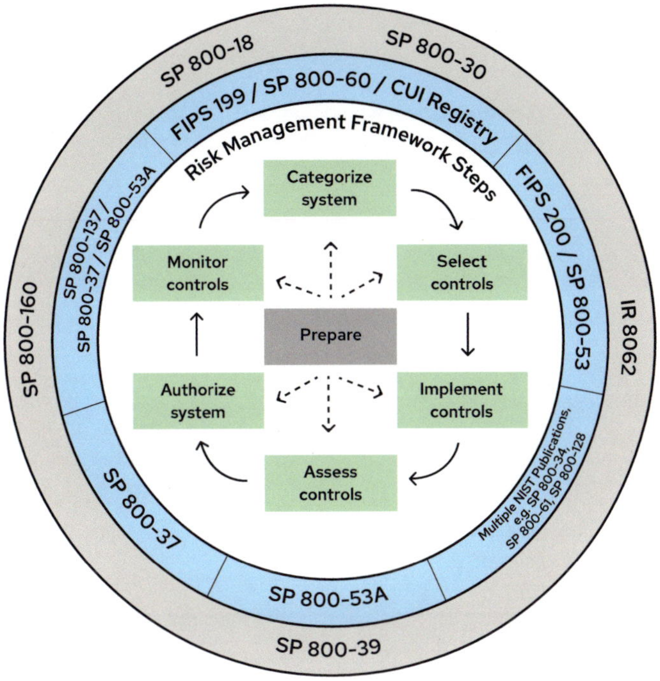

Figure 1.2: NIST Risk Management Framework Steps

NIST Foundational Guidance

FIPS 199/200 Elements

Through its FIPS 199 and 200 publications, NIST has established foundational elements within risk management that speak to categorizing security risks and establishing *adequate security* for each of those levels. Together these publications establish a matrix that represents security scope through a catalog of control families (see Table 1.1 : NIST Control Families) and impact levels.

NIST Control Families		
Access Control (AC)	Awareness and Training (AT)	Audit and Accountability (AU)
Security Assessment and Authorization (CA)	Configuration Management (CM)	Contingency Planning (CP)
Identification and Authentication (IA)	Incident Response (IR)	Maintenance (MA)
Media Protection (MP)	Physical and Environmental Protection (PE)	Planning (PL)
Personnel Security (PS)	Risk Assessment (RA)	System and Services Acquisition (SA)
System and Communications Protection (SC)	System and Information Integrity (SI)	

Table 1.1: NIST Control Families

As a vendor, Red Hat uses FIPS 199 to orientate default security settings based on the defined impact levels :

	Potential impact		
Security objective	**Low**	**Moderate**	**High**
Confidentiality Preserving authorized restrictions on information access and disclosure, including means for protecting personal privacy and proprietary information. [44 U.S.C., SEC. 3542]	The unauthorized disclosure of information could be expected to have a **limited** adverse effect on organizational operations, organizational assets, or individuals.	The unauthorized disclosure of information could be expected to have a **serious** adverse effect on organizational operations, organizational assets, or individuals.	The unauthorized disclosure of information could be expected to have a **severe or catastrophic** adverse effect on organizational operations, organizational assets, or individuals.
Integrity Guarding against improper information modification or destruction, and includes ensuring information and non-repudiation and authenticity. [44 U.S.C., SEC. 3542]	The unauthorized modification or destruction of information could be expected to have a **limited** adverse effect on organizational operations, organizational assets, or individuals.	The unauthorized modification or destruction of information could be expected to have a **serious** adverse effect on organizational operations, organizational assets, or individuals.	The unauthorized modification or destruction of information could be expected to have a **severe or catastrophic** adverse effect on organizational operations, organizational assets, or individuals.
Availability Ensuring timely and reliable access to and use of information. [44 U.S.C., SEC. 3542]	The disruption of access to or use of information or an information system could be expected to have a **limited** adverse effect on organizational operations, organizational assets, or individuals.	The disruption of access to or use of information or an information system could be expected to have a **serious** adverse effect on organizational operations, organizational assets, or individuals.	The disruption of access to or use of information or an information system could be expected to have a **severe or catastrophic** adverse effect on organizational operations, organizational assets, or individuals.

Table 1.2: NIST Impact Levels

Readers charged with compliance-related responsibilities may find it helpful to understand which security control groups and associated impact level are required for their system.

Legal Requirements

For many organizations, meeting the required legal standards is an organizational imperative. Whether utilizing validated ciphers, achieving information assurance certifications, or complying with government mandates, the following sections refer to some of the most internationally recognized and mandated requirements that many organizations are required to adhere to.

Federal Information Processing Standard 140 (FIPS 140)

As defined in the United States Public Law 104-106, any cryptography used to protect *sensitive or valuable data* must undergo formal validation.

Developed by the National Institute of Standards and Technology (NIST), as part of the Cryptological Module Validation Program (CMVP), FIPS 140 is a United States Government standard that describes the cryptographic algorithms which may be used and how they are to be validated and certified.

Through various laws and regulations, the official position of the United States Government is that unvalidated cryptography provides no protection to information or data. In effect, the encrypted data using non-FIPS validated cryptography would be considered the same as plain text.

Between 1987 and 2002, a special provision allowed for United States Government agencies to waive the FIPS 140 validation requirements. Since the Federal Information Systems Management Act (FISMA) of 2002, a waiver can no longer be provided for cryptography that has not passed FIPS validation.

When a cryptographic module undergoes FIPS validation, an independent, third-party laboratory cryptographically verifies specific NIST-approved ciphers and hashes used in the system. When the third-party lab has completed its assessment, the results are reported to NIST for final approval, and then NIST issues certificates to the vendor indicating that the module has been validated. It is important to note that the validation is done against compiled binaries on specific types of hardware. This means that using the source code that contains the FIPS cryptographic ciphers and hashes and re-compiling the source code not only invalidates the NIST validation but any data encrypted with the recompiled edition is considered plain text.

OpenShift's FIPS 140 Strategy

As an aggregation of many elements, products are typically not FIPS 140 validated although specific cryptographic modules within the product can be FIPS validated. So, it is inaccurate to state that all of OpenShift, or even all of Red Hat Enterprise Linux, is FIPS validated.

An example of an accurate statement would be that an "OpenSSH Server, when deployed on Red Hat Enterprise Linux 7, is FIPS validated." It would not be accurate to make a broad, product-wide claim, such as "Red Hat Enterprise Linux is FIPS validated."

To meet the FIPS 140-2 cryptographic module requirements as established through the Federal Information Security Management Act (FISMA), OpenShift's guiding principle is to use the NIST-validated cryptographic modules found in Red Hat Enterprise Linux when RHEL is booted in FIPS mode. Please see sections below detailing the validation status of FIPS modules.

Current Usage of FIPS 140 Cryptography

The following FIPS 140-validated modules are available for use when OpenShift 4 is deployed on RHEL 7 :

Module name	NIST certificate	Functionality	Sunset / expiration
Red Hat Enterprise Linux (v7) GnuTLS Cryptographic Module	3571	GnuTLS is a secure communications library implementing the TLS and DTLS protocols. It provides a programming interface to access the secure communications protocols as well as APIs to parse and write X.509, PKCS #12, and other required structures.	11/24/2024
Red Hat Enterprise Linux (v7) Kernel Crypto API	3565	Provides services operating inside the kernel with various ciphers, message digests, and an approved random number generator.	11/14/2024
Red Hat Enterprise Linux (v7) Libreswan	3563	Provides IKE protocol key agreement services required for IPSec.	11/14/2024
Red Hat Enterprise Linux (v7) OpenSSL	3538	General purpose cryptographic library designed to provide FIPS-validated cryptographic functionality with the high level API of the OpenSSL library.	9/25/2024
Red Hat Enterprise Linux (v7) NSS	3270	The logical interfaces of this module consist of the PKCS #11 (cryptoki) API. This API is often used in authentication, such as for Multi-Factor Auth (MFA), PIV, and CaC.	8/28/2023
Red Hat Enterprise Linux (v7) OpenSSH Client	3067	Client-side component for an SSH protocol version 2 protected communication channel.	11/26/2022
Red Hat Enterprise Linux (v7) OpenSSH Server	3063	Server-side component for an SSH protocol version 2 protected communication channel.	11/13/2022

Table 1.3: FIPS-validated Red Hat Modules

Planned / In Progress Usage of FIPS 140 Cryptography

Implementation Under Test List

Per NIST, the Implementation Under Test (IUT) list "is provided as a marketing service for vendors who have a viable contract with an accredited laboratory for the testing of a cryptographic module." Or perhaps more directly, inclusion on the NIST IUT list means that Red Hat has placed an auditor on contract to begin formal evaluation, pending resource availability of the auditor to begin the validation work. Currently, the following Red Hat Enterprise Linux 8 (and thus Red Hat Enterprise Linux CoreOS) modules are on the NIST Implementation Under Test list :

Module name	Functionality	IUT Date
Red Hat Enterprise Linux 8 GnuTLS	GnuTLS is a secure communications library implementing the TLS and DTLS protocols. It provides a programming interface to access the secure communications protocols as well as APIs to parse and write X.509, PKCS #12, and other required structures.	10/21/2019
Red Hat Enterprise Linux 8 NSS	The logical interfaces of this module consist of the PKCS #11 (cryptoki) API. This API is often used in authentication, such as for Multi-Factor Auth (MFA), PIV, and CaC.	10/21/2019

Table 1.4: Red Hat Module Implementation Under Test Status

NIST publishes a complete registry of all modules, from all vendors, that are currently in the "Implementation Under Test" list. This is available at :

https://csrc.nist.gov/Projects/cryptographic-module-validation-program/Modules-In-Process/IUT-List

Modules in Process List

The Modules in Process (MIP) list contains cryptographic modules which are *actively* being reviewed by NIST. This is the last stage prior to formal FIPS validation. Currently, the following Red Hat Enterprise Linux 8 (and thus RHCOS) cryptographic components are on the NIST Modules in Process List :

Module name	Functionality
Red Hat Enterprise Linux 8 Kernel Cryptographic Module	GnuTLS is a secure communications library implementing the TLS and DTLS protocols. It provides a programming interface to access the secure communications protocols as well as APIs to parse and write X.509, PKCS #12, and other required structures.
Red Hat Enterprise Linux 8 libgcrypt	Libgcrypt is a general purpose cryptographic library originally based on code from GnuPG. This library provides symmetric and public key cryptography, hashing, key derivation, and several other functions.
Red Hat Enterprise Linux 8 OpenSSL	General purpose cryptographic library designed to provide FIPS validated cryptographic functionality with the high level API of the OpenSSL library.

Table 1.5: Red Hat Products under Active Review – Modules in Process

The NIST registry of Modules in Process can be found at : https://csrc.nist.gov/Projects/cryptographic-module-validation-program/Modules-In-Process/Modules-In-Process-List

Common Criteria

Common Criteria is a security-related certification for products that do "information assurance" work which, these days, includes nearly everything!

Unique security function requirements are applied to broad technology categories such as operating systems, routers, or virtualizations. Common

Criteria (CC) is an international standard (ISO/IEC 15408) that defines and specifies how to evaluate information systems and software. The Common Criteria process ensures that the product or solution provider meets established criteria through third-party review and evaluation. Topics of evaluation include system design, architecture, life cycle management, documentation guidance on secure deployment, and vulnerability assessment.

The *common* in Common Criteria refers to an international consortium of governments collaboratively creating mutually recognized standards. Common Criteria ensures Red Hat OpenShift 4 can be deployed into markets such as Australia, Canada, France, Germany, India, the United States, and several dozen others.

Within the United States, the National Policy Governing the Acquisition of Information Assurance (IA) and IA-Enabled Information Technology Products states that in order to acquire Commercial Off-the-Shelf (COTS) products (if there is an applicable protection profile) that product *must* have a Common Criteria certification. Additionally, Common Criteria evaluation and certification is needed for solutions to meet the full scope of NIST 800-53 Moderate and High targets.

Starting with Red Hat Enterprise Linux 8.1, 8.2, and every Extended Life Cycle (ELS) and Extended Update Support (EUS) release afterwards, RHEL 8 pursues Common Criteria certification. This means that versions of OpenShift 4 will benefit from the underlying Common Criteria standing provided by Red Hat Enterprise Linux 8 nodes.

Regulations and Policies

Those with compliance responsibilities within an organization have a full scope of regulations and policies that may need to be followed. There are many regulatory and policy requirements such as Section 508 that do have to be considered. However, an exhaustive treatment of such would be out of scope for this book. Below is a list of the more security-focused regulations and frameworks and may serve at minimum as a guide to understanding or researching what may be applicable for your industry, government or organization.

NIST 800-53

The National Institute of Standards and Technology (NIST) created a catalog of several hundred recommended security controls for governments and organizations to create and assess security and compliance requirements for their respective divisions and/or organizations. These controls are defined in the NIST Special Publication 800-53 (NIST SP 800-53). As previously mentioned in the NIST Foundational Guidance section, a subset of the 800-53 controls have been selected for information systems that are categorized as low, moderate, or high levels of heightened security. It is from these impact baselines (low, moderate, high) that the various U.S. Government agencies and organizations derive and map their respective compliance frameworks (FedRAMP, FISMA, Common Criteria, etc.) and profiles (low, moderate, high, etc.) for a product or an information system. This means that for OpenShift to be utilized in the U.S. Government, OpenShift and its components must meet the selected technical controls laid out in the NIST baseline profiles. Red Hat cannot choose which parts of the compliance framework to meet based on personal opinions. Red Hat must follow the guidelines set forth by the compliance framework.

Red Hat undertakes internal assessments of products against all NIST 800-53 controls, creates checklists, open sources the checklists, and submits those checklists against the various government compliance frameworks (FedRAMP, FedRAMP, FISMA, Common Criteria, etc.). Currently, only Red Hat Enterprise Linux meets the majority of the U.S. Government compliance framework requirements.

To facilitate reciprocity amongst the different international security standards bodies and frameworks, NIST has provided mappings and references to other frameworks (COBIT5, ISSA, and others) The Cloud Security Alliance also publishes the Cloud Controls Matrix which provides valuable insight related to control mapping.

The Australian Information Security Manual and the Essential Eight

The Australian government, under the direction of the Australian Cyber Security Centre (ACSC), publishes both the Information Security Manual (ISM) and a document known as the Essential Eight (E8). The Australian ISM represents another source of risk management guidance while the E8 is a prioritized baseline of mitigation strategies. Both are designed to be adopted for increased systems protection and defense against bad actors.

Effectively, the E8 introduces maturity levels that help gauge alignment with the overall strategies specified by the ACSC. In this regard the prioritization of importance is similar to the NIST security objectives and impact levels.

IPv6

IPv6 requirements have made their way into government acquisition language. Therefore, the United States Government has agreed on a common interoperability test for IPv6 hosts, routers, and network protection devices called USGv6. IPv6 implementations are tested by independent labs to make sure they all work together.

For the latest status of IPv6, and any other US Government certification, refer to the "Government Standards" article on the Red Hat Customer

Portal : https://access.redhat.com/articles/2918071#usgv6-tested-product-list-7

Configuration Baselines

Through participation in the United States' National Cybersecurity Center of Excellence (NCCoE), Red Hat collaborates with NIST via the National Checklist Program. Defined by NIST 800-70, the NIST National Checklist Program is the United States Government repository of publicly available security checklists (or benchmarks) that provide detailed low-level guidance on setting the security configuration of operating systems.

Red Hat configuration baselines submitted to the NIST National Checklist contain the following :

- ***Security Content Automation Protocol (SCAP) Data Streams***
  Red Hat publishes human-readable configuration guidance as eXtensible Configuration Checklist Description Format (XCCDF), and machine-parsable pass/fail content in the Open Vulnerability Assessment Language (OVAL). This data can be consumed by any NIST SCAP Validated Product, such as OpenSCAP, Tenable, Qualys, SPAWAR SCC, and many other tools.

- ***NIST 800-53 Security Requirements Traceability Matrix***
  Often called an SRTM or SRM, this content maps specific configuration actions (such as how to enable TLS) to specific NIST 800-53 controls. These tables are often used to demonstrate recommended configuration actions to satisfy a NIST 800-53 control and include manual processes that third-party auditors can use to verify that a control has been implemented.

- ***Ansible and/or MachineConfig Templates***
  To support automation-driven workflow, and ensure systems are installed directly into a compliant state, automation content such as Ansible Playbooks and/or MachineConfig templates are provided.

The full listing of Red Hat's NIST National Checklist program entries, which include baselines such as the Australian Essential 8, the Defense Information Systems Agency Security Technical Implementation Guides (DISA STIGs), and the Health Insurance Portability and Accountability Act (HIPAA), can be found at :

https://nvd.nist.gov/ncp/repository?authority=Red+Hat&startIndex=0

2. Red Hat Enterprise Linux CoreOS Security

Red Hat Enterprise Linux CoreOS (RHCOS) is the operating system base for OpenShift Container Platform (OCP). As a lightweight and purpose-built operating system, it is based on Red Hat Enterprise Linux 8 and uses the same kernel, code, open source development process, and ships with a specific subset of RHEL software packages.

RHCOS is built and supported for use in OpenShift 4 clusters. Its primary goal is to provide a secure operating system platform for running Kubernetes, OpenShift services, and the containerized workloads running on the aggregated platform.

This chapter breaks down RHCOS security features into several areas that largely follow a cognitive journey from understanding toward action. First, it covers how core components are designed to provide a secure and efficient container platform. Next, it describes the entry points for adding security features to nodes. After that, it steps through specific tasks for adding available security features. And finally, it explains how to manage ongoing security tasks with topics such as troubleshooting and upgrading nodes.

RHCOS Design

RHCOS represents the next generation of single-purpose container operating system technology. Created by the same development teams that created Red Hat Enterprise Linux Atomic Host and CoreOS Container Linux, RHCOS combines the quality standards of Red Hat Enterprise Linux (RHEL) with automated, remote upgrade features from Container Linux.

RHCOS is supported only as a component of OpenShift Container Platform 4 for all OpenShift Container Platform machines. It is the only supported operating system for the OpenShift Container Platform control plane or master machines. While RHCOS is the default operating system for all cluster machines, some of the cluster is composed of compute nodes, which are also known as worker nodes. These may require certain flexibility in design to enable certain workload types. To accommodate such scenarios, worker nodes can be created that use RHEL as their operating system, instead of RHCOS.

There are two general ways RHCOS is deployed in OpenShift Container Platform 4 :

- If the cluster is installed on infrastructure that the cluster provisions, RHCOS images are downloaded to the target platform during installation, and suitable Ignition config files, which control the RHCOS configuration, are used to deploy the machines. This approach represents the installer-provisioned installation model.
- If the cluster is installed on a local infrastructure, follow the installation documentation to obtain the RHCOS images, generate Ignition config files, and use the Ignition config files to provision the machines. This model is the approach associated with user-provisioned infrastructure.

Key RHCOS Features

The following list describes key features of the RHCOS operating system :

- ***Based on RHEL***
  The underlying operating system consists primarily of RHEL components. The same quality, security, and control measures that support RHEL also support RHCOS. For example, RHCOS software is in RPM packages, and each RHCOS system starts up with a RHEL kernel and a set of services that are managed by the systemd init system.

- ***Controlled immutability***
  Although it contains RHEL components, RHCOS is designed to be managed more tightly and indirectly than a default RHEL installation. Management is performed remotely from the OpenShift Container Platform cluster. On set up, RHCOS machines have only a few system settings which can be modified. This controlled immutability allows an OpenShift Container Platform to store the latest state of RHCOS systems in the cluster, so it is always able to create additional machines and perform updates based on the latest RHCOS configurations.

- ***CRI-O container runtime***
  RHCOS contains features for running the OCI- and libcontainer-formatted containers that Docker requires. It does this by incorporating the CRI-O container engine instead of the Docker container engine. CRI-O focuses on features needed by Kubernetes platforms. In this approach, CRI-O can offer specific compatibility with different Kubernetes versions. CRI-O also offers a smaller footprint and reduced attack surface than is possible with container engines that offer a superset beyond Kubernetes-centric features. Since the OpenShift Container Platform is really Kubernetes, it benefits from these features as well. At the moment, CRI-O is only available as a container engine within OpenShift Container Platform clusters.

- ***Set of command line container tools***
  For tasks such as building, copying, and otherwise managing containers, RHCOS replaces Docker with a compatible set of container tools. The *podman* command supports many container runtime features, such as running, starting, stopping, listing, and removing containers and container images. The *skopeo* command can copy, authenticate, and sign images. The *crictl* command can be used to work with containers and pods from the CRI-O container engine. While direct use of these tools in RHCOS is discouraged, they can be used for debugging purposes.

- ***rpm-ostree upgrades***
  RHCOS features transactional upgrades using the rpm-ostree system. Updates are delivered by means of container images and are part of the OpenShift Container Platform update process. When deployed, the container image is pulled, extracted, and written to disk, then the bootloader is modified to boot into the new version. The machine will reboot into the update in a rolling manner to ensure cluster capacity is minimally impacted.

- ***Updated through Machine Config Operator***
  In OpenShift Container Platform, the Machine Config Operator handles operating system upgrades. Instead of upgrading individual packages, as is done with Yum upgrades, the *rpm-ostree* command delivers upgrades of the OS as an atomic unit. The new OS deployment is staged during upgrades and goes into effect on the next reboot. If something goes wrong with the upgrade, a single rollback and reboot returns the system to the previous state. RHCOS upgrades in OpenShift Container Platform are performed during cluster updates.

Everything in a Container

For RHCOS systems the layout of the rpm-ostree file system has the following characteristics:

- `/usr` is where the operating system binaries and libraries are stored and is read-only. Red Hat does not support altering this.

- `/etc`, `/boot`, `/var` are writable on the system but only intended to be altered by the Machine Config Operator

- Files written to these paths are persisted.

- `/usr/local` is a symlink to `/var/usr/local`. Software may be placed in `/usr/local/{bin,sbin}`. Depending on the path settings, RHCOS may not use these paths. As such, it is not recommended that administrators rely on these paths.

- Some content in `/boot`, is managed by `rpm-ostree` for Kernel and boot loader settings

- The bootloader configuration is managed by `rpm-ostree`. The Machine Config Operator can set kernel parameters for machine pools

- Various paths in `/` are symlinks to `/var`:

    - `/root` -> `/var/roothome`

    - `/opt` -> `/var/opt`

    - `/srv` -> `/var/srv`

- `/var/lib/containers` is the graph storage location for storing container images

RHCOS is not intended to be run outside of an OpenShift Cluster. Conceptually, RHCOS is the base layer of OpenShift Container Platform 4. As a member of the cluster, RHCOS is managed by and upgraded through the cluster. In order to run software, admins for RHCOS should use containers. Due to the unique filesystem layout, managed, and atomic updates, RHCOS is incompatible at the host level with most non-containerized applications.

An immutable operating system is one where the state does not persist between reboots. RHCOS is not an immutable operating system because state may persist. The *rpm-ostree* command may be used to override and change the underlying ostree image. RHCOS does have elements of immutability that are controlled by the OpenShift Cluster. This controlled immutability refers to the machine operating system content that is delivered from Red Hat which includes the kernel, initramfs, packages, and the default configuration. The Machine Config Operator ensures that each node maintains the required configuration from the cluster view.

Machine Config Operator

OpenShift 4 is an operator-driven platform. This approach allows specific operators such as the Machine Config Operator (MCO) to take a declarative approach to cluster component life cycle management. This effectively allows the automated management of cluster updates that range from the kernel to services higher in the stack. The MCO is the component that joins RHCOS and the OpenShift Cluster together.

MachineConfig resources provide the interface to thread OS configuration through the cluster from bootstrap to cluster upgrades.

Some specific configuration options are abstracted into higher-level knobs within MachineConfigs such as kernelType to enable the real-time kernel or kernelArguments. Configuration for the container runtime and the kubelet can be handled with their respective precursor objects, ContainerRuntimeConfigs and KubeletConfigs, which are translated into MachineConfigs by dedicated controllers.

Notably, MachineConfigs contain a section for defining files, units, and certain user configurations which follow the CoreOS Ignition configuration format. Indeed, MachineConfigs provide the basis for the Ignition payload delivered to nodes on first boot. Additional files and configurations can be added or modified on existing nodes through MachineConfig objects. This symmetry between first-boot and subsequent updates makes RHCOS configuration consistent across a pool of nodes.

Ignition

The first boot agent driving RHCOS is Ignition. From Ignition's Github page :

Ignition is the utility used by CoreOS Container Linux, Fedora CoreOS, and RHEL CoreOS to manipulate disks during the initramfs. This includes partitioning disks, formatting partitions, writing files (i.e. regular files, systemd units), and configuring users. On first boot, Ignition reads its configuration from a source of truth (remote URL, network metadata service, hypervisor bridge, etc.) and applies the configuration.

During installation, the installer dynamically creates Ignition profiles to setup and install RHCOS and OpenShift. While Ignition configuration files can be used to change the behavior of the bootstrap, it should only be done when necessary, such as to enable hardware or set targeted settings.

A Word on Agents

Many information security programs choose and require local agents to implement certain functions of the program. There are a wide variety of agent types available from commercial and community providers that add security controls to Linux-based systems. Additionally, many cloud providers also have agents that perform a pantheon of actions. Functions such as configuration management, state management, audit, authentication, logical access control, and monitoring are normally presumed to be available for a Linux system.

It is important to understand that the scope of agent use here is for RHCOS as the platform operating system. Security services deployed higher in the stack that target Kubernetes and workloads are not addressed here.

RHCOS promotes an expectation of certain consistencies intended to add rigor to certain aspects of operations and security. The use of third-party agents within RHCOS is considered to be an anti-pattern within the RHCOS security architecture. This generally prompts an information security program policy decision to use an appliance-like strategy as a starting perspective to manage RHCOS. Furthermore, many agents expect a traditional file system layout and may fail to work on RHCOS; this is true even of agents that work on RHEL 8. Notably, the kernel module location under RHCOS is read only. When an agent installation is necessary, it should be containerized.

Modifying RHCOS Security Settings

Because Red Hat OpenShift 4 was designed to be simple to install and secure out of the box, a major goal was to lock down workers and control plane nodes. Nodes that veered from default settings are at risk of creating security vulnerabilities and becoming difficult to upgrade. As a result, OpenShift 4 :

- ***Discourages direct RHCOS modification***
  The classic practice by Linux administrators to log in to a node and add software packages or change configuration files, does not scale well in a cloud-first, container-first workflow under ongoing engineering by DevOps practitioners. Direct low-level manipulation of disposable workers also puts systems at risk of having changes overwritten by upgrades or operators.

- ***Encourages enhancements to nodes in pools***
  As much as possible, all worker and control plane nodes need to be configured the same. OpenShift offers ways of applying changes to all similar nodes at once using operators. Adding changes in this way is also more scalable, since changes made in this way will be applied to new nodes as well.

That said, there are times when security requirements demand that modifications be made to the RHCOS systems in OpenShift 4 clusters. As a rule, any security modifications should be kept to a minimum and implemented at the cluster level, whenever possible. With that rule in mind, there are several entry points where modifications to OpenShift 4 worker and control plane nodes might be considered.

Security Modifications at Installation Time

During installation, RHCOS provides opportunities to add security settings that need to be in place before the cluster starts or immediately after the first boot. Some of these settings are currently only supported with bare metal OpenShift 4 installs while others can be done during installations where a cloud provider or other environment provides the infrastructure.

Bare Metal Installation

Bare metal installation is considered more laborious than cloud-based installations. With cloud-based installations, the OpenShift Installer can drive installation using APIs to provision infrastructure and the installation environment for RHCOS is consistent for each installation; these features are often lacking in bare metal installations.

Installer-Provisioned Infrastructure Installation

For installer-provisioned installations in OpenShift 4, there is an opportunity to interrupt the *openshift-install* procedure to add a manifest file. Although this should be done thoughtfully, any configuration file can be modified and applied to all worker nodes or control plane nodes using a feature called Ignition. The Ignition configs are put in place for when each system first boots. The same Ignition configs can also be used after the cluster comes up to modify nodes through MachineConfigs, using the Machine Config Operator (MCO).

Examples of the kinds of security-related modifications which may be enabled during installer-provisioned infrastructure installations include FIPS mode, cloud disk encryption (encrypted EBS), and cloud encryption services provided through cloud providers (e.g. AWS, GCP, Azure). There are components that can be modified for final installation such as RHCOS configuration files via Ignition configs, the implementation risk of these components can vary. It is recommended to evaluate the risks based on each organizations' best practices or requirements.

Security Modifications Post-installation

Once the OpenShift 4 cluster is up and running, making changes directly to RHCOS systems in the cluster can be done easily using the Machine Config

Operator (MCO). Unlike configuration done on bare metal installs, features added through the MCO are saved by the cluster. MCO features are applied immediately to existing nodes, and to any nodes added in the future. Likewise, there are other operators that can be used to manage specific security features with similar expectations of application.

Machine Config Operator

Using the Machine Config Operator ensures that SSH keys, configuration files, systemd unit files, kernel arguments, audit enablement, and other features can be added. These changes can be chosen to apply to worker pools and control plane nodes. The format of the MachineConfigs are the same format used during installation.

Adding Security Services

If the hosting data center or cloud provider requires agents or other services to be running on each node, the following items can be created :

- Kubernetes DaemonSet: DaemonSets are designed to run a pod on all nodes in the cluster, although they can be limited to selected nodes based on a specific nodeSelector. DaemonSets are particularly useful for such events as logging, virus scans, file integrity checking, and cluster storage on each node. Before using a Kubernetes DaemonSet, please see Chapter 3: Container Security. Proposed DaemonSet usage should be examined for security impact, placed under risk management, and logical controls should be selected to use minimal security permissions.

- OpenShift Operator: Operators allow a practitioner to phrase a security solution as a deployable, maintainable service that leverages the system availability of OpenShift. Security function version checks and upgrades are managed in the same way as other OpenShift services.

In general, the two approaches can be used if it is acceptable to start the service after the CRI-O container engine starts up. A common pattern in Kubernetes practice is to run security-based daemonsets, or custom OpenShift Operators, as privileged (i.e. as root) pods. It is recommended that after containerizing the services, that :

- The pod is set to run where needed

- Consider endpoints, ports, and the level access

- Ensure that host mounts are kept to a minimum

- Use service accounts for permission binding. For example, if the service needs access to a specific device on the node, the service should be run with that permission set.
- Think at scale. The RHCOS node is a member of the cluster. A focus on individual nodes can lead to unsustainable practices that make maintenance, upgrade, and audit more difficult.

Tasks for Accomplishing Security Goals

The goal of RHCOS is to be part of the OpenShift Container Platform. In contrast, most other Operating Systems form the foundations on which a universe of services could be built upon. As a result, RHCOS makes some very opinionated choices regarding human-interface interactions : Human intervention should not be required for the day-to-day operation of RHCOS.

Only exceptional circumstances, such as disaster recovery, should require a human to engage with RHCOS itself. RHCOS design supports creation of services that allow practitioners to minimize this interaction and better characterize the organizational service management strategy. Thus, the services run under the aegis of OpenShift and its immediacy of control and vigilance. As such, the number of entry points into the cluster during intervention events can be minimized.

Some OpenShift security enhancements must be done before the OpenShift cluster first boots such as during an OpenShift install, while building the cluster, or during a bare metal OS install. Other tasks can be done after the cluster is up and running. The following sections describe the two different types of tasks.

RHCOS Security During Cluster Installation

The RHCOS design approach attempts to minimize feature decision requirements during boot and early user space. Only two features – FIPS mode and Full Disk Encryption (FDE) – are considered pre-first boot of the cluster operations. After the cluster has been bootstrapped, the cluster can further drive all other node level changes.

FIPS Mode

In order to ensure compliance, FIPS mode must be enabled before cluster nodes first boot and should not be disabled once enabled. Moreover, once a cluster has been installed, FIPS mode must remain on for the life of the cluster, and for any newly introduced nodes, lest a weak key is generated and used. FIPS cannot be enabled after installation or turned off and back on as it will cause problems across the nodes and cluster. This can present itself as odd errors among systems in a cluster performing cryptographic transactions between each other.

Systems built in a non-FIPS state are unsafe for use if FIPS mode is enabled after installation. Such systems should be prevented from entering or otherwise discarded from the cluster.

During the first boot of RHCOS, the system performs a number of cryptographic operations. Per the FIPS standard, any cryptographic material must be only created and used with FIPS-validated modules. If a non-FIPS system is bootstrapped and then FIPS is enabled, any previously generated cryptographic material must be re-generated which would disrupt the functioning of the cluster.

These requirements also apply to bootstrap nodes.

These practices ensure that the cluster meets the objectives of an organizational FIPS-compliance audit. Only CMVP FIPS-validated cryptographic modules are enabled before the initial system boot. OpenShift does not support changing the FIPS mode setting after installation.

From the perspective of RHCOS, FIPS mode is enabled through an embedded Machine Config Object. During node (worker or master) installation :

- A module in the initramfs fetches the embedded Ignition specification
- The embedded MCO specification is checked for `fips: true`
- If false, the machine continues to boot
- If true, the machine's `fips=1` bootloader argument is added, and the machine immediately reboots
- Upon reboot,

  ```
  update-crypto-policies --set FIPS --no-reload
  ```

  is run in the `initramfs`

It is important to note that FIPS mode is enabled before any cryptographic material is persisted. If necessary, security practitioners should create audit automation validation to ensure the desired end state and cryptographic material usage requirements are met.

Setting FIPS Mode

To generate an `install-config.yaml` file, run :

```
$ ./openshift-install create install-config --dir=install
```

Then edit `install-config.yaml` and set `fips: true`.

Full-disk Encryption

Starting with OpenShift 4.3, RHCOS supports full-disk encryption for the system disk. As implemented, RHCOS disk encryption is FIPS compliant if FIPS mode is enabled. RHCOS disk encryption will use the AES256-CBC block cipher. This cipher is named in various places on the system and in config files as **cbc(aes)**, **aescbc**, **aes cbc** and similar.

By default, RHCOS boots with no encryption enabled. Currently, the only two ways that disk encryption is supported is either with TPM2 and a Tang server.

Disk Layout

LUKS (Linux Unified Key Setup) is the Linux standard for implementing disk encryption. With OpenShift 4.3, the on-disk layout for RHCOS was changed to store the root filesystem in a LUKS container. For example :

```
# lsblk --output name,type,label,FSTYPE,UUID
NAME      TYPE LABEL        FSTYPE       UUID
sda       disk
|-sda1    part boot         ext4         1ff4569d-80fa-4f36-9f63-
43775847c1e9
|-sda2    part EFI-SYSTEM   vfat         1B80-D8C2
|-sda3    part
`-sda4    part crypt_rootfs crypto_LUKS 00000000-0000-4000-a000-
000000000002
```

On initial boot, RHCOS will look for a LUKS filesystem with the UUID of `00000000-0000-4000-a000-000000000002` as a candidate for applying encryption.

Note : This disk layout is expected to change in a future RHCOS release. Please check the current OpenShift documentation.

No Encryption

If the user has not opted into full-disk encryption, the LUKS container is ignored. In this case, a device-mapper linear target is set up that by-passes the LUKS header. The device mapper name `coreos-luks-root-nocrypt` indicates that encryption has been turned off.

```
$ sudo dmsetup table
coreos-luks-root-nocrypt: 0 32471007 linear 252:4 32768
```

If the root-file system is mounted with the device name `coreos-luks-root-nocrypt`, the file-system is NOT encrypted.

Encryption

```
cryptsetup
```

Passphrases should meet organizational quality standards for password creation. LUKS libcryptsetup is linked to libpwquality in all Red Hat-based distributions. This means organizational standards and controls for libpwquality usage (i.e. user password quality checks in RHEL) will likely already exist in mature Linux-centric Information Security Programs, and those controls would apply here as well.

OpenShift does not support any attended boot. As such, when disk encryption is used RHCOS will discern the passphrase from either a TPM2 or a Tang Server using Clevis.

During the initial install boot, the system :

- Determines if FIPS mode is needed (updates if enabled)
- Checks for a Clevis Pin. If no Pin is found, then the encryption setup will be skipped
- Generates ephemeral and random passphrases
- Applies encryption
- Binds the LUKS Header to a Clevis Pin
- Continues to boot normally

During a regular boot, RHCOS :

- Looks for the LUKS partition with a label of `crypt_rootfs`
- Checks the LUKS header for a LUKS token with `clevis`
- Calls Clevis to unlock the disk

A failure during the encryption, Clevis binding, or opening of an encrypted file system is detected, RHCOS will drop to a rescue console. The only recourse for failure to apply encryption is to re-provision a node.

Since encryption setup skips on a failed Clevis pin and boot continues, security practitioners should create validation to ensure the desired state exists afterward.

Currently, RHCOS does not support updating the Clevis configuration or re-binding to a different key store.

For encrypted nodes, the bound passphrase can be read by `oc debug`.

<u>Clevis</u>

Clevis is an open source project and a component of Red Hat Enterprise Linux 8 that enabled `Network Bound Disk Encryption (NBDE)`. Clevis implements a distributed encryption mechanism using a McCallum-Relyea Exchange. The process is designed so that neither the client nor the server store knowledge of the key itself.

Simply put, a McCallum-Relyea Exchange means that the server is the only one that can rediscover the key material, and the client is able to recalculate what the server rediscovered without a direct key transmission or the client's own key retention. The client is anonymous to the server, and the server stores no data. With Clevis, a **pin** is used to query a back end for completing the McCallum-Relyea Exchange. RHCOS supports two pins, TPM2 and Tang. During the initial boot, RHCOS looks for the presence of a file delivered via the Machine Config Operator called `/etc/clevis.json`. For example :

```
$ cat << EOF > ./99_openshift-worker-tpmv2-encryption.yaml
apiVersion: machineconfiguration.openshift.io/v1
kind: MachineConfig
metadata:
  name:  clevis-config
  labels:
    machineconfiguration.openshift.io/role: worker
spec:
  config:
    ignition:
      version: 2.2.0
      storage:
```

```
          files:
            - contents:
                source: data:text/plain;base64,e30K
                filesystem: root
                mode: 420
                path: /etc/clevis.json
EOF
```

A similar MachineConfig can be created with the master role to target master nodes.

Machine Config Pools can optionally be used to bind encryption to a subset of worker nodes. See : https://github.com/openshift/machine-config-operator/blob/master/docs/custom-pools.md for information on creating custom pools.

Mixed modes are also possible. For example, both TPM2 and Tang servers can be on the master nodes.

TPM2

Due to simplicity, binding disk encryption to a TPM2 device is the preferred encryption schema. In the example above, the Clevis binding is to a TPM2 device. `data:text/plain;base64,e30K` is decoded as `{}` (empty curly brackets).

Tang

In order to provide network-bound disk encryption, RHCOS supports Tang. In this security mechanism, the disk will be encrypted, and the boot will fail unless the RHCOS can connect to the remote Tang Server.

Tang is a server for binding data to network presence. It makes a system containing data available when the system is bound to a certain secure network. Tang is stateless and does not require TLS or authentication. Unlike escrow-based solutions where the server stores all encryption keys and has knowledge of every key ever used, Tang never interacts with any client secrets, so it never gains any identifying information from the client.

The Clevis pin for Tang uses one of the public keys to generate a unique, cryptographically-strong encryption key. Once the data is encrypted using this key, the key is discarded. The Clevis client should store the state produced by this provisioning operation in a convenient location. This process of encrypting data is the provisioning step. See : https://access.redhat.com/documentation/en-us/red_hat_enterprise_linux/8/html/security_hardening/configuring-automated-unlocking-of-encrypted-volumes-using-policy-based-decryption_security-hardening

To bind RHCOS to Tang, the IP or DNS name of the server and a thumbprint of the server are needed. Thumbprint can be used in two ways :

```
$ echo secret | clevis-encrypt-tang '{"url": "http://<HOST>"}'
The advertisement contains the following signing keys:
MXDt77HSEXcuFL1CReL2VsQPHKg
Do you wish to trust these keys? [ynYN]
```

In the case above, `MXDt77HSEXcuFL1CReL2VsQPHKg` is the thumbprint to be used. Conversely, `tang-show-keys` can be used on the Tang server.

With the Tang Thumbprint in hand, it needs to be base64 encoded in a JSON document. For example :

```
$ cat << EOF > ./99_openshift-tang-encryption.yaml
apiVersion: machineconfiguration.openshift.io/v1
```

```
kind: MachineConfig
metadata:
   name: clevis-config
   labels:
   matchExpressions:
      - {key: machineconfiguration.openshift.io/role, operator:
In, values: [worker,worker]}
spec:
  kernelArguments:
    - rd.neednet=1
    - ip=dhcp
  config:
    ignition:
      version: 2.2.0
      storage:
        files:
          - contents:
              source: data:text/plain;base64,$(base64 -w '{"url":
"http://tang.example.org", "thp": "<THUMBPRINT>"')
              filesystem: root
              mode: 420
              path: /etc/clevis.json
EOF
```

Note that the specific MachineConfig for Tang must :

- Include two kernel arguments for `rd.neednet=1` and `ip=dchp`
- A base64 encoded JSON document

Since Clevis uses the Tang binding in the initramfs, DHCP is required since there are no supported methods to persist non-DHCP IP addresses as kernel command line arguments.

Performance

Encryption is impacted by situations where the disk latency is noticeable to the encryption service. Red Hat Engineering has determined that attempting full-disk encryption on network-backed disks, such as Amazon EBS and Azure root disks, `etcd` would fail to provision in the specified timeout.

Before enabling full-disk encryption, security practitioners should empirically verify availability of sufficient CPU, low disk latency, and high networking bandwidth.

RHCOS Network Configuration Security

RHCOS itself does not require networking. However, when deployed in the context of OpenShift Container Platform, networking is required. By default, RHCOS is configured to use DHCP to obtain both networking information and network identity. Either RHCOS or the network address provisioning scheme will need to be altered to accommodate a requirement for static addressing.

Network Configuration Behavior

If RHCOS is running in a cloud-based environment, then RHCOS is designed to work with the cloud to obtain both identity and networking information. Otherwise, DHCP should provide a hostname.

Hostname

In the case of self-hosted installations, DHCP should provide the hostname. If the hostname is not provided via DHCP, network identity is inferred.

If the hostname is NOT set, then it will discern its hostname in the following order :

- `/etc/hostname`
- DHCP lease
- systemd-hostnamectl's transient hostname, if set
- using a reverse PTR lookup

Under the following circumstances, it is recommended to set the hostname via Ignition :

- multiple interfaces served via DHCP that provide a hostname
- statically-configured network interfaces

Please see Red Hat Enterprise Linux CoreOS Architecture for related documentation.

Non-DHCP Network Configuration

For any environment without DHCP, Kernel Arguments (Kargs) and Ignition must be used to set a persistent hostname.

Linux supports invoking network settings via the Grub prompt. This experience is less than ideal, and Red Hat is actively working on an improved solution. Please check the current documentation on when setting network information via the kernel command line.

RHCOS Security After the Cluster is Up

As much as possible, post-deployment changes to RHCOS nodes should be done at the cluster level. Direct changes to RHCOS nodes should not be accomplished by logging in to a node and adding software packages or editing configuration files. Once an OpenShift cluster is up and running, most direct changes to RHCOS nodes should be done by applying MachineConfig objects to worker or master nodes.

Post-deployment security-related activities for RHCOS include adding kernel modules that are applied when the RHCOS nodes boot and modifications to security-related configuration files. To illustrate modifying a configuration file, the procedure below changes the location of the time server used to sync the chronyd service on each node. Both kernel arguments and RHCOS configuration file changes can be applied to the nodes through MachineConfigs.

Add a Kernel Argument to RHCOS Nodes

Some security features need to be done by passing arguments to the kernel when an RHCOS node boots. There are kernel arguments that enable tradeoffs between security and system availability.

One example of a kernel-related argument that can have an impact on RHCOS security is **pti**. Turning on the kernel page-table isolation kernel argument (pti=on) hardens the kernel to prevent bypassing kernel address space layout randomization (KASLR), while mitigating the Meltdown security vulnerability.

Kernel arguments can also be used to disable physical ports, such as Universal Serial Bus (USB) and Firewire (IEEE 1394). Input/output (I/O) devices include, for example, Compact Disk (CD) and Digital Video Disk (DVD) drives. Physically disabling or removing such connection ports and

I/O devices help prevent exfiltration of information from information systems and the introduction of malicious code into systems from those ports/devices.

The following procedure enables kernel page-table isolation symmetric multi-threading on all worker nodes in a cluster. Substituting **master** for **worker** would apply that change to master nodes instead. Once done, the kernel argument is appended to the end of the existing kernel arguments. Run the following procedure on an OpenShift 4.3 or later cluster as a user with admin privileges.

1 To see the current MachineConfigs, type :

```
$ oc get MachineConfig
NAME                                GENERATEDBYCONTROLLER
IGNITIONVERSION CREATED
00-master                           25bb6aeb58135c38a66... 2.2.0
        6h57m
00-worker                           25bb6aeb58135c38a66... 2.2.0
        6h57m
01-master-container-runtime         25bb6aeb58135c38a66... 2.2.0
        6h57m
01-master-kubelet                   25bb6aeb58135c38a66... 2.2.0
        6h57m
01-worker-container-runtime         25bb6aeb58135c38a66... 2.2.0
        6h57m
01-worker-kubelet                   25bb6aeb58135c38a66... 2.2.0
        6h57m
99-master-b93e3bc8-a298-4d23... 25bb6aeb58135c38a66... 2.2.0
        6h57m
99-master-ssh                       25bb6aeb58135c38a66... 2.2.0
        6h57m
99-worker-c2a65f30-b05c-46aa... 25bb6aeb58135c38a66... 2.2.0
        6h57m
99-worker-ssh                       25bb6aeb58135c38a66... 2.2.0
```

```
        6h57m
rendered-master-0e026742499d... 25bb6aeb58135c38a66... 2.2.0
        6h57m
rendered-worker-38ca73bcfcca... 25bb6aeb58135c38a66... 2.2.0
        6h57m
```

2 Add the kernel argument to a MachineConfig entry in a file and name that file so that it is inserted in an appropriate place in the list of MachineConfigs. For example, `20-worker-ption.yaml`:

```
apiVersion: machineconfiguration.openshift.io/v1
kind: MachineConfig
metadata:
  labels:
    machineconfiguration.openshift.io/role: worker
  name: 20-worker-ption.yaml
spec:
  config:
    ignition:
      version: 2.2.0
  kernelArguments:
    - pti=on
```

3 Use `oc create` to add the kernel argument to all worker nodes in the cluster:

```
$ oc create -f 20-worker-ption.yaml
```

4 To see the new machine config, type:

```
$ oc get MachineConfig
NAME                        GENERATEDBYCONTROLLER   IGNITIONVERSION
```

```
 CREATED
00-master                          25bb6aeb58135c38a66...   2.2.0
          6h57m
00-worker                          25bb6aeb58135c38a66...   2.2.0
          6h57m
01-master-container-runtime        25bb6aeb58135c38a66...   2.2.0
          6h57m
01-master-kubelet                  25bb6aeb58135c38a66...   2.2.0
          6h57m
01-worker-container-runtime        25bb6aeb58135c38a66...   2.2.0
          6h57m
01-worker-kubelet                  25bb6aeb58135c38a66...   2.2.0
          6h57m
20-worker-ption.yaml                                        2.2.0
             6s
99-master-b93e3bc8-a298-4d23... 25bb6aeb58135c38a66...   2.2.0
          6h57m
```

5 Check that the worker nodes have rebooted and are available :

```
$ oc get nodes
ip-10-0-131-171.us-east-2.compute.internal
Ready         worker    7h15m    v1.16.2
ip-10-0-137-96.us-east-
2.compute.internal          Ready         master    7h24m    v1.16.2
ip-10-0-151-140.us-east-2.compute.internal
Ready         worker    7h16m    v1.16.2
ip-10-0-158-218.us-east-2.compute.internal
Ready         master    7h24m    v1.16.2
ip-10-0-163-217.us-east-2.compute.internal
Ready         master    7h24m    v1.16.2
ip-10-0-167-252.us-east-2.compute.internal
Ready         worker    7h16m    v1.16.2
```

6. List the contents of the `/proc/cmdline` file on one of the worker nodes, to make sure the kernel argument has been applied:

```
$ oc debug node/ip-10-0-131-171.us-east-2.compute.internal
Starting pod/ip-10-0-131-171us-east-2computeinternal-debug ...
To use host binaries, run `chroot /host`
If you don't see a command prompt, try pressing enter.
sh-4.2# cat /host/proc/cmdline
BOOT_IMAGE=(hd0,gpt1)/ostree/rhcos-
9a8c2fd60f5219ecf823c685ed70097b8c55bb8b0d43e4192737ea791863091
8/vmlinuz-4.18.0-147.3.1.el8_1.x86_64 rhcos.root=crypt_rootfs
console=tty0 console=ttyS0,115200n8 rd.luks.options=discard
ostree=/ostree/boot.1/rhcos/9a8c2fd60f5219ecf823c685ed70097b8c5
5bb8b0d43e4192737ea7918630918/0 ignition.platform.id=aws pti=on
```

Change a Configuration File on RHCOS Nodes

The procedure for applying any configuration file to an RHCOS node is basically the same, regardless of which file is applied. The following procedure describes how to replace the `chrony.conf` file so that one could change settings or assign a different time server in the chronyd service. Apply the change using a MachineConfig, and it will be deployed to all worker or master nodes.

1. To create the contents of the chrony.conf file and encode it as base64, do the following:

```
$ cat << EOF | base64
server clock.example.com iburst
driftfile /var/lib/chrony/drift
makestep 1.0 3
rtcsync
logdir /var/log/chrony
```

```
EOF
c2VydmVyIGNsb2NrLnJlZGhhdC5jb20gaWJ1cnN0CmRyaWZ0ZmlsZSAvdmFyL2x
pYi9jaHJvbnkv
ZHJpZnQKbWFrZXN0ZXAgMS4wIDMKcnRjc3luYwpsb2dkaXIgL3Zhci9sb2cvY2h
yb255Cg==
```

2 Replacing the base64 string with the one created earlier, as shown in the following example. In this example, the file is added to all worker nodes :

```
$ cat << EOF > ./50_workers-chrony-configuration.yaml
```

```
apiVersion: machineconfiguration.openshift.io/v1
kind: MachineConfig
metadata:
  labels:
    machineconfiguration.openshift.io/role: worker
  name: workers-chrony-configuration
spec:
  config:
    ignition:
      config: {}
      security:
        tls: {}
      timeouts: {}
      version: 2.2.0
    networkd: {}
    passwd: {}
    storage:
      files:
      - contents:
          source: data:text/plain;charset=utf-
```

```
AvdmFyL2xpYi9jaHJvbnkvZHJpZnQKbWFrZXN0ZXAgMS4wIDMKcnRjc3luYwpsb
2dkaXIgL3Zhci9sb2cvY2hyb255Cg==
          verification: {}
        filesystem: root
        mode: 420
        path: /etc/chrony.conf
  osImageURL: ""
EOF
```

3 Make a backup copy of the configuration file.

4 This file could either be used during OpenShift installation or via the MCO after the cluster is running. If the cluster is not up yet, generate manifest files, add this file to the openshift directory, and continue to create the cluster. If the cluster is already running, apply the file as follows:

```
$ oc apply -f ./50_workers-chrony-configuration.yaml
```

As noted earlier, this procedure can be repeated for any file to add to every worker or master node in a cluster.

Ongoing RHCOS Security Issues

Once an OpenShift cluster is up and running, there are ongoing tasks which can be done to ensure the underlying RHCOS systems remain secure. A few elements of the underlying design of OpenShift 4 should help approach these topics:

- ***Troubleshooting***
  Because OpenShift 4 is designed to be managed from the cluster itself, directly logging in to a node, typically using ssh, is not recommended. Instead there are both web-based (the OpenShift console) and command-line (oc command) methods for troubleshooting the security of RHCOS nodes.

- ***Upgrading***
  RHCOS technologies, such as rpm-ostree, provide a different upgrade technique than typical RPM software package upgrades using yum and dnf. Instead, RHCOS upgrades are done by delivering a new ostree layer (via a container) to overlay the existing deployment.

Troubleshooting RHCOS Security

To troubleshoot RHCOS systems in an OpenShift cluster, the OpenShift web console or the `oc` command may be used. This is supportive of a rapid incident intervention strategy. Other means of accessing RHCOS nodes in a cluster, which are discussed later, should be used primarily to troubleshoot nodes that are inaccessible from the cluster.

Using the Web Console to Troubleshoot

After an OpenShift cluster is up and running, a URL to the cluster's web console and credentials for logging in are presented in the CLI output of the installer.

Once logged in to the console, issues associated with each node can be found in a variety of ways. In particular, the Compute sections in the left navigation menu offer RHCOS node information, as illustrated in Figure 2.1 :

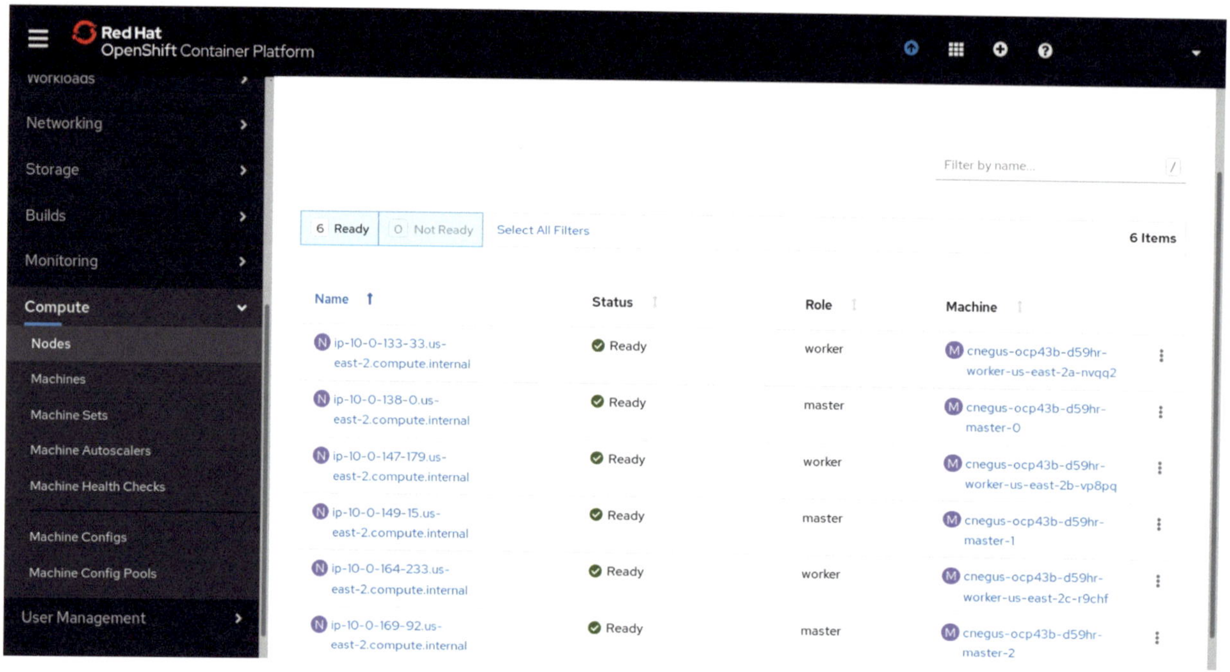

Figure 2.1: Troubleshoot RHCOS Systems from the OpenShift Console Compute Area

From the `Nodes` selection, the names of the nodes assigned to the cluster appear, while the `Machines` section helps identify the purposes of each node (such as whether it is a worker or master node).

For security purposes, `Machine Health Checks` is available. Turning on health checks creates reporting of the security state of each machine. Checking the Machine Configs and Machine Config Pools reveals how the machines are configured.

Troubleshooting Nodes from the Command Line

The oc command is the primary tool for interacting with the nodes in an OpenShift cluster. With oc, issues can be pursued by listing available nodes, viewing logs, checking pod activity, and creating and deleting Kubernetes components.

Use `oc adm must-gather` to gather a variety of logs and resources from the cluster and drop them into a `must-gather*` directory on the local system. In particular, `host_service_logs` files provide insights into critical host-specific services, such as kubelet and crio :

```
$ oc adm must-gather
```

If security issues with a node are suspected, its workload can immediately be moved, and it can be isolated from further use until an investigator decides it is usable again or chooses to delete it. To isolate a node from accepting new workloads and drain the node in preparation for shutdown, use :

```
$ oc adm cordon <yournode>
$ oc adm drain <yournode>
```

At this point, a new node could be spun up to replace the old one. If the node issue is resolved, the current one may be made available again via `oc adm uncordon`.

Troubleshooting with Direct Shell Access to Nodes

Deeper debugging of a node might require direct access to that node from a shell. Direct user access to OpenShift RHCOS nodes by a privileged user is normally *strongly discouraged*. If something goes critically wrong with a node, the recommended course of action is to bring up a new node and remove the broken one. Times when responders may want direct access to a node, however, include :

- ***Recurring problem analysis***
  If developers experience recurring problems requiring node-specific troubleshooting data, they may need privileged access via a shell, so they can interactively run commands such as `sosreport`, `strace`, or `tcpdump` to examine what is happening.

- ***Cluster inaccessibility***
  If the master nodes are inaccessible, `oc` commands will not be able to access the cluster for troubleshooting, intervention, or repair. Logging in directly to a node may be a viable alternative to deleting the cluster and starting over.

- ***Incident response root cause analysis***
  The node is taken offline and analyzed to determine its causative role or to correlate events in a network-oriented incident.

- ***Forensics***
  The node is taken offline, and a shell is required for forensic analysis.

Different access topology strategies that allow direct privileged access to nodes include :

- Direct : The `oc debug` command opens a container on a node with root privileges via a shell

- Via Bastion : Setting up a bastion host requires additional work but makes it easier to audit privileged activities performed on cluster nodes.

Privileged Shell Access with `oc debug`

Using the `oc debug` command as the kubeadmin user provides shell access to an RHCOS node. Before setting out on this course, there are a few risk elements to consider:

- Because the kubeadmin user has root (privileged) access to the nodes, the kubeadmin account should be protected in the same manner as root. See the *kubeadmin User* section of Chapter 5: Identity and Access Management, to consider how to lock down this account and make use of its privileges only in emergencies.
- While an audit can record the user invoking oc debug, there is no user-specific auditing done of privileged activities once root shell access to the node is established.

Once a privileged user understands the risks of using `oc debug`, that command is used to debug a node as follows:

1. Get the name of the node to access:

```
$ oc get nodes
```

2. Use oc debug to connect to the node, replacing `<yournode>` with the name of the node to access:

```
$ oc debug node/<yournode>
        Starting pod/ip-10-0-136-20us-east-2computeinternal-
debug …
To use host binaries, run `chroot /host`
If you don't see a command prompt, try pressing enter.
sh-4.2#
```

This command starts a pod that runs the support-tools container and opens a shell inside that container. The node's root file system is available from `/host` within that container.

3. Use `chroot` to open a bash shell that looks directly at the node's root file system :

```
sh-4.3# chroot /host bash
[root@ip-10-0-136-20 /]#
```

4. Run `toolbox` to pull in a container that has a large set of debugging tools someone can use to troubleshoot the node :

```
[root@ip-10-0-136-20 /]# toolbox
        Trying to pull registry.redhat.io/rhel8/support-tools
           ...Getting image source signatures
Copying blob fd8daf2668d1 done
Copying blob 1457434f891b done
        ...
```

At this point, any available troubleshooting can be run from the node or the toolbox so that they act on the `/host` directory. Tools can be temporarily installed. Some examples of useful troubleshooting commands include :

- sosreport – This collects data about the configuration and ongoing activities on the node for use in diagnosing problems or for passing on to a support organization for help
- tcpdump – This displays data from network interfaces on the node
- strace – This can trace system calls and signals on a running process

- fdisk – This displays, and allows, changes to information about disk partitions
- lsof – show open files and network ports

Setting up a Bastion Host

By creating a bastion host with access to the RHCOS nodes on the cluster, it is possible to have a more secure and auditable way to gain access to those nodes. A bastion host can be set up to :

- Have separate login accounts for everyone accessing the bastion host
- Log who has accessed the bastion host
- Create user-specific keys to provide some level of log correlation
- Log across multiple nodes

Red Hat offers some guidance for setting up a bastion pod (https://access.redhat.com/solutions/4073041) and deploying a bastion host for OpenShift 4 on AWS (https://access.redhat.com/solutions/4057081).

RHCOS Upgrades

Security practitioners are generally required to mitigate risk via consistently applied OS updates. This ensures vulnerabilities are mitigated ("patched") and components work correctly. By managing the OS as part of the cluster, the **Machine Config Operator** can apply upgrades automatically in a coordinated fashion, minimizing the impact on the running cluster.

Red Hat delivers timely RHCOS updates to clusters as part of the OpenShift release payload. Thus, RHCOS upgrades move consistently in lock step with cluster upgrades and share the same versioning and cadence. This ensures RHCOS releases are in sync with cluster components. For example, the container runtime (CRI-O) version needs to remain compatible with the Kubernetes version used by the Kubernetes api-server. OpenShift promises these compatibilities remain when an update arrives with the rpm-ostree system. To ensure supply chain integrity, only release payloads with verified signatures are applied to clusters.

Since MachineConfigs are highly flexible, custom MachineConfigs added by a cluster admin may interact with the built-in MachineConfigs in unknown ways during upgrades.

Cluster operators should track certain types of customized changes, so they may be re-examined for impact during a change management review. This is especially true when dealing with crio and kubelet configs since changes to those configs can affect the cluster functionality. If a cluster has custom MachineConfigs that :

- overrides something in the base MachineConfigs
- depends on a file or service defined in an OpenShift-provided MachineConfig
- depends on a specific package installed via the OpenShift Image or cluster

...then upgrades should be cautiously applied.

To ensure a smooth upgrade :

1. Roll out updates slowly, across various clusters and across nodes.
2. For extra caution, pause the relevant MachineConfigPool before upgrade, run upgrade, check the rendered MachineConfigs after the MachineConfig Controller updates them (confirm they were upgraded by looking at the controller-version hash annotation on them).
3. Look over both the base MachineConfigs and the rendered MachineConfigs for the relevant pool to make sure they look correct.
4. Unpause the MachineConfigPool to roll out updates to the nodes.

3. Container Security

Linux containers are fundamental enablers of digital transformation initiatives. Microservices architecture and cloud-native application experts recommend that cloud-native applications are packaged, deployed, and managed as container images, with the help of container orchestrators such as OpenShift.

As an essential construct for logical separation of workloads, containers and associated security features provide the compartmentalization needed to enhance isolation and protection for both workloads and hosts. The security capabilities derived from the Linux kernel are specified and blended to achieve the desired security posture. Best practices suggest that the resulting security configurations inherently do well at protecting the host and workloads from each other.

Container and host security capabilities come from four large areas :

- *Linux namespaces* create a partitioning of system resources, forming the logical boundaries around the structure of the container
- The *secure computing (seccomp)* feature provides a way to filter system call availability within a container

- *Linux capabilities* allow the reduction of privileges that would normally be allowed within the context of the "root" user

- *Security-Enhanced Linux (SELinux)* enforces mandatory access control for system processes, services, files, and network resources. Working upstream with the National Security Agency, Red Hat introduced SELinux in its Red Hat Enterprise Linux 4 product more than 15 years ago.

This chapter will describe how to manage and orchestrate the implementation of the features and capabilities provided by the facilities described above.

Describing Linux Containers

To understand how containers affect security, multiple perspectives need to be considered :

- From the operating system (OS) perspective, a container is just a process that runs within a sandbox isolated from processes running outside of its sandbox. A Linux host creates this sandbox using standard kernel features such as namespaces, control groups, and SELinux.

- From a system administrator perspective, a container is an application that is portable across different environments. This application is deployed, unchanged, on different cloud providers, bare-metal servers, and virtualized servers.

- From a developer perspective, a container is a way to package an application together with all its dependencies. Containers provide a universal packaging format that is not dependent on the programming language runtime.

Many IT professionals compare containers to virtual machines (VMs) because both technologies provide isolation and universal packaging. The following figure compares traditional applications, running as regular, non-sandboxed processes, with some applications running on containers and others running on VMs.

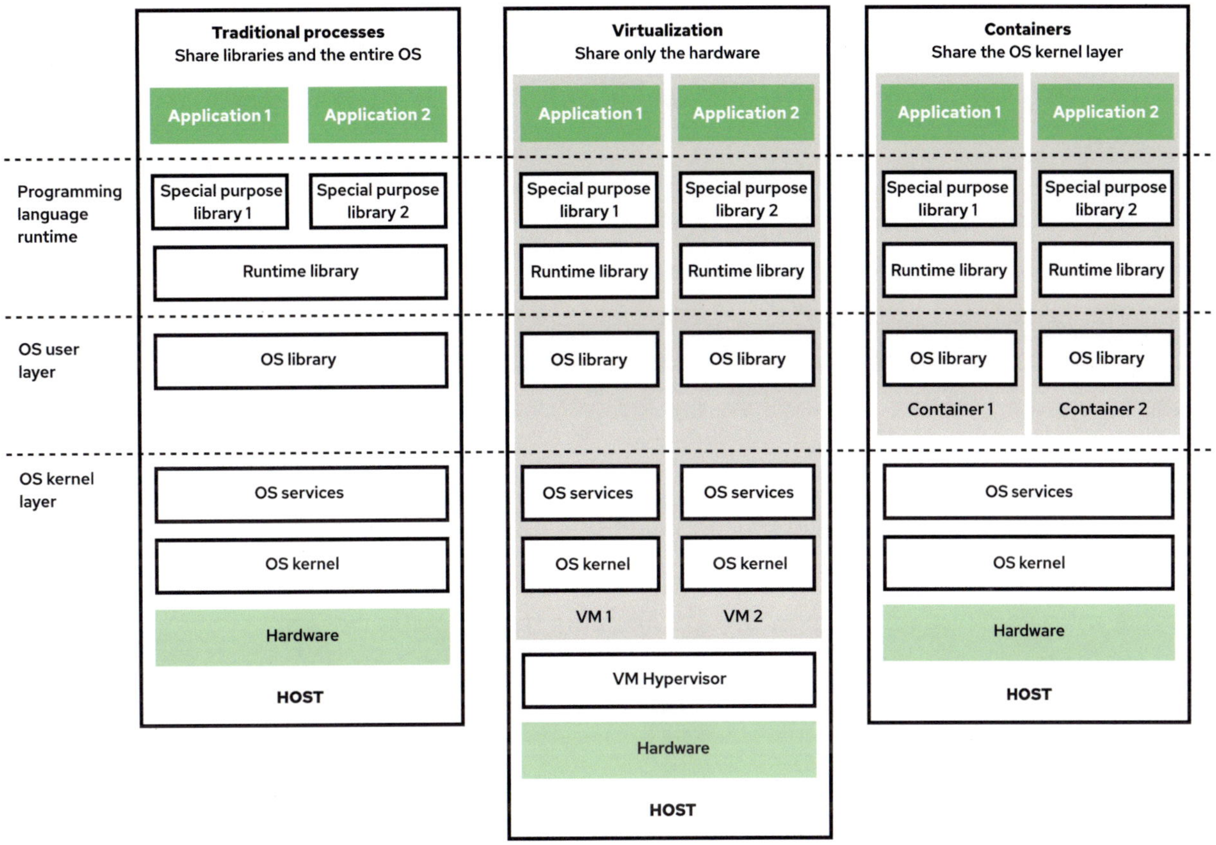

Figure 3.1: The Workload and Infrastructure Evolution to Containers

Containers split the traditional packaging of an operating system into a kernel layer and a user layer. The OS kernel layer runs on the host and includes kernel and operating system services such as networked file system and time synchronization clients. The OS user layer includes operating system libraries such as the glibc and tools such as the Bash shell.

A container runs a minimal user layer tailored for that specific application. All containers share the OS kernel layer from the host. Containerized applications still invoke system calls against the host layer and OS service APIs using the same mechanisms as traditional applications. With containers, there is no intermediate layer that adds overhead.

Comparing Containers and Virtual Machines for Application Isolation

Both containers and virtual machines (VMs) isolate applications so that vulnerabilities from one application do not affect other applications sharing the same host. Most organizations cannot update the OS kernel layer for security fixes quickly enough to respond to breaches because they first need to ensure that the applications continue to work under the new releases.

The host OS can be updated without breaking a containerized application because most applications do not depend on a specific OS kernel and OS service release. They depend on the OS libraries that provide access to kernel system calls and to the APIs of OS services. Unlike a VM, a container doesn't include its own kernel, limiting the container's attack surface.

Container images enable faster continuous integration (CI) and continuous delivery (CD) pipelines because building container images is faster than building VM images, and containers start faster than VMs. This allows organizations to more frequently deploy production and reduces time on security fixes.

Creating Linux Containers with a Container Engine

A container engine provides a set of tools for tasks such as creating container images and starting containers. CRI-O is the container engine of OpenShift. As an implementation of the Kubernetes CRI (Container Runtime Interface), CRI-O enables the use of OCI (Open Container Initiative) compatible runtimes.

CRI-O is the default container engine for OpenShift 4, replacing Docker, which was the default in OpenShift 3.11. From a security standpoint, CRI-O was developed to :

- ***Align with Kubernetes releases***
  By aligning with Kubernetes releases, updates to CRI-O are always done with the sole purpose of working better with the current Kubernetes release.

- ***Have a reduced attack surface***
  The scope of CRI-O is tied to the Container Runtime Interface (CRI). By not including extra features for direct command-line use or other orchestration facilities, CRI-O's footprint is smaller and vulnerabilities are reduced.

- ***Improve performance***
  A smaller feature set encourages better performance among the supported features.

- ***Allow the inclusion of different container runtimes***
  Currently, OpenShift supports the runc container runtime. However, as other runtimes become available for full support, such as the Kata Containers runtime, they can be supported by CRI-O.

Most interaction with CRI-O is done by managing containers from the OpenShift cluster. However, for advanced security issues, there are ways to tune CRI-O or access CRI-O directly.

CRI-O Architecture

CRI-O is not supported as a stand-alone container engine and must be used as the container engine for OpenShift. To run containers without OpenShift use `Podman` on a RHEL host.

The Figure 3.2 shows the various OpenShift components and their role in the creation of a pod. Please note that the directories `/container/image` and `/container/storage` are given as an example and may differ depending on specific deployments. By default, for OpenShift deployments, CRI-O storage is under `/var/lib/containers`.

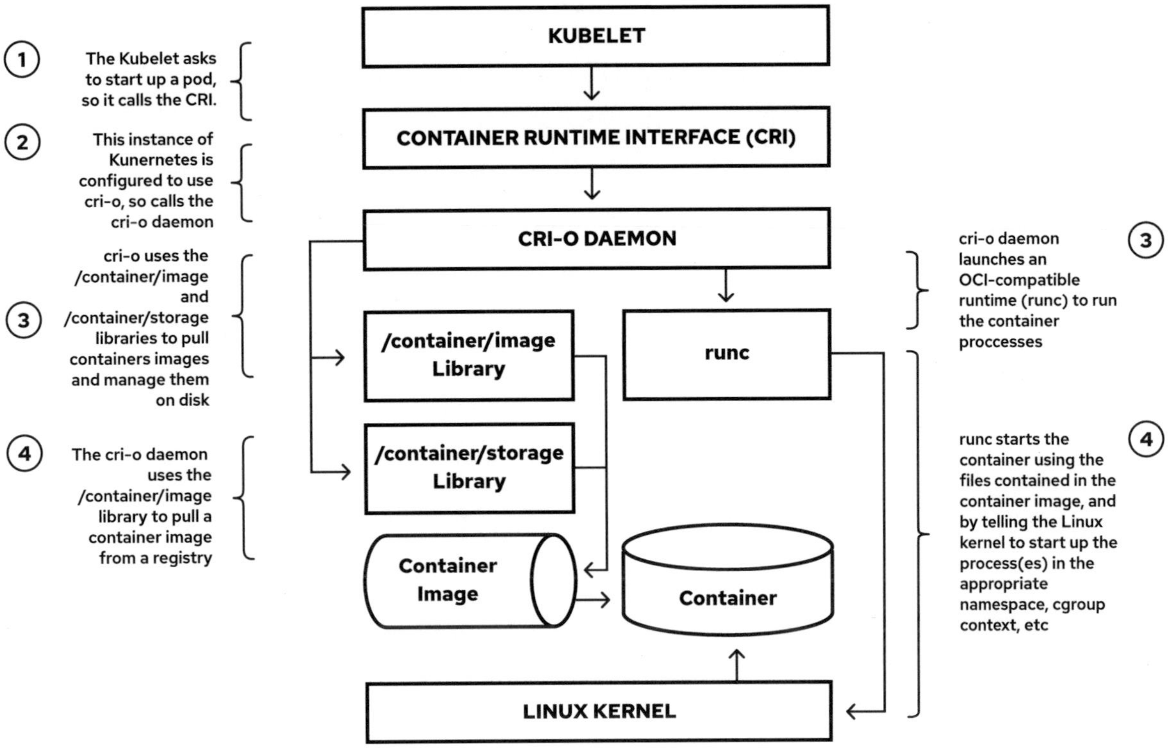

Figure 3.2: CRI-O Interface with Kubernetes

CRI-O supports FIPS-Mode, in that it configures the containers to know that they are running in FIPS mode.

Tuning CRI-O

While direct tuning of CRI-O is not encouraged, adaptation of CRI-O to meet advanced security needs can be done by modifying the contents of the `/etc/crio/crio.conf` file. In crio.conf set such things as PID limits to set the maximum number of processes allowed in a container. See Chapter 2 : Red Hat Enterprise Linux CoreOS Security for information on how to use a MachineConfig to change an RHCOS configuration file.

Accessing CRI-O Directly

Just as CRI-O tuning is not encouraged, neither is direct access to CRI-O. However, for debugging purposes, access CRI-O directly using the `crictl` command from any OpenShift node. For example, on an OpenShift node list running containers and see logging messages for a specific container as follows :

```
# crictl ps
49f7832d3c4b9 quay.io/openshift-release-dev/ocp-v4.0-art-
dev@sha256…


     5 hours ago    Running    openvswitch    0b989143485eb


# crictl logs 49f7832d3c4b9
```

Other features in the crictl command can be used to manage containers and container images on an OpenShift node. For examples of other uses of crictl, see the crictl page on Github. A blog from Dan Walsh further details the complementary relationship between crictl and Podman tools: https://www.openshift.com/blog/crictl-vs-podman

Container Security in the Linux Kernel

The part of a container engine that effectively starts and monitors containers is the container runtime. runc is the container runtime of OpenShift.

A container runtime leverages a number of Linux kernel features to start a container :

- The main feature is namespaces. Namespaces create the sandbox that isolates a process from other processes running outside of the sandbox. Namespaces provide, among other things, a segregated view of the process table, host file system, and network.

- Another important feature is control groups (Cgroups). Sandboxed processes are regular processes managed by the host kernel sharing host hardware resources, such as memory and CPU. Control groups enforce limits on process consumption of CPU slices, memory pages, and I/O capacity, preventing a single process from using up all the host capacity for itself.

- Though not strictly necessary to create a sandboxed process, SELinux, capabilities, and seccomp complement namespaces and control groups to prevent a process from breaking its confinement and interfering indirectly with other processes in the same host.

Other software packages, such as operating system service managers, systemd, and web browsers including Firefox, use some of the same kernel features to run processes inside a sandbox. Linux containers are just one specific scenario, though more general in purpose, of creating sandboxed processes.

The main role of a container engine is to make it easier to leverage these features by, for example, providing high-level command-line tools and programming libraries that interface with a container runtime and container registries. Without a container engine, a systems administrator would need to manage each of these kernel features individually, using low-level OS commands which would be very time-consuming and error-prone.

A container runtime is, in essence, a helper that starts processes inside a set of control groups and namespaces, under restricted SELinux contexts, capabilities set, and seccomp settings.

A container runtime keeps track of the processes it started and assigns them a container ID. These container IDs have meaning only to the container runtime that created them. They have no meaning to the kernel.

A container engine also provides troubleshooting features such as starting new processes under the same sandbox as an existing container. These are useful for running diagnostic tools inside a container to inspect the state of containerized processes and interface with file systems and networks in the same way that the container does.

Figure 3.3 shows four broad areas of security parameters that can be applied to containers. These areas will be covered in detail in the following sections.

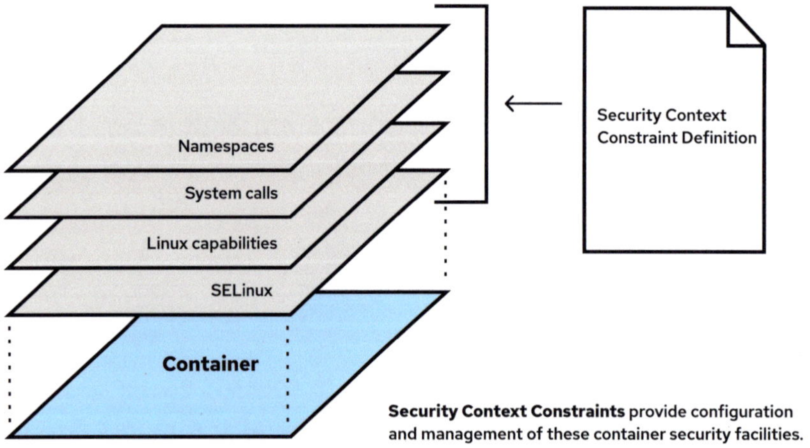

Figure 3.3: Security Context Facilities

Describing Linux Namespaces

Linux namespaces functionality is a kernel feature that provides resource abstraction for processes. It is a way to change a process view of the system. A process inside a namespace only sees the resources associated with that namespace.

Linux namespaces provide an isolation level for several kinds of resources : Process Identifier (PID), Inter-process Communication (IPC), network, UNIX Time Sharing (UTS), mount points, control groups (cgroups), and user. For example, processes in a network namespace have their own network stack and cannot see network resources such as interfaces and listening ports from other namespaces or the host system.

By providing that resource isolation layer, the Linux namespaces are an essential part in the implementation of containers.

Introducing the Linux Namespaces Types

The Linux kernel provides the following namespaces :

PID : Processes in a PID namespace have their own process ID number space. The first process in the namespace gets the PID 1. From outside, the ps command still shows those processes, but the kernel maps the PID in the namespace to a PID on the host system.

IPC : IPC namespaces isolate the System V IPC (interprocess communication) resources. A process in an IPC namespace can only see and use the IPC objects in that namespace.

Network : Processes in a network namespace have their own network resources, such as devices, IP stacks, firewall rules, and routing tables. Network namespaces enable the building of virtual networks.

UTS : A UNIX Time Sharing namespace isolates the host name and domain name. In this way, each namespace can have a custom host name. Changing the hostname inside the namespace does not change the hostname on the host system.

Mount : Processes in a mount namespace can only see the mount points in that namespace. They cannot interact in any way with the mount points from the host system or another mount namespace. Mount namespaces abstract a complete file system view.

Cgroup : The system exposes the cgroups as a directory hierarchy under `/sys/fs/cgroup/`. Cgroup namespaces restrict the view of that directory hierarchy. This way the processes in a cgroup namespace cannot get any information on the resource limits set to other processes on the system. Notice that one set limits on resources at the cgroup level; cgroup namespaces only restrict the view of the directory hierarchy.

User : User namespaces isolate the user and group identifiers. A process inside a user namespace appears with a user ID (UID) and a group ID (GID) that can be different on the host system. This is especially useful to give root access to a process inside a container. Outside the container, the system maps the process to an unprivileged user account. This way, a vulnerable process that needs to run as root can do so inside its user namespace. If it manages to escape the namespace, it only has the rights of the associated unprivileged user account. User namespaces are already available in host tools such as Podman but are not yet implemented in Kubernetes.

A process can belong to different namespace types at the same time. It can belong to a PID namespace which has its own process ID number space, and to a network namespace and an IPC namespace.

Managing Resources with Cgroups

Control groups (or Cgroups for short) are a way of limiting access to system resources.

Some of the different resources that can be limited are :

- blkio – Sets limits on the available bandwidth to and from block devices
- cpu – Sets limits on the available CPU time
- cpuset – Sets limits on the available CPUs and memory regions in NUMA systems
- memory – Sets limits on the available memory
- freezer – Task in this cgroup are suspended

These subsystems are also known as *resource controllers* or controllers. OpenShift uses control groups to fairly distribute the available resources between tenants. Cgroups also protect container processes from being overrun by rogue or greedy processes.

Linux Capabilities

Traditionally, in Linux, there are two kinds of user identities : privileged and non-privileged, with the root user being the privileged account that can do anything. This absence of granularity has been problematic as processes that need to perform any administrative tasks run as the privileged root account and, in the absence of other protection mechanisms, can do anything. Therefore, Linux provides capabilities – groups of superuser's powers that can be selectively enabled or disabled to limit the power the root user normally has. One can indeed think of the root user in the traditional sense as possessing all existing capabilities.

Many containerized applications only need a subset of the root privileges, for example a container running an httpd server might need to bind to port 80, the rest of its operations can be performed as a non-root user. In terms of capabilities, the http server does need the `CAP_NET_BIND` capability even when running as root in order to bind to a privileged port. On the other hand, there is no reason most containers need to set the system time, which normally root would have allowed, so there is no need for them to have the `CAP_SYS_TIME` capability.

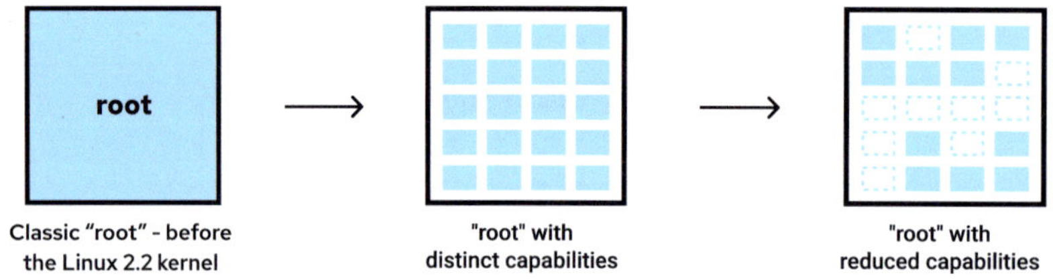

Figure 3.4: Understanding Root's Reduction in Capabilities

The classic behavior of the root user (illustrated in the first box of Figure 3.4) saw all capabilities enabled – this reflects the root user's capabilities before the introduction of the Linux 2.2 kernel. The second box indicates that with the Linux 2.2 kernel the notion of root privileges were split into distinct units called *capabilities*. An overview of all available capabilities can be found in the "capabilities" manual page.

The capabilities of a running container on a RHEL host can be viewed by running `podman inspect $container`. Notice that the default capability set doesn't include `CAP_SYS_ADMIN`, because if a malicious actor or process took control of the container, `CAP_SYS_ADMIN` would easily allow access to the host kernel. For example, the process to mount file systems could be used to remount one of the read-only file systems such as the `/sys` filesystem, as read-write because the `CAP_SYS_ADMIN` was improperly added to the container.

When running containers locally with Podman, a capability might be added or dropped from the default set using the `--cap-add` or `--cap-drop` parameters, respectively. For example, one can run `ntpd` in a container and allow it to set the system time by running :

```
$ sudo podman run -d --cap-add SYS_TIME ntpd
```

With OpenShift, capabilities are added or removed relative to the default set that the container runtime provides and can be set in the `securityContext` attribute of a container. Note that there also exists a `securityContext` attribute on the pod level.

While the container level `securityContext` generally overrides the pod level `securityContext`, it also has some extra fields of which capabilities is one.

With that in mind, let's schedule a pod that drops the `CAP_SYS_CHOWN` capability, and even though it runs as root, it's not permitted to change ownership of the `/tmp` directory. Using a pod definition such as :

```
$ cat pod-drop-caps.yaml
apiVersion: "v1"
kind: Pod
metadata:
  name: caps-test
spec:
  containers:
        - name: caps-container
            image: registry.access.redhat.com/ubi8/ubi
            command: ["/bin/sh"]
            args: ["-c", "chown bin.bin /tmp; ls -ld /tmp"]
            securityContext:
```

```
                capabilities:
              drop:
              - CHOWN
  restartPolicy: Never
$ oc create -f pod-drop-caps.yaml
pod/caps-test created
$ oc logs caps-test
uid=0(root) gid=0(root) groups=0(root)
chown: changing ownership of '/tmp': Operation not permitted
drwxrwxrwt. 1 root root 6 Mar 31 14:54 /tmp
```

Security Context Constraints (SCCs) provide the facility that controls security capabilities allocation during pod creation. This is what prevents a user from arbitrarily adding powerful privileges such as CAP_SYS_ADMIN.

In SCC instances, there are three fields related to capabilities :

- `requiredDropCapabilities:` These capabilities will always be dropped and cannot be added
- `allowedCapabilities:` These capabilities can be added. There are two special values `null` and `*` that can be added. `Null` means that no additional capabilities can be added and `*` means that any capability can be added.
- `defaultAddCapabilities:` These capabilities will be added to the pod unless the pod explicitly drops them

Regular users are restricted by the SCC/restricted SCC which has the relevant attributes set to the following values :

```
allowedCapabilities: null
defaultAddCapabilities: null
requiredDropCapabilities:
```

```
- KILL
- MKNOD
- SETUID
- SETGID
```

This means that the user constrained by the restricted SCC cannot gain any new capabilities. Let's try this out by running a pod that would gain the CAP_SYS_ADMIN capability, essentially becoming root.

```
$ oc whoami
user1
```

With a pod :

```
apiVersion: "v1"
kind: Pod
metadata:
  name: caps-test
spec:
  containers:
        - name: caps-container
            image: registry.access.redhat.com/ubi8/ubi
            command: ["/bin/sh"]
            args: ["-c", "cat /proc/1/status"]
            securityContext:
                capabilities:
              add:
      - SYS_ADMIN
  restartPolicy: Never
```

This results in an error before the pod is even created:

```
$ oc create -f pod-add-caps.yaml
Error from server (Forbidden): error when creating "pod-add-
caps.yaml": pods "caps-test" is forbidden: unable to validate
against any security context constraint: [capabilities.add:
Invalid value: "SYS_ADMIN": capability may not be added]
```

By default, in OpenShift, only the **privileged** SCC allows capabilities to be gained, but all SCCs allow capabilities to be dropped. Learn more about SCCs later in this chapter and in the official OpenShift documentation.

Secure Computing (seccomp) Profiles

Typically, a container or an OpenShift pod runs a single application that runs one or a set of well-defined tasks. Therefore, the application usually requires only a small subset of the underlying operating system kernel APIs – for example, a container running an httpd server has no business calling the `mount(2)` system call. At the same time, all containers on the host, which might run many different applications, share the same kernel which is used by the host itself (using the previous example, the host surely does need the mount syscall) and would have access to the whole kernel API.

To limit the attack vector of a subverted process running within a container, the *seccomp* (secure computing mode) Linux kernel feature can be used to limit the process running in a container to only call a subset of the available system calls. Both Podman and OpenShift ship with default seccomp profiles that are used for a container unless otherwise specified. The default profiles cut the number of available syscalls substantially, from over 300 available in Linux kernel 5.x, to roughly half. That number is still more than a typical application would use.

Let's show seccomp in action. With Podman on a RHEL host, the default seccomp policy is stored at `/usr/share/containers/seccomp.json`, optionally overridden by `/etc/containers/seccomp.json`. Our example application will be just `ls /`, which can be initiated with `podman run fedora:latest ls /`. As the next step, we're going to modify the default seccomp policy and remove the `stat()` system call, which is what ls used to learn the details about the `/` directory. Copy the file `/usr/share/containers/seccomp.json` to another location, remove the `stat(1)` call, and run the Podman invocation again, this time pointing at the edited policy:

```
$ cp /usr/share/containers/seccomp.json /tmp/seccomp.json
$ vim /tmp/seccomp.json # remove the stat call
$ podman run --security-opt seccomp=/tmp/seccomp.json -it
fedora:latest ls /
```

This command would now fail because the new seccomp profile no longer allows the ls binary to execute the `stat(1)` syscall. Even though this is a negative example, we brought a well-functioning application and broke it with a too restrictive policy, and hopefully it illustrates the point:

```
$ podman run --security-opt seccomp=/tmp/seccomp.json -it
fedora:latest ls /
ls: cannot access '/': Operation not permitted
```

In OpenShift, any pod annotated with `seccomp.security.alpha.kubernetes.io/pod` would use the seccomp profile specified in value of the annotation. The annotations are checked by the SCC admission controller against the current SCC linked to the current user's role. If the seccomp profile is allowed for this user, the kubelet runs the pod on a node with the specified seccomp profile. Note that the profile definition file must exist on the node where the pod is scheduled.

To put it all together, in order to schedule a pod with a custom seccomp profile, one needs to:

- Make sure the seccomp policy exists on the node. The default directory for the seccomp profiles is at `/var/lib/kubelet/seccomp/`
- Make sure the profile is allowed in an SCC linked to the role of the user scheduling the pods
- Annotate the pods with the desired seccomp profile

Let's try the same example as we showed earlier with Podman, this time in an OpenShift environment. Copy the default CRI-O seccomp profile (`/etc/crio/seccomp.json`) from one of the cluster nodes to your local system. To do this, open a debug session, then copy the file from the debug pod to your local system :

```
$ oc debug node/ip-10-0-164-156.ec2.internal
```

With the debug session still active, from a second shell, log in to the cluster (`oc login`), then copy the file to the local system :

```
$ oc cp \ default/ip-10-0-164-156ec2internal-
debug:host/etc/crio/seccomp.json .
$ cp seccomp.json seccomp-nostat.json
$ vim seccomp-nostat-json # remove the “stat” system call
$ diff -u  seccomp.json seccomp-nostat.json
--- seccomp.json              2020-04-09 21:11:56.410394097
+0200
+++ seccomp-nostat.json    2020-04-09 19:57:20.113819802 +0200
@@ -318,7 +318,6 @@
                                 "socketcall",
                                 "socketpair",
                                 "splice",
-                                  "stat",
                                 "stat64",
```

```
                                    "statfs",
                                    "statfs64",
```

Next, using MachineConfig, upload the file to `/var/lib/kubelet/seccomp/seccomp-nostat.json`. Follow the Machine Config Operator documentation, just substitute the content and the paths.

Once the file is there, create a pod using a profile such as the one below :

```
apiVersion: "v1"
kind: Pod
metadata:
  name: seccomp-test
  annotations:
        seccomp.security.alpha.kubernetes.io/pod:
"localhost/seccomp-nostat.json"
spec:
  containers:
        - name: seccomp-container
            image: registry.access.redhat.com/ubi8/ubi
            command: ["/bin/ls", "/"]
  restartPolicy: Never
```

If the pod is run now, the ls command will fail, because it's not allowed to execute the `stat(1)` system call :

```
$ oc create -f pod-seccomp.yaml
$ oc get pods
NAME                   READY   STATUS          RESTARTS   AGE
seccomp-test           0/1         Error           0
         42m
$ oc logs seccomp-test

ls: cannot access '/': Operation not permitted
```

In addition to the `localhost/path/to/profile` annotation value, there exists a reserved value `runtime/default` that will make sure that the pod uses the default policy of the CRI-O runtime. It is recommended that either the runtime default or a more restrictive policy is used.

It should be noted that no security technology exists in isolation; rather they are layered. Seccomp profiles coexist with Linux capabilities; for example, it is possible to allow a certain syscall on condition that a process also has a capability set. It is possible to allow certain syscalls only if a process has a capability set:

```
{
  "names": [
    "delete_module",
    "init_module",
    "finit_module",
    "query_module"
  ],
  "action": "SCMP_ACT_ALLOW",
  "args": [],
  "comment": "",
  "includes": {
    "caps": [
      "CAP_SYS_MODULE"
    ]
  },
  "excludes": {}
};
```

For example, the above permits the process to call the `init_module or delete_module` system calls, but only if the calling process also has the `CAP_SYS_MODULE` capability.

Writing seccomp profiles for an application can be tedious and often requires deep knowledge of the application in addition to the programming language or framework. As an example, the developer must be aware that a framework that sets up a network server to accept connections would translate into calling the `socket(2)`, `bind(2)`, and `listen(2)` system calls. On the one hand, writing a seccomp policy that is too loose might leave some syscalls wide open. On the other hand, write a seccomp policy that is too tight and the application would fail with errors such as, *Permission denied*. Since most real-world seccomp profiles would probably err on the side of being a little loose, it is important to layer security protections to make sure that if a malicious actor bypasses one layer, such as seccomp, they would be stopped by another layer, such as the capabilities or SELinux.

Unfortunately, currently there are no tools or operators provided by OpenShift that would help develop the seccomp profiles. There are some third-party tools, or alternatively, the developer might want to trace the calls made by their application in a CI pipeline through tools such as eBPF and continuously augment their seccomp policy. A talk by Dan Walsh on the topic outlines some of the available options.

Security-Enhanced Linux

Security-Enhanced Linux started as a project within the National Security Agency (NSA) to bring *mandatory access control* (MAC) to Linux. Since its introduction, subsequent SELinux development has been a joint effort between the NSA, Red Hat, and the community of SELinux developers. Given the availability of many other facilities that can improve the security and isolation of containers, SELinux presents as an integral component that ensures containers embrace the mandatory access control posture. In this regard, SELinux enhances the container security experience by truly separating containers from each other while protecting the host in an intuitive manner.

Basic Concepts

As other authors have already mentioned, SELinux is a *labeling system*. This means that everything in Linux has a label :

- Processes
- Files
- Directories
- System objects

Policy rules control access between processes and objects, e.g. a process labeled **container_t** can access files labeled **container_file_t**.

With SELinux enabled, everything is denied unless there is a rule that explicitly allows it. This makes for a very solid security policy.

Labels for objects are called **SELinux contexts**, and contexts themselves are composed of user, role, type, and security level. Something to keep in mind when writing policies is that it is normal to specify that a certain SELinux **type** can interact with another SELinux **type**. It is not common to specify the full context of an object. So, a container running on a node would have an SELinux context as follows :

System_u :system_r:container_t:s0:c667,c123

Where :

- **system_u** is the user
- **system_r** is the role

- **container_t** is the type; this is also sometimes referred to as **domain**
- **S0 :c667, c123** is the security level or MCS label

Unconfined Domains

Normally, in Red Hat systems, every provided RPM package comes with an SELinux policy which enables the process to run securely. If installing a binary out-of-band that normally won't come with an SELinux policy, run that binary with an `unconfined domain` (`unconfined_t`). This type is allowed to do almost anything in the system and should normally not be used for daemons. Instead, this is meant to allow users to interact with the system without SELinux blocking them.

SELinux in Containers

While SELinux wasn't designed specifically to address container security, there was already previous work done on securing virtual machines. Similar concepts were taken into use and were adapted towards securing containers.

One important thing to consider is that all containers are started, by default, with the label, `container_t`. This is a predefined label that already has a policy attached to it. It is already very constrained, which makes it a great default!

For practical usage, containers with the `container_t` can :

- Read, write, and execute files labeled `container_file_t`
- Read and execute files labeled `usr_t`, which are files in `/usr`

- Read files labeled `etc_t`, which are files under `/etc`
- Bind to any unused port on the host

There are other capabilities and details for this label, but these are better left as implementation details.

Normally, any process running as `container_t` would be able to interact with any file labeled `container_file_t`; this behavior would then imply that containers can interact or meddle with each other's files. It would then be possible for a container to tamper with another container's sensitive data, which is undesirable. Fortunately, there is another mechanism that protects containers from attacking each other, and these are the *MCS labels*.

MCS stands for Multi-Category Security and it comes from Multi-Level Security. In practical terms, each container gets assigned its own MCS label, and so only they can access objects with a matching MCS label. They can, however, access objects that don't have a category set.

Let's take a look at a quick example :

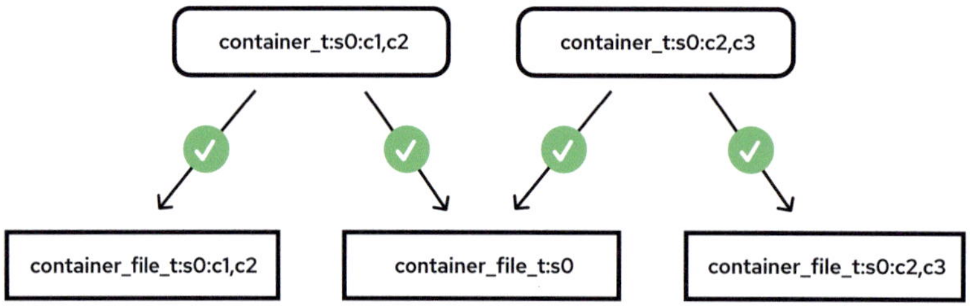

Figure 3.5: Multi-Category Security Labeling for Containers

In this case, we have two containers :

- Both containers use the default `container_t` label
- They're both trying to access files with the `container_file_t` label
- `container_t:s0:c1,c2` has a matching MCS label as `container_file_t:s0:c1,c2` granting it access
- `container_t:s0:c1,c2` cannot access `container_file_t:s0:c2,c3` because the MCS label doesn't match
- Both `container_t:s0:c1,c2` and `container_t:s0:c1,c2` can access `container_file_t:s0` since that file doesn't have a category set. In such cases, the file can be shared between containers

Podman

Let's solidify the concepts that we outlined a little while ago.

To find out whether a Podman installation supports SELinux labeling, do the following :

```
$ podman info | grep -i selinux
          +SYSTEMD +SELINUX +APPARMOR +CAP +SECCOMP +EBPF +YAJL
```

Let's run a simple container with Podman :

```
        $ podman run -ti registry.access.redhat.com/ubi8/ubi
/bin/bash
```

In another terminal, let's now inspect that container :

```
$ podman ps
```

```
CONTAINER ID  IMAGE
        COMMAND        CREATED             STATUS
         PORTS  NAMES
3fdf4f63ab82  registry.access.redhat.com/ubi8/ubi:latest
 /bin/bash  2 minutes ago  Up 2 minutes ago
        priceless_jones

$ podman inspect 3fdf4f63ab82 | jq ".[0].MountLabel"
"system_u:object_r:container_file_t:s0:c116,c225"

$ podman inspect 3fdf4f63ab82 | jq ".[0].ProcessLabel"
"system_u:system_r:container_t:s0:c116,c225"

$ podman inspect 3fdf4f63ab82 | jq -r ".[0].State.Pid" |
xargs ps uZ
LABEL                                       PID TTY          STAT
TIME COMMAND
system_u:system_r:container_t:s0:c116,c225 777931 pts/0 Ss+
 0:00 /bin/bash
```

Let's now create a container that bind-mounts a directory that's shared between containers :

```
$ mkdir container-public
        $ echo "This is accessible by all containers" >
container-public/text.txt
        $ podman run -ti -v=./container-public/:/public:z
registry.access.redhat.com/ubi8/ubi /bin/bash
[root@14feb9b28937 /]# cat /public/text.txt
This is accessible by all containers
```

The `-Z option` at the end of the volume declaration told Podman to relabel that directory in such a way that it's shared between containers. We can verify this in another terminal :

```
$ ls -Z container-public/
system_u:object_r:container_file_t:s0 text.txt
```

We can easily spawn another container that mounts that directory and takes that file into use :

```
$ podman run -ti -v=./container-public/:/public:z
registry.access.redhat.com/ubi8/ubi /bin/bash
[root@eeaf7d80f49a /]# cat /public/text.txt
This is accessible by all container
```

What happened in the background is that Podman re-labeled the directory to use the `container_file_t` domain with the MCS label `s0`.

Let's now spawn another container that mounts a directory with a non-shared MCS label :

```
$ mkdir container-private
$ echo "This is private" > container-private/text.txt
$ podman run -ti -v=./container-private/:/private:Z
registry.access.redhat.com/ubi8/ubi /bin/bash
[root@e42033efb780 /]# cat private/text.txt
This is private
```

In another terminal :

```
$ podman ps
CONTAINER ID  IMAGE
        COMMAND         CREATED                 STATUS
        PORTS  NAMES
e42033efb780  registry.access.redhat.com/ubi8/ubi:latest
 /bin/bash  42 seconds ago  Up 41 seconds ago
        hungry_jones
$ podman inspect e42033efb780 | jq ".[0].MountLabel"
```

```
"system_u:object_r:container_file_t:s0:c329,c433"
$ ls -Z container-private/
system_u:object_r:container_file_t:s0:c329,c433 text.txt
```

As we can see, Podman relabeled the file with the appropriate MCS label that matches the one the container has set.

So, what happens if we spawn another container that bind-mounts that same directory?

```
$ podman run -ti -v=./container-private/:/private:Z
registry.access.redhat.com/ubi8/ubi /bin/bash
[root@bf0aae021337 /]# cat /private/text.txt
This is private
```

The container was able to read the file. So, what happened? Let's look at this a little closer.

```
$ ls -Z container-private/
system_u:object_r:container_file_t:s0:c275,c578 text.txt
$ podman inspect bf0aae021337 | jq ".[0].MountLabel"
"system_u:object_r:container_file_t:s0:c275,c578"
```

As we can see, Podman relabeled the directory, and it's now private to the new directory. So, what happened to the previous container we had?

```

[root@e42033efb780 /]# cat private/text.txt
cat: private/text.txt: Permission denied
```

Since the directory was relabeled, the first container (e42033efb780) doesn't have access to that file anymore. Effectively making it private for the second container (bf0aae021337).

Kubernetes

Kubernetes has the option to assign SELinux labels to containers. This is part of the normal pod specification and no special extensions are needed for this. OpenShift, being a Kubernetes distribution, will take these specifications into use and they will be executed by CRI-O which is the Container Runtime Interface (CRI) that's installed, by default, in OpenShift.

SELinux settings live under the `SecurityContext` section of the pod's specification file. The SELinux options for the container can be set as follows:

```
apiVersion: v1
kind: Pod
metadata:
  name: my-pod
spec:
  containers:
  - name: my-container
    image: registry.access.redhat.com/ubi8/ubi:latest
    command: ["/bin/bash"]
    args: ["-c", "while true; do sleep 2; done"]
    securityContext:
      seLinuxOptions:
        type: container_t
        level: s0:c275,c578
    volumeMounts:
    - name: priv-dir
      mountPath: /container-private
  restartPolicy: Never
  volumes:
```

```
  - name: priv-dir
    emptyDir: {}
```

There are some things to note from this :

- Even if the API allows it, there is no need to set the `user` and `role` parameters of the `seLinuxOptions`.
- In this case, the type (domain) `container_t` specified is already the default that's used by CRI-O. Specifying any other type is possible, but it has to be installed on the host.
- We specified a level (MCS label) of `s0:c275,c578` which effectively makes the volume private for that specific container.
- To use a specific context, given the declarative nature of Kubernetes, explicitly tell Kubernetes to use that context.

Let's dig into what's going on here! And, for this, we need to log into the host and check :

```
sh-4.4# crictl ps --name my-container
CONTAINER                  IMAGE

           CREATED                      STATE                        NAME
                    ATTEMPT                      POD ID
d2f39c15bcc0b
         registry.access.redhat.com/ubi8/ubi@sha256:1f0e6e1f451f
f020b3b44c1c4c34d85db5ffa0fc1bb0490d6a32957a7a06b67f    3
minutes ago            Running                      my-container
          0                        4f29c6b1c4d75

sh-4.4# crictl inspect d2f39c15bcc0b
{
  "status": {
```

```
        "id":
"d2f39c15bcc0beda6ec67c35828216745a2c32edd19333a12b8c56d3b39c84
0f",
        "metadata": {
          "attempt": 0,
          "name": "my-container"
        },
        "state": "CONTAINER_RUNNING",
…
"mounts": [
          {
            "containerPath": "/container-private",
            "hostPath": "/var/lib/kubelet/pods/12387098-3b5a-
4ab6-9a26-4d5cf971acf3/volumes/kubernetes.io~empty-dir/priv-
dir",
            "propagation": "PROPAGATION_PRIVATE",
            "readonly": false,
            "selinuxRelabel": false
          },
…
sh-4.4# cd /var/lib/kubelet/pods/12387098-3b5a-4ab6-9a26-
4d5cf971acf3/volumes/kubernetes.io~empty-dir/
sh-4.4# ls -lZ
total 0
drwxrwxrwx. 2 root root
system_u:object_r:container_file_t:s0:c275,c578 6 Apr  8 15:02
priv-dir
```

What we did here was looked for our container running on the system, checked the directory created to fulfill that volume mount, and verified that the directory has the MCS label we specified in the `level parameter`.

There is a caveat for SELinux relabeling volumes in Kubernetes. Given that operations on the host could potentially damage the deployment, the CRI won't attempt to relabel a `hostPath`.

If we want a directory to be shared within containers, we can specify that as follows :

```
seLinuxOptions:
  level: s0
```

OpenShift has some extra levels of security and automation when it comes to the usage of SELinux relabeling. This depends on the Security Context Constraint that the service account used to spawn the pod that it is able to use. We'll talk more about this in subsequent sections.

How does SELinux Protect me from Attacks?

While SELinux is not included in some Kubernetes distributions, its inclusion in OpenShift has provided protection from several major CVEs. For instance :

- CVE-2015-3627 – Insecure opening of file-descriptor 1 leading to privilege escalation
- CVE-2015-3630 – Read/write proc paths allows host modification and information disclosure
- CVE-2015-3631 – Volume mounts allow LSM profile escalation
- CVE-2016-9962 – RunC Execution Vulnerability
- CVE-2019-5736 – Execution of malicious containers allows for container escape and access to the host file system

The reason it has protected the host in so many instances is the labeling system itself. Containers run with a `container_t` domain. Even if a container escape would happen (and it can), the `container_t` doesn't have permission to access other files on the host, so any actions that the attacker might try to execute on other labels will be blocked.

Writing Policies with udica

Why?

While the default policy already provides a very secure default and can handle most cases, there are times where the default policy is too restrictive, and other times where it's too loose.

Scenario #1:

While deploying a log forwarding solution, there is a need to mount the host's log directory (`/var/log`). `container_t` doesn't allow access to the logging directory (which has a `var_log_t` type). Relabeling `/var/log` is not an option because other components wouldn't be able to write to their logs. This would break the system. So, in this case, the default policy is too restrictive for the scenario.

Scenario #2:

`container_t` gives the container permission to listen on any port on the host, however, there is a need in this case to add permission to just listen on ports labeled with `http_port_t`. To restrict the container to only allow permission to listen for traffic on standard HTTP ports (e.g. 80, 8080, 443), the default policy is too permissive.

udica

udica is a project that aims to assist developers with writing policies for their containers in a faster and more intuitive manner. Instead of having to write policies from scratch, udica relies on a concept called *block inheritance*, where blocks of ready-made policy are available for use to develop policies from. Udica also provides a utility that reads container definition and automatically generates a policy.

Let's look at an example :

We want to run a container that mounts the home directory as well as `/var/spool`, and that listens on port 21. Clearly, in this case, the default container policy will be too restrictive, so we wouldn't be able to use it. Let's give it a try :

```
$ podman run -v /home:/home:ro -v /var/spool:/var/spool:rw -p
21:21 -it registry.access.redhat.com/ubi8/ubi /bin/bash
[root@c2f7755ef5b8 /]# ls /home/
ls: cannot open directory '/home/': Permission denied
```

As expected, SELinux blocks us from accessing that directory.

Let's use udica to generate a policy :

```
$ podman inspect c2f7755ef5b8 | udica my_container
Policy my_container created!

Please load these modules using:
# semodule -i
my_container.cil /usr/share/udica/templates/{base_container.cil
,net_container.cil,home_container.cil}
```

```
Restart the container with: "--security-opt
label=type:my_container.process" parameter
```

After following the instructions that udica provides, it's simple to use the policy :

```
$ podman run -v /home:/home:ro -v /var/spool:/var/spool:rw -p
21:21 \
--security-opt label=type:my_container.process \
-it registry.access.redhat.com/ubi8/ubi /bin/bash
```

No relabeling needed!

This same process can be taken into use in OpenShift given that udica can also read CRI format through using `crictl inspect` command. It would be necessary to install the policy in each node of the cluster and subsequently take it into use as follows :

```
securityContext:
  seLinuxOptions:
    type: my_container.process
```

The process for using it with Kubernetes requires manual adaptation for now but Red Hat is working hard to make developers' lives easier. More automation will come in the near future.

Security Contexts Constraints

In Red Hat OpenShift Container Platform, Security Context Constraints (SCCs) restrict privileges for pods. This allows enforcement or relaxation of their capabilities, thus ensuring that running applications do not use privileges that they do not need. SCCs are similar to policies, which enforce certain actions or prevent others from a service or a user. By using SCCs, the level of privileges can be precisely controlled for the application and the user's applications, and if needed, give them more permissive or more restrictive privileges.

SCCs are OpenShift resources; they define a set of conditions (or rules) that a pod must satisfy in order to be created (or admitted in the cluster). An OpenShift Container Platform ships with a set of SCCs, from a restrictive policy that restricts the root user in pods and drops certain Linux capabilities, to a more permissive policy that allows the root user in pods, the usage of any UIDs and GIDs, and access to the container host file system.

By default, for authenticated users, resources deployed in a project inherit the restricted security context, which prevents applications from running as root and escalating privileges (`allowPrivilegeEscalation`). This security context also blocks certain capabilities, such as `mknod` or `setuid`, which further increases the security of the environment. If an attacker performs an exploit and breaks out of the container, they still do not have root access to the container's host.

Use SCCs to manage the following security settings :

Privilege mode

This setting allows or prevents the container from running in privileged mode, that is, having access to the underlying container host resources, such as hardware devices. This mode bypasses many restrictions, such as Cgroups, Linux capabilities, seccomp profiles, and usage of specific users or group IDs.

Privileges escalation

This setting enables or disables privilege escalation inside a container (the `allowPrivilegeEscalation` flag).

Linux capabilities

This setting allows addition or removal of Linux capabilities to and from containers. For example, dropping the `KILL` capability which prevents a user from killing processes they do not own.

Seccomp profiles

This setting allows specification of which Seccomp profiles are allowed to be used by the pod. Seccomp profiles in turn allow or block certain system calls. For example, block the `mount` system call to prevent the container from attempting to mount directories if it doesn't need to.

Volume types

This setting allows permitting or preventing certain volume types from being accessed by applications; this includes persistent volumes, configuration maps, and temporary directories (`empyDir`).

System control (Sysctl) settings

The Sysctl interface allows modification of kernel parameters at runtime. It allows tuning of the kernel in real time. Use this SCC setting to allow or prevent certain system controls from being executed.

Host resources

This set of settings allows permitting or prevention of a pod accessing the following host resources : IPC namespaces, host networks, host ports, and host PID namespaces.

Read-only root system

This setting allows making the root file system read-only. This prevents any changes and forces users to mount a volume if they need to store data.

User and group IDs

These settings allow restriction of the allocation of user and group IDs to a specific range. Those are useful settings for restricting users to a certain set of ID or GIDs.

SELinux labels

This setting allows definition of a SELinux label to the pods. OpenShift supports all available SELinux fields : user, role, type, and level.

File system groups

This setting allows definition of supplemental groups for the user, which is usually required for accessing a block device. This allows provision of adequate access to block storage, such as Ceph RBD, and iSCSI.

SCCs are OpenShift resources that can be listed with the `oc get scc` command

```
$ oc describe scc restricted
Name:                                                   restricted
Priority:                                               <none>
Access:
  Users:                                                <none>
  Groups:
system:authenticated
Settings:
  Allow Privileged:                                     false
  Allow Privilege Escalation:                           true
```

```
  Default Add Capabilities:                              <none>
  Required Drop Capabilities:
KILL,MKNOD,SETUID,SETGID
  Allowed Capabilities:                                  <none>
  Allowed Seccomp Profiles:                              <none>
  Allowed Volume Types:
configMap,downwardAPI,emptyDir,persistentVolumeClaim,projected,
secret
  Allowed Flexvolumes:                                   <all>
  Allowed Unsafe Sysctls:                                <none>
  Forbidden Sysctls:                                     <none>
  Allow Host Network:                                    false
  Allow Host Ports:                                      false
  Allow Host PID:                                        false
  Allow Host IPC:                                        false
  Read Only Root Filesystem:                             false
  Run As User Strategy: MustRunAsRange
    UID:                                                 <none>
    UID Range Min:                                       <none>
    UID Range Max:                                       <none>
  SELinux Context Strategy: MustRunAs
    User:                                                <none>
    Role:                                                <none>
    Type:                                                <none>
    Level:                                               <none>
  FSGroup Strategy: MustRunAs
    Ranges:                                              <none>
  Supplemental Groups Strategy: RunAsAny
    Ranges:                                              <none>
```

Managing SELinux Context with SCCs

SELinux contexts can be managed for the container's main process by using SCCs. The `SELinux Context` setting allows management of a strategy; the restricted SCC defines a strategy of `MustRunAs`, which forces the pods of the project to define an SELinux policy but does not define any values for SELinux contexts, which means that the project must define the options, such as user, role, type, and level. Failure to do so prevents pods from being created.

If a custom SELinux type needs to be used, either create a custom SCC that allows this type, or use the privileged SCC (and do not set the privileged option in the `securityContext`) since this would allow open setting of the security settings.

What is a Privileged Container?

In a few cases, there might be a need to deploy a container with fewer restrictions than the ones that are set by default. A privileged container is a container with all *capabilities* enabled, fewer seccomp restrictions, and uses a SELinux domain of `spc_t`.

One would normally set it up by setting the `privileged` flag in the `securityContext` section of the pod as follows :

```
securityContext:
  privileged: true
```

While it might seem simple and tempting to enable this (since it will work around any restrictions), using privileged containers is discouraged as it basically gives `full root capabilities` on the host. The container will have an SELinux context of `spc_t` which is equivalent to an unconfined domain, so SELinux won't be able to block `attacks` as it normally would.

Fortunately, OpenShift limits the ability of users to deploy privileged containers. This is done by limiting the usage of such containers through the privileged Security Context Constraints (SCC).

Container Image Security

This section outlines several approaches to make consuming container images safer. It does not go into detail on how to properly secure container images themselves. For information on how to build secure container images, see Chapter 9 : Securing CI/CD.

During development, it might be tempting to just run whatever arbitrary content gets the job done. But, with the ease that containers can be produced and published comes the risk of running dangerous content, either locally or in a cluster. There are several mitigation strategies that can be implemented :

- Establish a whitelist of allowed registries : This ensures that the container runtime can only pull images from certain sources
- Require that only fully qualified image names are used to reference images to prevent multiple container registries from becoming mixed up
- Verify signatures of container images to ensure containers were built by a trusted party

Registry Configuration Sources

There are two files that configure the properties of registries : `/etc/containers/registries.conf` and `/etc/containers/policy.json`. Even though the `registries.conf` file is also allowed to include a registries' blacklist, it is recommended that the list of registries is set in `policy.json` as the `policy.json` file gives greater flexibility and is supported by all container runtimes. The `registry.conf` file is then used to set any optional registries that accept unqualified names.

When running containers locally with Podman, go ahead and edit those two files. With OpenShift, the configuration method depends on what aspect needs to be configured. There is a `CustomResource` named `Image` that allows setting of allowed or blocked registries. There is only one instance of the resource using the reserved name **cluster**. This custom resource is rendered into the `registries.conf` and `policy.json` files by the `machine-config-operator`. Unfortunately, if anything else needs to be configured, such as registries without qualified names, or image signing set up, create the `registries.conf` and `policy.json` files manually and push them to the cluster as `MachineConfigs`.

Container Registry Whitelist

With OpenShift, the most straightforward way to configure a registry whitelist is to set the `allowedRegistries` attribute in the `image.config.openshift.io/cluster` resource. Even though the `Image.config.openshift.io` custom resource also supports setting up blacklists, a whitelist is always inherently safer.

Run `oc edit image.config.openshift.io/cluster` and make a list for allowed registries in the `registrySources.allowedRegistries` attribute, for example :

```
apiVersion: config.openshift.io/v1
kind: Image
# metadata omitted for clarity
spec:
  registrySources:
    allowedRegistries:
    - myregistry.com
    - registry.redhat.io
```

```
    - registry.access.redhat.com
status:
internalRegistryHostname: image-registry.openshift-image-
registry.svc:5000
```

This file would be rendered by the MCO into `/etc/container/policy.json` on the nodes with content along these lines:

```
{
   "default": [{"type": "reject"}],
   "transports": {
      "atomic": {
         "myregistry.com": [
            {"type": "insecureAcceptAnything"}
         ],
         "registry.redhat.io": [
            {"type": "insecureAcceptAnything"}
         ],
         "registry.access.redhat.com": [
            {"type": "insecureAcceptAnything"}
         ],
         "": [{"type": "reject"}]
      },
      "docker": {
         "myregistry.com": [
            {"type": "insecureAcceptAnything"}
         ],
         "registry.redhat.io": [
            {"type": "insecureAcceptAnything"}
         ],
         "registry.access.redhat.com": [
            {"type": "insecureAcceptAnything"}
         ],
```

```
            "": [{"type": "reject"}
            ]
        }
    }
}
```

As the container registry does not have a notion of what kind of a transport protocol the registry implements, the Machine Config Operator adds all entries for both the `atomic` and the `Docker` protocols. This might be significant if there is need to express more complex matching rules as each transport protocol evaluates the matches differently – and in this case, needs to push a particular version of the policy.json file instead of relying on rendering the file from the `image.config.openshift.io/cluster` object using MachineConfig objects.

More details about the matching details can be found in the policy.json manual page. Let's just point out two important pieces from the `policy.json`, as highlighted in the example above. The ones highlighted in red are the default policy for transports not explicitly mentioned and per-transport default policy. It is important that these defaults are set to reject and select transports, and that scopes of transports are enabled rather than the other way around.

Fully Qualified Image Names and Registry Search List

The registry search list can be used as a convenience feature in order to be able to pull container images using their short name. Consider these two calls :

```
$ podman pull ubi8/ubi:latest
$ podman pull registry.redhat.io/ubi8/ubi:latest
```

Clearly, the first one is easier to type, but with the second format, there is a greater degree of knowledge of where the image comes from. It is recommended that only fully qualified image names are used if more than one registry is allowed in the environment. For example, instead of `ubi8/ubi:latest` there is only an allowance to pull `registry.redhat.io/ubi8/ubi:latest`. The rationale behind this is that when a short name is used and the system is configured to use multiple registries, there exists the risk that an attacker might place an image with the same short name to a registry earlier in the search list, especially when using public registries. Any public registries should either not be allowed to pull with a short name at all or be at the very last position in the search list.

Configuration-wise, this boils down to only using trusted registries on a line starting with the `unqualified-search-registries` of the `/etc/containers/registries.conf` file, for example :

```
$ cat /etc/containers/registries.conf
unqualified-search-registries=['myregistry.com',
'registry.access.redhat.com']
```

In case only fully qualified names are to be allowed, just omit the `unqualified-search-registries` line from the file.

Image Signing

How to ensure that a container image about to be run has not been tampered with and is really what is intended to run? Container image signing helps with these issues as the signature is verified using a configured public key which can then be verified using the image from someone who possesses the corresponding private key. In addition, if the image were modified, the image signature would no longer match the image.

Each container registry for a container runtime can be configured to either allow running unsigned images, which is the default, or require that images be signed. Configuration-wise, requiring that an image be signed is set in `policy.json`. Unfortunately, there is no mechanism for configuring the image signing verification other than manually crafting the `policy.json` file. Taking the previous examples in mind, the following two snippets illustrate how to enable signature verification for `registry.redhat.io`:

```
{
    "default": [{"type": "reject"}
    ],
    "transports": {
        "atomic": {
            "myregistry.com": [
                {"type": "insecureAcceptAnything"}
            ],
            "registry.redhat.io": [
                {"type": "insecureAcceptAnything"}
            ],
            "registry.access.redhat.com": [
                {"type": "insecureAcceptAnything"}
            ],
            "": [{"type": "reject"}]
        },
        "docker": {
            "registry.redhat.io": [
                {
                    "type": "signedBy",
                    "keyType": "GPGKeys",
                    "keyPath": "/etc/pki/rpm-gpg/RPM-GPG-KEY-redhat-
release"
                }
```

```
            ],
            "myregistry.com": [
               {"type": "insecureAcceptAnything"}
            ],
            "registry.access.redhat.com": [
               {"type": "insecureAcceptAnything"}
            ],
            "": [{"type": "reject"}]
         }
      }
   }
```

The configuration mechanism that expresses the policy is complex. As shown, policy requirement (the value of the registry scope) is an array. When multiple policies are specified, all of them must match. The upstream manual page has a nice example that illustrates how to make sure that images in a registry mirror are signed, at the same time, by both the vendor of the images and the local authority that approves the images for mirroring :

```
{
  "default": [
    {"type": "reject"}
  ],
  "transports": {
    "atomic": {
      "hostname:5000/vendor/product": [
        {
          "type": "signedBy",
          "keyType": "GPGKeys",
          "keyPath": "/path/to/vendor-pubkey.gpg",
          "signedIdentity": {
            "type": "exactRepository",
            "dockerRepository": vendor-
```

```
hostname/product/repository"
          }
        },
        {
          "type": "signedBy",
          "keyType": "GPGKeys",
          "keyPath": "/path/to/reviewer-pubkey.gpg"
        }
      ]
    }
  }
}
```

Enabling FIPS Mode in a Container

To enable FIPS mode in a container running on Red Hat Enterprise Linux :

1. The host system must be switched into FIPS mode.

2. Mount the `/etc/system-fips` file on the container from the host.

3. Set the FIPS cryptographic policy level in the container :

```
$ update-crypto-policies --set FIPS
```

If using Red Hat Enterprise Linux 8.2 or later, an alternative method for switching a container to FIPS mode was introduced. It requires only using the following command in the container :

```
# mount --bind /usr/share/crypto-policies/back-ends/FIPS \
       /etc/crypto-policies/back-ends
```

4. Kubernetes Security

Kubernetes is the orchestration layer used to manage deploying container instances at scale. Kubernetes is used to :

- Determine which containers should be deployed to which hosts
- Manage shared resources such as network and storage
- Enable containers to discover each other and prevent containers from discovering each other
- Automatically scale application capacity to meet demand

Kubernetes is a large system with the ability to define policies at multiple layers of the system. This chapter will discuss how OpenShift secures the Kubernetes layer, including workloads deployed to the cluster, and provides recommendations for additional configurations.

OpenShift builds boundaries between user workloads through multi-tenancy. Multi-tenancy combines Role-Based Access Controls and network policies with container isolation at multiple levels (host, application, and service levels). While multi-tenancy separates user workloads, Admission Controllers form boundaries between the OpenShift API and components making requests to the API. Those features, along with operators, help automate and simplify security management of Kubernetes features.

Security-Focused Kubernetes Operations

High-level OpenShift operations provide ways of automating the otherwise manual process of setting up, modifying, and upgrading Kubernetes components. As a result, security professionals can more easily gain a broad overview of the health of a cluster while focusing less on the details of managing each Kubernetes component.

OpenShift Operators play a critical role in both the initial start-up and the on-going maintenance of those components. Specific operators are charged with performing upgrades for each node, as well as on particular low-level Kubernetes components. A range of health-check features in OpenShift allows monitoring and logging of events at both node and application levels while telemetry gathers data that lets Red Hat improve the health of your OpenShift clusters.

The Use of Operators

Although Kubernetes excels at managing applications, it does not specify or manage platform-level requirements or deployment processes. Neither does it include all the elements necessary for an enterprise platform, such as monitoring and logging. Powerful and flexible platform management tools and processes are important benefits provided by the OpenShift Container Platform.

OpenShift uses *operators* to manage the Kubernetes cluster components. Each operator manages a specific area of cluster functionality, such as cluster-wide application logging, management of the Kubernetes control plane, or the machine provisioning system.

Each operator provides a simple API for determining cluster functionality. OpenShift operators deploy platform components in the preferred, supported configuration.

An operator is a method of packaging, deploying, and managing a Kubernetes-native application. A Kubernetes-native application is an application that is both deployed on Kubernetes and managed using the

Kubernetes APIs with the `kubectl` tooling. Operators create application-specific custom controllers which allow the platform to use *Kubernetes to manage Kubernetes.*

OpenShift ensures that the platform components are deployed and managed as declared by the operator. When configuration changes are supported, those changes are made through the operator for the individual component. If an unsupported configuration change is made, the operator will reset the component back to the supported configuration (leveraging the declarative nature of Kubernetes). This allows operators to manage configuration drift. If an unsupported configuration change is made, the operator will reset to the supported configuration.

Cluster Upgrades

The cluster manages upgrades to the machines through the Cluster Version Operator, the Machine Config Operator, and a set of individual operators. The scope also includes updates and upgrades to the host operating system.

Updates to OpenShift are managed by the cluster administrator. Patches are delivered through the same mechanism. The Machine Config Operator updates nodes in a rolling fashion, with zero cluster downtime for well behaving applications, making it easier to keep the cluster up to date with the latest fixes. All platform operators watch for drift and reset any unsupported configuration changes.

Cluster Incident and Event Management

The health and availability of a cluster is part of its security posture. OpenShift includes a variety of capabilities to automatically evaluate and manage cluster health.

Machine Health Checks

Cluster administrators can configure and deploy a machine health check to automatically repair damaged machines (worker nodes). This process is not applicable to clusters where machines are manually provisioned. Advanced machine management and scaling capabilities can only be used in clusters where the machine API is operational. The controller that observes a MachineHealthCheck resource checks for the status that has been defined.

If a machine fails the health check, it is automatically deleted and a new one is created to take its place. When a machine is deleted, a machine deleted event is noted. To limit disruptive impact of the machine deletion, the controller drains and deletes only one node at a time. If the number of unhealthy machines exceeds the maxUnhealthy threshold in the targeted pool of machines, remediation stops so that manual intervention can take place. For more information see https://docs.openshift.com/container-platform/4.3/machine_management/deploying-machine-health-checks.html

Cluster Monitoring

Cluster monitoring services are deployed to all nodes. OpenShift Container Platform includes a preconfigured, preinstalled, and self-updating monitoring stack that is based on the Prometheus open source project. It provides monitoring of cluster services and includes a set of alerts to immediately notify the cluster administrator about any occurring problems through a set of Grafana dashboards. The cluster monitoring stack is only supported for monitoring and metrics gathering of OpenShift Container Platform clusters.

Cluster Logging

When the cluster logging operator is installed, logging services are deployed to all nodes. OpenShift includes the option to deploy a logging operator. The cluster logging services are based upon Elasticsearch, Fluentd, and Kibana (EFK). The collector, Fluentd, is deployed to each node in the OpenShift Container Platform cluster. It collects all node and container logs and writes them to Elasticsearch (ES). Kibana is the centralized, web UI where users and administrators can create rich visualizations and dashboards with the aggregated data for log analysis. For more information, see Cluster Logging in the OpenShift documentation.

Audit

OpenShift event auditing and host auditing services are deployed to all nodes. As an API-driven system, OpenShift audits cluster events by default. Events allow the OpenShift Container Platform to record information about real-world events in a resource-agnostic manner. They also allow developers and administrators to consume information about system services in a unified way.

Project audit data is available to project administrators and cluster audit data is available to cluster administrators. OpenShift platform services connect to the built-in monitoring solution in OpenShift. An alert dashboard is available. Best practice is to configure your cluster to forward all audit and log events to a Security Information and Event Management (SIEM) system for retention and analysis. Additional information about auditing is available in Chapter 7 : Auditing. For a list of events, see the List of events documentation.

Remote Telemetry and Health Monitoring

In a connected cluster, telemetry services are deployed to all nodes. The OpenShift Container Platform collects anonymized aggregated information about the health, usage, and size of clusters and reports it to Red Hat via two integrated components : Telemetry and the Insights Operator. This information allows Red Hat to improve the OpenShift Container Platform and to react to issues that impact customers more quickly. This also simplifies the subscription and entitlement process for Red Hat customers and enables the Red Hat OpenShift Cluster Manager service to provide an overview of the clusters and their health and subscription status. A cluster that reports data to Red Hat via Telemetry and the Insights Operator is considered a connected cluster.

This continuous stream of data is used by Red Hat to monitor the health of clusters in real time and to react as necessary to problems that impact our customers. It also allows Red Hat to roll out the OpenShift Container Platform upgrades to customers to minimize service impact and continuously improve the upgrade experience. This debugging information is available to Red Hat Support and engineering teams with the same restrictions as accessing data reported via support cases. All connected cluster information is used by Red Hat to help make OpenShift Container Platform better and more intuitive to use. None of the information is shared with third parties.

The Telemetry and the Insights operator can be disabled. For more information see About Remote Health Monitoring.

Securing Platform Services

Described below are the individual Kubernetes platform services that need to be managed by OpenShift.

Access to the Cluster

For users to interact with the OpenShift Container Platform, they must first authenticate to the cluster. OpenShift includes an integrated OAuth server for token-based authentication. The authentication layer identifies the user or service associated with requests to the OpenShift Container Platform API. The authorization layer then uses information about the requesting user or service to determine if the request is allowed. Detailed information about authentication and authorization can be found in Chapter 5 : Identity and Access Management Security.

Internal connections to the API server are authenticated by X.509 certificates. External access to the API server is managed by the ingress controller. Best practice is to separate access to the API server from access to workloads running on the cluster. This can be achieved by configuring separate ingress controllers for each type of access.

Control Plane

The control plane is composed of master nodes. OpenShift services, such as the API Server, etcd, Controller, Scheduler, etc., run only on these master nodes. These control plane services manage workloads on the compute nodes, which are also known as worker nodes. A default OpenShift 4 cluster must include three master nodes to ensure that a quorum for etcd is maintained.

Most of the control plane components are deployed as static pods. Static pods are managed by the kubelet and are always bound to one kubelet on a specific node. The kubelet automatically creates a mirror Pod on the API server for each static pod. This means that the pods running on a node are visible on the API server but cannot be controlled from there which minimizes the attack surface. Security secrets for control plane components such as the Kubernetes apiserver, etcd, the controller manager, and the scheduler are stored with their respective static pod configurations in the /etc/kubernetes/static-pod-resources/*/secrets directory on its host. Secrets for the control plane components are automatically managed and rotated by OpenShift.

API Server

The OpenShift API server is managed by the apiserver operator. The API server is served over HTTPS with authentication and authorization, and the secure API endpoint is bound to 0.0.0.0 :6443. The API server cannot be configured to listen on any other port. If needed, configure the load balancer in front of the API to listen on any custom port and redirect requests to the expected port 6443.

The default API server uses the certificate from the Ingress Controller. Clients outside of the cluster will not be able to verify the API server's certificate by default. This certificate can be replaced by one that is issued by a CA that clients trust. When deployed in a public cloud, the API server can and should be configured to only be accessed from a private zone.

OAuth Server

OpenShift includes an embedded OAuth server for authentication and Role-Based Access Control (RBAC) for authorization. Additional information about how OpenShift manages authentication and authorization is available in Chapter 5 : Identity and Access Management Security.

etcd

etcd stores the persistent master state while other components watch etcd for changes to bring themselves into the specified state. etcd also stores kubernetes secrets. Given its importance to the functioning of the cluster, security for the etcd datastore is built into OpenShift.

The cluster etcd is managed by the cluster etcd operator. etcd is automatically deployed on each of the 3 master nodes. Its pod specification file is created on control plane nodes at `/etc/kubernetes/manifests/etcd-member.yaml`. The kubeconfig file for `system:admin` (`admin.conf`) is stored in `/etc/kubernetes/kubeconfig`.

OpenShift uses X.509 certificates to provide secure communication to etcd. OpenShift configures these automatically. OpenShift does not use the etcd-certfile or etcd-keyfile flags.

OpenShift supports data at rest encryption of the etcd datastore but it is up to the customer to configure. The AES-CBC (Cipher Block Chaining) cipher is used with the keys stored and automatically rotated on the filesystem of the master. Encryption of the etcd datastore can be enabled post-installation against a running system. For more information on etcd encryption please see the section in Chapter 8 entitled Etcd Datastore Encryption.

Scheduler

Pod scheduling is an internal process that determines placement of new pods onto nodes within the cluster. The scheduler watches new pods as they get created and identifies the most suitable node to host them. It then creates bindings (pod to node bindings) for the pods using the master API. The default scheduling behavior is managed with the OpenShift kube-scheduler-operator.

Cluster administrators may wish to influence the behavior of the scheduler in order to simplify auditing of regulatory requirements. For example, if an organization's policy requires that applications with certain types of sensitive data only be deployed to specific physical nodes. This can be done by making use of the following advanced pod scheduling methods. Each one addresses a different use case so it's important to understand what behavior is desired. Important to note is that a combination of methods may be required in order to achieve the desired outcome.

Note : The scheduling operator's default behavior can be changed by creating or editing the scheduler policy ConfigMap in the openshift-config project. However, it is not recommended. The techniques listed below are preferred.

Node Selectors

Node selectors are used when there are specific resources that must be scheduled on specific nodes.

With node selectors, a label is applied to the node and all services that need to be scheduled on those nodes need to be configured with the corresponding node selector. Node selectors can be configured on a cluster level, project level or pod level for desired granularity.

If a node selector is specified in conjunction with a resource and there are no available nodes with that selector label, those resources will not be schedulable. On the contrary, if a node selector is not specified within a resource, those resources can still be scheduled on the nodes with a selector label.

Taints and Tolerations

Taints and tolerations are used when the desired outcome is to prevent resources from being scheduled on specific nodes by default unless otherwise necessary. When a taint is applied to a node, all resources will be repelled from that node *unless* it is configured with a toleration that allows it to be scheduled there.

Controller Manager

The Controller Manager Server watches etcd for changes to objects such as replication, namespace, and service account controller objects, and then uses the API to enforce the specified state. The kube-controller-manager is managed with the cluster Controller Manager Operator. In other words, the controller manager, in combination with the other cluster operators ensures that the declared state for objects in the cluster is maintained.

Ingress Controller

The Ingress Controller and wild card DNS are managed with the ingress operator. An Ingress Controller is configured to accept external requests and proxy them based on the configured routes. This is limited to HTTP, HTTPS using SNI, and TLS using SNI, which is enough for web applications and services that work over TLS with SNI. By default, the OpenShift Container Platform uses the Ingress Operator to create an internal CA and issue a wildcard certificate that is valid for applications under the `.apps sub-domain`. The default ingress certificate can be replaced. After replacing the certificate, all applications, including the web console and CLI, will have encryption provided by a specified certificate. See the Replacing default ingress certificate documentation. More information about the Ingress Operator can be found in Chapter 6: Network Security.

Console

The OpenShift Container Platform web console is a user interface accessible from a web browser. Administrators can use the web console to manage and monitor the status of the cluster. Developers can use the web console to visualize, browse, and manage the contents of projects. Modify the OpenShift Container Platform web console to set a logout redirect URL or disable the console.

Recommendation : Specify the URL of the page to load when a user logs out of the web console. Specifying a logoutRedirect URL allows users to perform a single logout (SLO) through the identity provider to destroy their single sign-on session. See https://docs.openshift.com/container-platform/4.3/web_console/configuring-web-console.html

Instructions on disabling the web console is available here : https://docs.openshift.com/container-platform/4.3/web_console/disabling-web-console.html

Kubelet

The kubelet runs on each node in the cluster and registers each node with the API server. The kubelet is installed as part of RHEL CoreOS and runs as a systemd service. OpenShift automatically generates and rotates the certificates for the kubelet to serve HTTPS traffic.

CRI-O Container Runtime

OpenShift uses CRI-O as the container runtime. CRI-O is run as a systemd service on each node in the cluster and is installed as part of RHEL CoreOS. CRI-O is a lightweight, Kubernetes-specific runtime with a reduced attack surface. CRI-O is versioned with Kubernetes. More information about CRI-O is available in Chapter 3 : Container Security.

Multi-tenancy

OpenShift enables multi-tenancy in a single cluster through the use of container isolation at the host level, application, and service isolation via OpenShift projects, in combination with Role-Based Access Control (RBAC) and network policies. Container multi-tenancy and RBAC are described in detail in Chapter 5 : Identity and Access Management Security. Network policies are described in Chapter 6: Network Security. This discussion of multi-tenancy will focus on the use of OpenShift projects.

Projects and Kubernetes Namespaces

OpenShift Projects are Kubernetes namespaces with additional annotations such as Multi- Category Security (MCS) labeling provided in SELinux. OpenShift projects allow a group of users to organize and manage their cluster resources (objects, policies, constraints, and service accounts) in isolation from other groups or cluster resources. Each project scopes its own set of objects, policies, constraints, and service accounts. OpenShift projects are the central vehicle by which access to resources for regular users is managed. Unlike upstream Kubernetes, the OpenShift projects (Kubernetes namespaces) are configured and deployed by default to enable multi-tenancy.

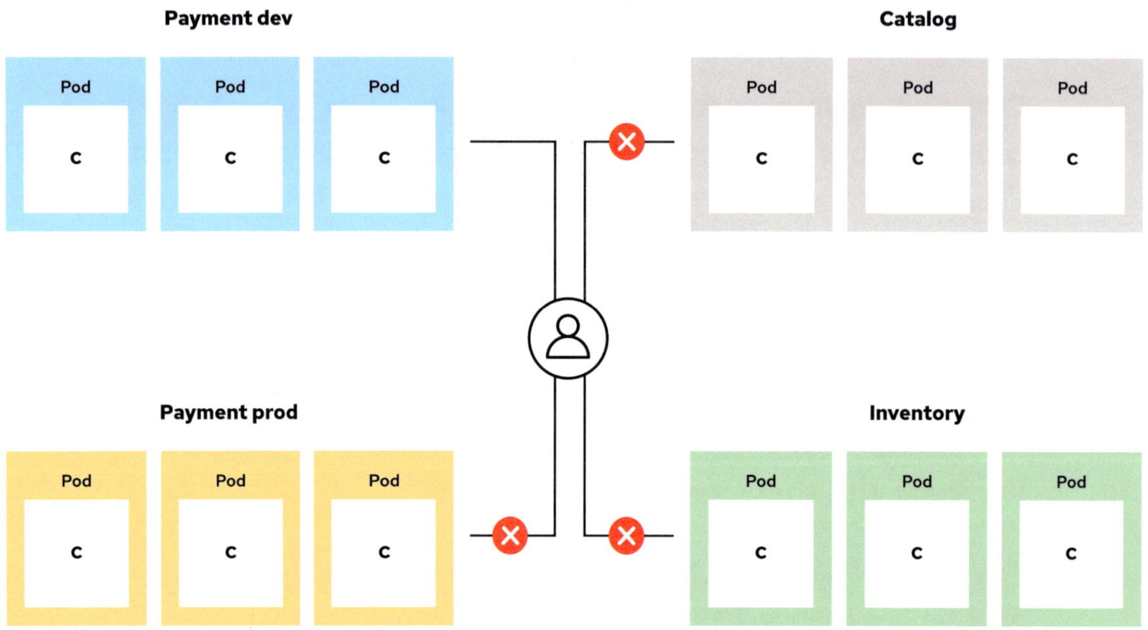

Figure 4.1: OpenShift Project/Namespace Isolation

Users or groups can be given access to projects by cluster administrators or project administrators but may also be delegated to create their own projects. Users or groups are only allowed to see the content in the projects to which they are assigned and are given specific roles within projects. These roles are referred to as local role bindings and determine what actions are allowed within those projects. Figure 4.2 illustrates the relationship between projects and local role binding.

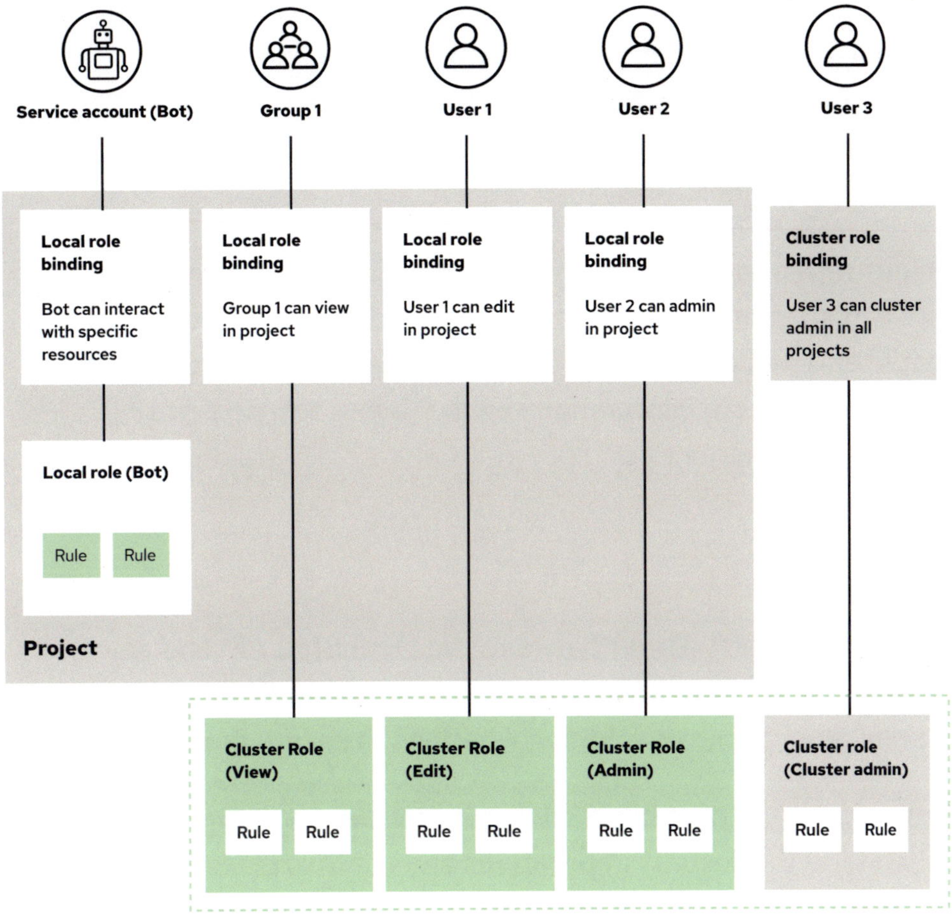

Figure 4.2: Role-Based Access Control (RBAC) within OpenShift Projects

Communication between pods in a project or between pods in separate projects is managed through network policies. Network policies are discussed in detail in the Network Security chapter.

Project Quotas

A resource quota, defined by a ResourceQuota object, provides constraints that limit aggregate resource consumption per project. It can limit the quantity of objects that can be created in a project by type, as well as the total amount of compute resources and storage that may be consumed by resources in that project. Cluster administrators can set and manage resource quotas on a per project basis, and developers and cluster administrators can view them. For more information see the Quota setting per project documentation.

Cluster administrators can also manage resource quotas across multiple projects with a multi-project quota. Resources used in each selected project are aggregated and that aggregate is used to limit resources across all the selected projects. For more information see the Quota setting across multiple projects documentation.

Admission Controllers

Admission Controllers form a layer between the OpenShift API and any request made to the API. Admission controllers can validate or mutate objects on admission, providing additional options to secure the cluster.

Learning how admissions controllers are set up, by default, in OpenShift helps to understand the security implications and controls placed on Kubernetes components. Security Context Constraints and Service Accounts define these limitations. Other constraints answer such questions as "when should a new version of an image be pulled when a local version is available" and "how are kubelets limited in the pods and nodes they can modify."

Security Context Constraints

The Security Context Constraints (SCCs) admission controller is used to restrict pod access in a similar way to restricting user access with RBAC. Pod SCCs are determined by the group that the user belongs to as well as the service account if one is specified. SCCs are enabled by default in

OpenShift and cannot be turned off. SCCs allow administrators to control many pod configurations including:

- The SELinux context of the container
- Whether a pod can run privileged containers
- The use of host directories as volumes

OpenShift SCCs support the same level of controls as Pod Security Policies (PSPs). While PSPs have the concept of ordering policies, it is not yet as complete as SCCs prioritization feature. Red Hat continues to work with the Kubernetes community on Pod Security Policies.

When a request is placed, admission will use the following approach :

- Retrieves all available SCCs
- Generates field values for all undefined SCC settings
- Validates against the available constraints

If a matching set is found, the pod is accepted. Otherwise, it is rejected.

SCC's priority field affects the ordering when attempting to validate a request by the admission controller. A higher priority SCC is moved to the front of the set when sorting. When the complete set of available SCCs are determined, they are ordered by :

- Highest priority first, `nil` is considered a `0` priority

- If priorities are equal, the SCCs will be sorted from most restrictive to least restrictive

- If both priorities and restrictions are equal, the SCCs will be sorted by name

By default, worker nodes and pods that run on worker nodes receive an SCC type of *restricted*. The restricted SCC ensures pods cannot run as privileged and must run as a user in a preallocated range of UIDs. It requires a pod to run with a preallocated MCS label. It also ensures that pods cannot mount host directory volumes and that the pod cannot connect directly to the host's network.

There are eight default SCCs in OpenShift, and they *should not be modified*. Modifying the default SCCs are not covered in our test matrices and will break upgrades. Instead of modifying the default SCCs, create a custom SCC. SCC management requires the role of cluster-admin. To view a list of SCCs:

```
$ oc get scc
NAME                AGE
anyuid              3h51m
hostaccess          3h51m
hostmount-anyuid    3h51m
hostnetwork         3h51m
node-exporter       3h50m
nonroot             3h51m
privileged          3h51m
restricted          3h51m
```

More information about a specific SCC can be viewed by :

```
$ oc describe scc <scc-name>
```

See Creating Security Context Constraints to see a procedure for creating a security context constraint from the command line.

There are several SCCs that trigger the admission controller to look for preallocated values from a namespace when no ranges are defined in the pod specs. More information about the preallocated SCC values can be found in About preallocated Security Context Constraints values in the OpenShift documentation.

Service Account

The goal of the Service Account admission controller is to implement the automation of service account management. In OpenShift, Service Accounts (SA) allow a service to directly access the API. Service accounts can be granted roles just as a regular user. Since the use of service accounts is required in each project to run builds, deployments, and other pods, three default service accounts are automatically created for each project.

The SA name is derived from the project, and its access is isolated and restricted to its project namespace. It is not recommended to remove the SAs created by default, even if there will not be any builds in that project, as cluster behavior cannot be guaranteed. Since SAs are scoped to the project level, removing them is not necessary.

As soon as a service account is created, two secrets are automatically added to it :

- An API token
- Credentials for the OpenShift Container Registry

The system ensures that service accounts always have an API token and registry credentials. The ServiceAccount token authenticator is configured with serviceAccountConfig.publicKeyFiles. OpenShift automates key rotation for platform components. By default, the ServiceAccount controller is enabled and cannot be turned off.

AlwaysPullImages

The goal of the AlwaysPullImages controller is to require pods to always pull images from the registry (requiring authentication) as opposed to pulling images from local cache if available.

In OpenShift, the default configuration is to set the imagePullPolicy to `always` when the tag is latest. Otherwise, the imagePullPolicy is set to IfNotPresent.

Always pulling images ensures that users are not using locally cached images and are using updated and authenticated images before a pod is started.

NamespaceLifecycle

The goal of the NamespaceLifecycle controller is to prevent the creation of resources in a namespace that is in a terminating state. It also protects the default, kube-system and kube-public namespaces by blocking their deletion. This controller is enabled by default in OpenShift and should not be disabled, as it protects the integrity of the namespace termination process.

NodeRestriction

This limits the number of Node and Pod objects a kubelet can modify. Enabling the NodeRestriction controller ensures that kubelets only be allowed to modify their own Node API objects and the Pod API objects that are deployed to their node. This controller is enabled by default in OpenShift and cannot be changed.

AlwaysAdmit

If enabled, the alwaysAdmit admission controller allows all pods in the cluster. This controller is disabled by default in OpenShift and cannot be enabled. It has also been deprecated by the Kubernetes community as it behaves as if there were no controller.

EventRateLimit

The goal of the EventRateLimit controller is to limit the rate at which the API server accepts requests. Some organizations recommended this controller to alleviate the potential issue of flooding the API server with requests. However, the kubelet has since been fixed to send fewer events. Therefore, this controller cannot be enabled in OpenShift 4.

In future Kubernetes releases, API priority and fairness (which is alpha in Kubernetes 1.18) will be used to limit the rate at which the API server accepts requests.

5. Identity and Access Management Security

The concept of identity is used to uniquely identify an actor in an OpenShift cluster. It defines *who the actor is*. Identity is represented as a user but, from a security standpoint, there are different types of users defined at different levels to take into consideration.

The actions a user is allowed to perform in the cluster depends on their unique identification determined via methods such as role-based access control (RBAC). An identity can also be used to audit what actions a user performed at some point in the past.

To help manage and secure users at different levels of an OpenShift cluster, this chapter differentiates between user accounts typically associated with a person (regular user accounts) and those used primarily for infrastructure and non-interactive workloads (system accounts, service accounts, and virtual system users). Security-related identity and access management concerns focus on how users are authenticated and how privileges associated with each account are assigned and managed.

Types of Users

When it comes to direct use and management of an OpenShift cluster, there are regular users (who typically run workloads and may do some administration) and system users (who can interact with the API). The kubeadmin user is the first user created on an OpenShift cluster and requires special attention since it holds superuser privileges. User accounts that function behind the scenes include service accounts and virtual system users.

Regular Users

A *user* most commonly represents a real person who interacts with the OpenShift cluster in some way. Since management of OpenShift is performed via the OpenShift API itself, this includes both administrators of the cluster as well as regular users of the cluster who use it to run their workloads.

System Users

At times, individual infrastructure services and components need to interact with the OpenShift API. *System users* are used to identify these components which allow their permissions to be defined via policy.

Service Accounts

Service accounts are specialized user objects that are intended for infrastructure and other non-interactive workloads, and cannot be managed externally. Every OpenShift project contains a default set of service accounts, and it is possible to create new service accounts as needed.

Any pod running with a service account automatically gets a secret for its service account mounted under `/var/run/secrets/kubernetes.io/serviceaccount/token`. If the serviceAccount field of podSpec is not specified then the default project service account is used.

This secret can be used from inside of the pod as an access token to authenticate the API. OpenShift Roles and ClusterRoles can be bound to a service account in the same way as a normal user, thus defining the authorization policy of the workload. Service accounts also need permissions to use certain SCCs which can influence the security settings of a pod.

Virtual System Users

In some special cases, OpenShift uses *virtual system users*. These users are not backed by a real identity from an identity provider (IdP) or OpenShift object. Virtual system users are hard-coded and reserved for infrastructure component use. They appear with a `system: prefix` (such as `system:admin`, `system:node:foo`). Many of these virtual users are defined in the subject fields of X.509 client certificates in use by control plane components to uniquely identify the component.

Anonymous User

Anonymous users are represented by the virtual system user `system:anonymous`. This user is added to the request by the Kubernetes authentication layer for requests that have failed authentication or did not provide any authentication credentials. This is intended mostly to identify a failed request to the rest of the API layers and does not grant any access. See also the Virtual Groups section of this chapter.

Kubeadmin and other Superuser Account

When an OpenShift cluster is first installed, a special `kubeadmin` user is provided to bootstrap the initial cluster configuration. This user is all-powerful and should be thought of as a `root` user for the cluster.

From a security perspective, `kubeadmin` should only be used to configure an identity provider and grant the `cluster-admin` role to at least one regular user. Using `kubeadmin` to interact with the cluster beyond this post-installation bootstrapping is bad practice, as it can make it difficult or impossible to determine who performed specific actions, particularly when the user is shared by multiple people.

Disabling the `kubeadmin` user after a new administrator is configured is strongly recommended. *Note that this is an irreversible operation!* It is highly recommended that the new administrator is tested first to be sure it is working properly. Disable the `kubeadmin` user by deleting the `kubeadmin` secret while logged in as a user with the `cluster-admin` role as follows:

```
$ oc delete secrets kubeadmin -n kube-system
```

Emergency Access

As part of the OpenShift installation process, the installer provides a `kubeconfig` file that is designed to be used for backup or emergency admin access. This is useful in situations where login to the cluster via an identity provider is not working properly as authenticating with the `kubeconfig` does not require OAuth to authenticate.

The `kubeconfig` contains a client certificate and private key that provides superuser access to the cluster. As such, it is very important to carefully protect the `kubeconfig` immediately after cluster installation by storing it in a secure offline location or as read-only in an online encrypted location that meets security requirements.

The default location for the kubeconfig is `<installation-directory>/auth/kubeconfig`. Authenticating to the cluster with the `kubeconfig` token can be done by:

- Passing the file as a flag when running oc commands :

```
$ oc --config=<path>/<to>/kubeconfig
```

- Or exporting it to the current shell session

```
$ export KUBECONFIG=<path>/kubeconfig
```

Once access has been restored to the cluster, place the `kubeadmin kubeconfig` file back into protected storage.

User Provisioning

In most cases, the people who will be interacting with a cluster already have user accounts defined centrally in a system of record such as an LDAP server. It is desirable (and often required per security policy) to have all authentication and user management handled in the centralized system of record.

While OpenShift Container Platform has *user objects*, they are not intended to be used as a primary identity source. User objects should be thought of as profiles used for assigning authorization and representing a user of the API within the platform.

For regular users, OpenShift provides a variety of external integration options via identity providers in the built-in OAuth server. Configuring an identity provider is the first thing to do after deploying a cluster, as OpenShift only provides a privileged `kubeadmin` user at install time. It is highly recommended to configure an external identity provider and remove the `kubeadmin` user after granting the `cluster-admin` role to a real user from that identity provider.

When choosing an identity provider, it is important to consider the identity-related security requirements with regards to :

- Authentication method strength
- Password policies
- Account controls (lockout, etc.)

By default, OpenShift automatically provisions a user object for a user when they log in for the first time via an identity provider. It is possible to change this behavior by configuring the mapping method for your identity provider. For example, the `lookup` mapping method can be used to require users to be manually provisioned in OpenShift before they will be allowed to log in. This setting is useful when successful authentication to the identity provider should not automatically confer access to OpenShift cluster resources.

Groups

Groups are a convenient construct provided to logically aggregated identities for the purposes of managing permissions in a maintainable way. Managing cluster permissions will be described in more detail in the Authorization section of this chapter, but it is important to understand what is possible with group management in OpenShift.

OpenShift provides the ability to define groups locally within the cluster. This can be a good place to define cluster-specific groups. Membership is managed via the `oc` CLI or the Console.

LDAP Group Synchronization

OpenShift also provides the ability to synchronize external groups from an LDAP server, dynamically provisioning them into OpenShift. Using LDAP groups allows access to OpenShift cluster resources to be managed from updates made directly to the LDAP server which is commonly used to centrally control access to applications and systems within an enterprise. Configuring LDAP group synchronization is a complex topic, as the exact configuration varies depending on the LDAP Deployment. See the official OpenShift documentation for details on how to configure LDAP synchronization for the environment.

Note that synchronizing groups from LDAP does not require an LDAP server to be used as the identity provider in OpenShift. This allows the parallel use of an identity provider that provides stronger authentication than the password-based authentication that the LDAP provider provides while still using groups from LDAP for authorization.

Both local groups and LDAP groups can be mixed together, allowing the most common cluster access to be managed via LDAP and locally defined cluster-specific groups defined in OpenShift to augment access granted via LDAP groups. This is useful when the administration of LDAP groups is handled by a different group of people than the administration of the OpenShift cluster.

If the environment uses an LDAP server, it is most likely used for more than just accessing the OpenShift cluster. It is possible to synchronize only a subset of groups from LDAP to OpenShift. From a security perspective, it is ideal to only synchronize groups that are to be used for controlling access to the cluster. This can be achieved in the `LDAP sync` configuration by setting the LDAP search `baseDN` and `filter` to restrict the entries found, as well as using whitelist and blacklist files to define exceptions.

When synchronizing groups from LDAP, it is important to know that the removal of groups in LDAP will not, by default, remove the associated group from OpenShift. The process of *pruning* groups is performed separately from the normal synchronization process by using the `oc adm prune groups` command. Ensure regular pruning of groups if LDAP groups are to be deleted as a method of removing access to the OpenShift cluster.

When synchronizing groups from LDAP, it is up to the cluster administrator to determine how often to perform the synchronization. From a security standpoint, it is important to consider how quickly authorization changes are to take effect when group membership changes. OpenShift will not know about changes to LDAP group membership until synchronization is run.

Virtual Groups

OpenShift Container Platform also provides for virtual groups used for authorization purposes. The most common of these are the `system:authenticated` and `system:unauthenticated` groups. Virtual groups are managed automatically by OpenShift.

Cluster Node Users

We have not mentioned users at the cluster node level. This is intentional, as regular management of the underlying RHCOS cluster nodes is designed to be performed via the OpenShift API itself. The only users that exist on an RHCOS OpenShift node are *root* and *core*. The core user is a member of the *wheel* group, which gives it permission to use `sudo` for running privileged commands. Adding additional users at the node level is highly discouraged.

Direct Access via oc debug

Direct node access is only intended to be used for troubleshooting and emergency purposes. By default, the only way to access a shell on a node in an OpenShift cluster is via the `oc debug node/<node>` CLI command. It is important to note that this provides a shell logged in as root on the node. This is only available to users with the `cluster-admin` role whose use should be limited as much as possible. Note that auditing the actions taken on a node via `oc debug node` will require audit logging to be configured. Additionally, logs from the cluster will need to be correlated to determine which real user performed the actions on the node. The audit logs on the node will only indicate that actions were performed by the root user. See Chapter 7 : Auditing for more details.

Direct Access via SSH

Though discouraged, SSH access to the nodes can be enabled to allow for emergency access and debugging. The RHCOS nodes are running `sshd` with `root` login disabled by default. To allow SSH access, MachineConfigs can be used to add SSH public keys to the core user's `authorized_key` configuration.

Using separate SSH keys per administrator is recommended, as it allows for auditing of the session which can be tied back to the specific SSH key used to authenticate. To do this, modify the existing MachineConfigs on the cluster. First, get a copy of MachineConfig for the node type to be updated :

```
$ oc get machineconfigs | grep ssh
99-master-ssh
                  2.2.0              2d18h
99-worker-ssh
                  2.2.0              2d18h
```

```
$ oc get machineconfigs 99-worker-ssh -oyaml > add-ssh-key-
worker.yaml
```

Modify the MachineConfig yaml file to add additional SSH public keys after as desired :

```
apiVersion: machineconfiguration.openshift.io/v1
kind: MachineConfig
metadata:
  labels:
    machineconfiguration.openshift.io/role: worker
  name: 99-worker-ssh
spec:
  config:
    ignition:
      version: 2.2.0
    passwd:
      users:
      - name: core
        sshAuthorizedKeys:
        - |
          ssh-rsa …
        - |
          ssh-rsa …
```

Apply the updated MachineConfig yaml file, and the Machine Config Operator will apply the configuration and reboot the nodes :

```
$ oc apply -f add-ssh-key-worker.yaml
machineconfig.machineconfiguration.openshift.io/99-worker-ssh
configured
```

If SSH is used to access one of the RHCOS nodes, the node will be annotated by the MachineConfigDaemon to flag that it has been accessed.

This can be monitored to detect if any nodes are accessed via SSH. The following annotation will be seen when running `oc describe` for a node that has been accessed via SSH :

```
machineconfiguration.openshift.io/ssh=accessed
```

Additionally, a good practice is to use *bastion hosts* when access to the RHCOS nodes via SSH is needed. The bastion hosts can be configured to meet more stringent authentication and auditing requirements.

If necessary, it is also possible to configure the System Security Services Daemon (SSSD) on the RHCOS nodes via a MachineConfig to allow a centralized identity source such as an LDAP server to be used. See Chapter 2 : Red Hat Enterprise Linux CoreOS Security for more details on the security considerations related to direct node access.

Authentication Overview

Authentication refers to the process that OpenShift performs upon receiving an API request in order to verify that the requestor (user) is who they claim to be. A request typically includes a user signed token or other identifying credentials that are validated by the API server's authentication layer. If the user's authentication attempt succeeds, the API server modifies the request to include the user's information and passes it along to the authorization layer.

In Kubernetes, the default is simple X.509 certificate verification, token files, and user passwords. To augment the default authentication, configure an identity provider via an OAuth server.

Kubernetes Authentication Layer

The Kubernetes authentication layer involves a stack of authentication methods. Individual authentication methods can offer differing degrees of trust verification (such as a password in a file versus a cryptographically signed token). The authenticators provided by Kubernetes out-of-the-box are the simple cases (X.509 certificate verification, token file). Integrating other authentication methods usually involves more complicated configuration. To address this, by default, OpenShift includes an integrated OAuth server.

The OAuth protocol provides a flexible framework for authenticating users against different external identity providers. The end result of a successful authentication is an access or bearer token that can be used for a period of time to subsequently authenticate the API without the need to provide the initial authentication credentials again.

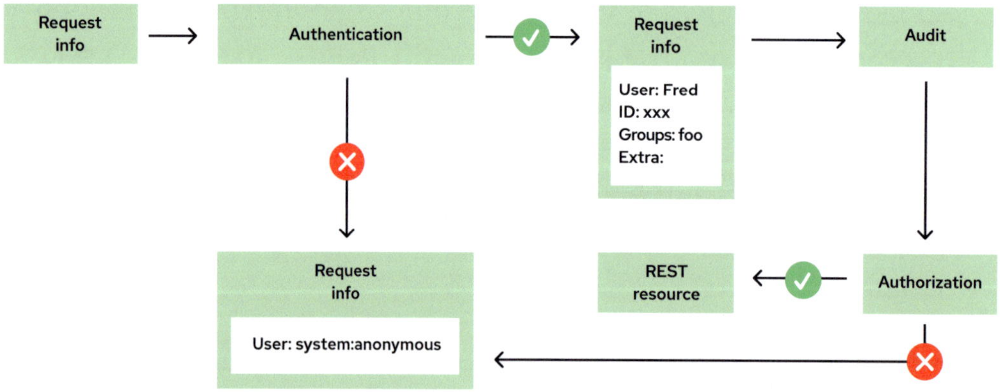

Figure 5.1 shows the layers that a request moves through inside of the API server. Note that the Authentication layer is concerned with verifying access tokens directly, and does not handle the actual user login process. Instead, the API server redirects an unauthenticated request to the internal OAuth

server, where the actual login process begins. We will outline this process in more detail below.

OAuth

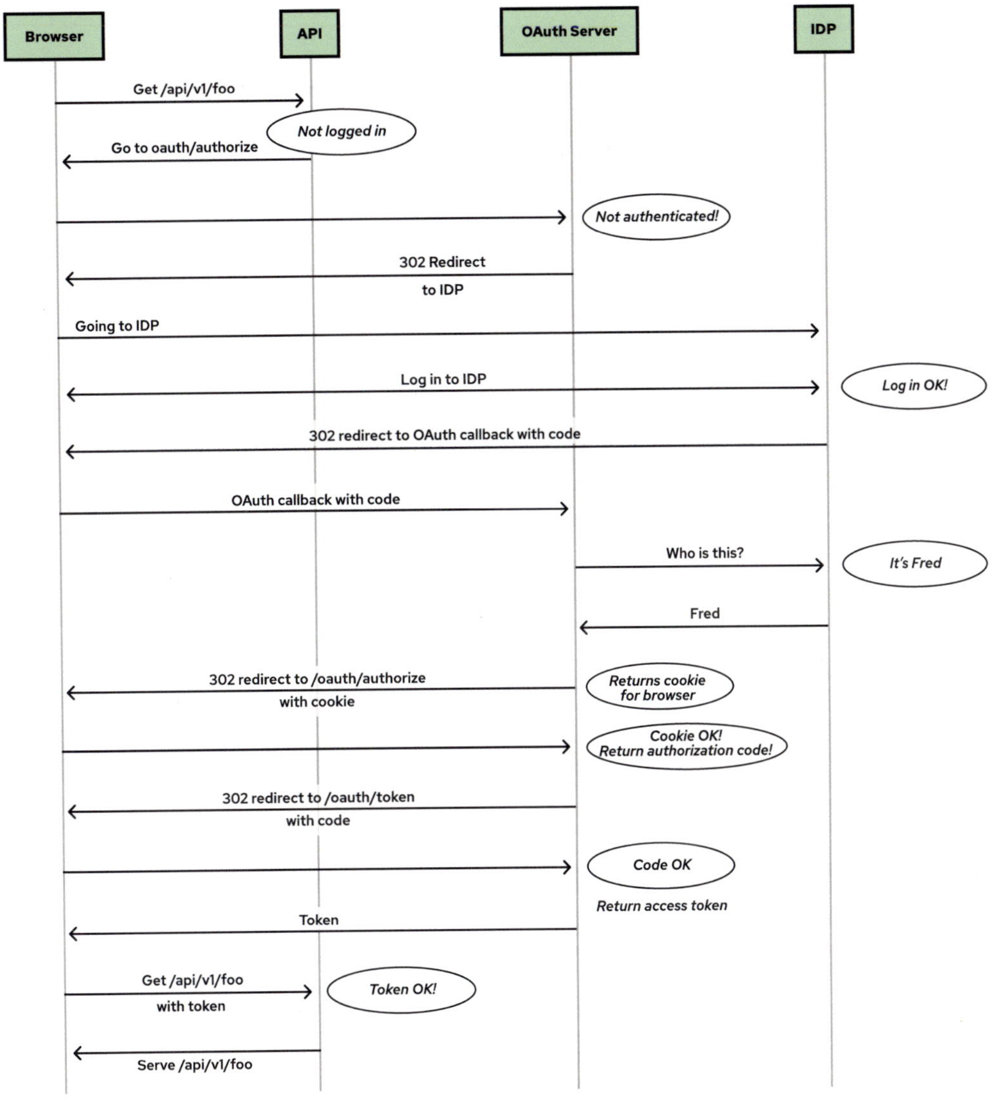

Figure 5.2: Browser-based OAuth Login Flow

Figure 5.2 shows an example of the OAuth flow on OpenShift when logging in using a web browser. The flow is controlled by a series of redirects and moves in a few general stages:

- Initial requests to the API by unauthenticated users are redirected to the OAuth server

- The OAuth server redirects the browser to the identity provider to authenticate. Typically, the browser is directed to a login prompt where user credentials are provided. At this stage, the browser interacts independently with the identity provider, and advanced authentication methods (such as 2-factor authentication) can take place according to what is configured and supported by the identity provider.

- Once authenticated to the identity provider, the browser follows a series of redirects in order to exchange an OAuth *authorization code* for a signed and encrypted browser cookie and access token. The use of a cookie allows a browser session to request new access tokens without requiring a user lookup from the identity provider each time.

The flow shown in Figure 5.2 can vary slightly depending on the IDP and user-agent capabilities. For example, while the illustrated flow would redirect to a GitHub identity provider login page, an LDAP identity provider would redirect to a custom login page served by the OAuth server. The `oc` command provides another variant, where the OAuth server serves a WWW-Authenticate challenge in exchange for an authorization code.

The OpenShift OAuth server supports both the standard authorization code and implicit grant types. For typical client usage of OpenShift, such as console and `oc` logins, the grant type is selected automatically (as well as the `client_id` and other required fields) to form the proper OAuth requests and follow redirects as needed. If the requests are manually formed (through curl, etc.), see the following documentation links for more information on the required request fields and endpoints :

- Understanding Authentication
- Configuring the Internal OAuth Server

A Note about Identity Provider Users and Authentication

The verification of the user credentials (authentication via an identity provider, mapping of the identity provider user, and so on) happens during the early OAuth process and not during the API server's validation of the access token. As a result, user management actions on the identity provider (such as deleting a user or adding a group) will not impact or invalidate an active bearer token from a previous authentication (see below about token lifetime).

Consider how soon authorization-related changes are required to be made to an identity provider to take effect in the OpenShift cluster when configuring the token lifetime. Future improvements to OpenShift, such as Keycloak integration, will allow more control over bearer token policy.

Authentication Methods

There are various ways to manage authentication tokens that can change the tokens lifetime or get rid of the token altogether. Tokens can also be delegated from one user to another.

OAuth Access Tokens

An access token (opaque to the client) is the result of a successful authentication. The access token is used in the HTTPS request to the API as an `Authorization: Bearer <xx>` header.

Access Token Lifetime

By default, the access token lifetime is 24 hours. This can be configured using the steps described in configuring the internal OAuth server's token duration. The decision to shorten or lengthen the token lifetime will depend on the use case. Shorter tokens will require more frequent authentication attempts, providing a possible hit in performance, but can decrease the impact of a leaked token.

Access Token Revocation

An active access token can be revoked manually by the administrator. To revoke an active access token, perform the following :

1. Get a list of active tokens in order to identify which token to revoke :

```
$ oc get oauthaccesstokens
```

2. When the token to revoke has been identified, delete the token :

```
$ oc delete oauthaccesstoken/name
```

This can be useful if access to the cluster for a specific user needs to be revoked.

Another way that a token is revoked is by a user manually performing a logout. For example, having the user run the following command will revoke access to the cluster using their existing token :

```
$ oc logout
```

Always having users logout when they are done working with OpenShift is a best practice. Unfortunately as of this writing, this is a manual process with no native way of auto-logging out users due to inactivity.

Service Account Tokens

Service Account tokens use the JSON Web Token (JWT) format and are signed using HMAC SHA256 (512-bit key) and encrypted using AES-256 (256-bit key). Service Account tokens never expire and do not refresh on their own. In order to refresh a Service Account token, delete the secret referenced in the Service Account :

```
$ oc get sa/default -o jsonpath='{range .secrets[*]}{.name}
{"\n"}{end}'
default-token-6j295
default-dockercfg-rfk45

$ oc delete secret/default-token-6j295
secret "default-token-6j295" deleted
```

After deletion, a new secret will automatically be generated and the Service Account token updated :

```
$ oc get sa/default -o jsonpath='{range .secrets[*]}{.name}
{"\n"}{end}'
default-dockercfg-rfk45
default-token-4n4pc
```

X.509 Certificate

OpenShift utilizes the Kubernetes built-in X.509 certificate authenticator for authentication of the cluster-admin user as well as control-plane components. The cluster-admin `kubeconfig` that is generated at install time contains a private key and certificate that is signed by an internal certificate authority (CA). OpenShift configures the API server to use this CA to validate the user certificate sent during TLS negotiation. If the CA validation of the certificate is successful, the request is authenticated and user information is derived from the certificate subject fields.

Since the OpenShift internal CA is not exposed beyond the cluster, attempting to use client certificates to authenticate normal users through the API is not recommended. An external CA would require signing and creating certificates out-of-band and would lose the ability to revoke the user's certificate. It is not currently possible to replace the CA that the API trusts for this purpose.

Token Delegation

There is a form of token delegation that offers the ability to delegate a subset of permissions to another user by generating a token with *scopes*. See skoping tokens for details on how to offer a subset of permissions from one user to another.

This feature has limited use for most workloads since the ability to create scoped tokens is restricted to the cluster-admin user. If used, token delegation should be used with care as it is possible to give a token scoped to a role with privileged access which in turn would provide escalating access to a cluster resource or the entire cluster.

Integrating with External Identity Providers

OpenShift supports a variety of OAuth identity providers, each providing a different degree of assured trust. The choice of identity provider depends on factors such as what is available in the environment and the desired level of security. See the OpenShift documentation for a full list of supported identity providers.

Where possible, choose to use an OAuth or OIDC-based identity provider (GitLab, OIDC) over the HTPasswd, LDAP or BasicAuthentication, as they provide stronger authentication methods.

Alternatively, the RequestHeader identity provider can be used to tie into SAML and Microsoft SSPI systems and can be configured to operate against custom identity solutions by using an Apache reverse proxy and custom Apache modules. For examples of this type of identity provider configuration, see Configuring a request header identity provider.

Using a custom RequestHeader identity provider may also be used for advanced identity use cases such as configuring a smartcard like CAC or PIV or configuring One Time Passwords (OTP). There are a few aspects to understand :

1. Custom RequestHeader identity providers may not work with the OpenShift client.
2. Smart Cards are not supported.
3. What can and cannot be done depends heavily on the identity provider.

For example, an identity provider, Red Hat IdM accessed via LDAP can be configured to accept a `password+pin` One Time Password response from the OpenShift web or client login.

Using the OpenShift client configured with a Red Hat IdM identity provider :

```
$ oc login -u=<username> -p=<password><hotp/totp_pin>
```

Again, this is heavily dependent on the identity provider's capability with no guarantees of success or supportability.

LDAP Identity Provider

Although using LDAP as an identity provider can provide a convenient way to plug into commonly used existing infrastructure, there are some drawbacks to be aware of.

Configuring an LDAP IdP potentially requires importing an LDAP bind DN and password into OpenShift which has the permissions to perform lookups against the LDAP tree. An LDAP administrative account should not be used for this purpose, as OpenShift only needs to perform read operations as this user. Distribution of admin credentials in this way is highly discouraged and disallowed in many environments. If an appropriate user does not exist, it is recommended to create an LDAP user for use by the OpenShift OAuth server with the appropriate permissions.

Additionally, the LDAP IdP performs an LDAP simple bind operation to authenticate the user, which transmits the user password to the LDAP server for authentication. If using an LDAP IdP, ensure that TLS is enabled in the IdP configuration to protect user passwords in transit.

Keep in mind that using TLS to communicate with the LDAP server still requires that users of the cluster provide their LDAP password to OpenShift. From a security perspective, this is not ideal since LDAP passwords are generally used for multiple applications within an enterprise that may have no relation to the OpenShift cluster. To avoid the potential for user LDAP passwords to be leaked, it is recommended to choose a different IdP that does not rely on password-based authentication.

Keep in mind that the LDAP identity provider does not need to be used in order to gather groups from LDAP, since syncing groups to OpenShift involves an admin running the group sync command at regular intervals instead of relying on IdP configuration. In some environments, it might be beneficial to use an IdP other than LDAP for user authentication while relying on LDAP only for group information.

Authorization

While authentication is meant to verify a user making a request, authorization is still needed to ensure that the user has permission to make the requested action. Figure 5.3 illustrates the flow of authentication and authorizations steps in OpenShift.

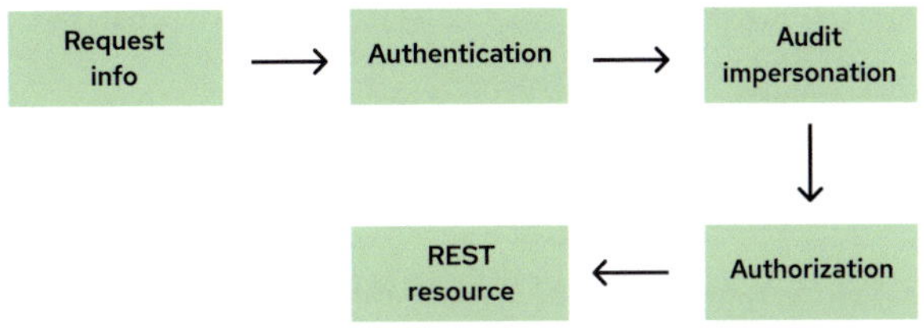

Figure 5.3: The Request Moving Through the Authentication and Authorization Layers

After authentication, the OpenShift API request is passed along (with the asserted User info) to the Kubernetes authorization layer (after a visit to the Audit layer). This layer is responsible for ensuring that the user has been granted permissions, by policy, to perform the requested action against the requested resource. Although the Kubernetes authorization layer is pluggable, OpenShift does not allow customization here, and only uses the Role-Based Access Control (RBAC) authorization type.

RBAC Overview

Authorization in OpenShift is managed using role-based access control (RBAC). OpenShift takes a *deny-by-default* approach to RBAC. Roles can be defined by *grouped-together* rules that represent allowed actions on objects within the cluster. These roles can then be applied to users and groups via role bindings.

Roles are maintained in a hierarchy, allowing for the definition of cluster-wide roles as well as project-specific (local) roles. RBAC evaluation takes this hierarchy into account, checking cluster-wide roles first, then local roles. This allows the cluster-wide roles to be augmented or overridden at the project level if necessary.

Role bindings are also maintained using the same hierarchy of *cluster* and *local* levels that are used by the roles themselves. This allows authorization to be scoped using common roles as roles defined at the cluster level can be used by a local binding to apply it to a specific project.

This section describes some recommended approaches to securely using RBAC. For a more thorough explanation of the fundamental concepts of RBAC, and the related oc commands for managing RBAC, see Using RBAC to define and apply permissions in the official OpenShift documentation.

Kubeadmin Usage

As mentioned in the Identity section above, the *kubeadmin* user is all-powerful within the cluster. Since it is not possible to restrict the kubeadmin account via RBAC, it is recommended to limit the usage of this account as much as possible, ideally disabling it completely after performing the initial identity provider configuration. For details on the procedure to disable kubeadmin, see the Kubeadmin and Other Super User Accounts section of this chapter.

Best Practices for RBAC Management

This section contains assorted best practices to configuring RBAC in the cluster.

Follow the Principle of Least Privilege

The most important advice is to follow the principle of least privilege and only grant the strictly required verbs to a role. While it is possible to use wildcards to grant access to all resources in an apiGroup or allow the role to use all verbs, it is always advisable to enumerate only the needed verbs and resources, especially if the role only needs read access.

Use ClusterRoles for Namespaced Resources with Caution

Roles scoped at a cluster level, i.e. ClusterRoles, should be used with extreme caution. Instead, using local roles to provide access at a namespace level offers more granular access. It is better to grant access to an explicit list of namespaces as opposed to the entire cluster. Otherwise, the ClusterRole might inadvertently open up access to resources in a namespace that the user does not need.

Make Use of the Predefined ClusterRoles

OpenShift 4 provides a set of predefined ClusterRoles. Defining custom roles instead of using the default ones can result in unexpected behavior as the predefined ClusterRoles are maintained and curated by the OpenShift team, with frequent patches and role updates. When defining a ClusterRole, it might be easy to forget about some resource or a verb, which might be difficult to debug or worse, it might be tempting to create a ClusterRole with more permission than is needed.

Don't Use the Default ServiceAccount, Use a Specific One Instead

While each namespace comes with a stock default serviceAccount, it is preferable to add a specific serviceAccount for a pod. This is both more explicit and enables better documentation and traceability back to the specific pod's serviceAccount. More importantly, the default service account is used unless an explicit serviceAccount is specified for a pod – in practice, extending the permissions for the default serviceAccount means that all pods that don't explicitly set a specific serviceAccount would inherit these extended permissions. This could result in unintended access being granted.

Manage Bindings via Groups as Much as Possible

When binding multiple subjects to a Role through a RoleBinding or a ClusterRoleBinding, it is preferable to include all the subjects in a group and refer to the group in the binding over individually listing the users. Having the set of users centrally defined as a group allows for easier review and management of the group, which is especially important if it's needed to remove a user's binding.

Review and Test Access

Because RBAC is the central way of managing access to a cluster, it is imperative to know who can do what. To display the RBAC configuration, it is possible to list the roles and bindings provided the user has the read permissions :

```
$ oc describe clusterrole.rbac
$ oc describe clusterrolebinding.rbac
$ oc describe rolebinding.rbac -n devproject
$ oc describe role.rbac --all-namespaces
```

The complete list of RBAC permissions might be overwhelming, so a good starting point might be to review any custom roles and evaluate their RBAC permissions :

- What can the role write to in the cluster?
- Can the role read or write to other resources in the cluster?
- Can the role read or write across namespaces?

Examining if any subjects have permissions to highly privileged default roles might provide administrators with an idea about the general level of RBAC access of the role to the cluster.

In addition to reviewing the RBAC rules, it is also possible to perform a dry-run of a request using the `auth can-i` oc plug-in. Let's see some examples :

- Can the current user create secrets in the current `namespace`?

```
$ oc auth can-i create secrets
Yes
```

- Can the current user create secrets in the namespace `default` ?

```
$ oc auth can-i create secrets -n default
no
```

The `auth can-i` plugin might also be combined with impersonation, which is a useful RBAC debugging tool for cluster administrators.

When do Authorization Changes take Effect?

Changes to both roles and local group membership instantly take effect, and the user is not required to re-login when their group membership changes. Note that since LDAP groups are periodically synchronized, the LDAP group membership would only come into effect on the next refresh. If synchronizing groups from LDAP, consider how quickly authorization changes need to take effect to meet security requirements and ensure that the synchronization schedule is treated accordingly.

Impersonation

Impersonation allows a user to temporarily act on behalf of another identity. This might be useful to grant a set of read-only permissions to a subject, but allow them to explicitly acquire elevated privileges by impersonating another subject with write permissions. This makes it harder to accidentally change cluster objects as the write access must be explicitly requested by impersonating the more powerful account.

Impersonation is recorded in Kubernetes audit logs. For example, if we allow members of a group to impersonate cluster-admin and a member of this group creates a secret using impersonation, the following request (abbreviated for clarity) appears in the Kubernetes audit log :

```
verb": "create",
  "user": {'
        "username": "user1",
        "groups": [
          "group1",
          "system:authenticated:oauth",
          "system:authenticated"
        ],
```

```
        "extra": {
          "scopes.authorization.openshift.io": [
            "user:full"
          ]
        }
  },
  "impersonatedUser": {
        "username": "cluster-admin",
        "groups": [
          "system:authenticated"
        ]
  },
  "objectRef": {
        "resource": "secrets",
        "namespace": "default",
        "name": "my-secret",
        "apiVersion": "v1"
  },
```

6. Network Security

The network is a major threat vector and is involved in most Information security attacks. Typically, such network attacks exploit system vulnerabilities or misconfiguration.

Some well-known network attacks are :

- Denial of Service (DoS) and Distributed Denial of Service (DDoS) attacks against any exposed component of an end-user service
- Man-In-the-Middle (MITM) attacks that intercept confidential information
- Automated continuous port scanning for break-in attempts

The adoption of cloud computing challenges the traditional perimeter security model that assumed relatively static and controlled workloads.

The concept of zero trust security has emerged to address new security challenges of cloud native architecture :

1. The cloud infrastructure is shared among workloads with different levels of trust
2. Applications are decomposed into interconnected containerized microservices increasing the attack surface
3. Continuous deployment of new software versions potentially changes the communication patterns

This chapter describes the networking design elements used in OpenShift that must be understood in order to address network security. The chapter first covers the networking concepts that are part of upstream Kubernetes. It then discusses the additional networking features brought by OpenShift to complement the basic Kubernetes capabilities.

This chapter covers the measures implemented by OpenShift to secure communication between the various components of each application deployed on the cluster.

Kubernetes Networking Concepts

In Kubernetes, network policies define the permissions pods must communicate with other pods and with network endpoints. The Container Network Interface (CNI) provides a framework for providing network connectivity to containers. Defining Ingress resources can create routes to allow cluster applications to be exposed outside of the cluster.

Network Policies

Controlling the traffic between pods is an essential part of securing their applications.

By restricting the service and endpoint connections, malicious activity can be prevented, and the impact of misbehaving application pods can also be limited. This prompts security practitioners to use a pod-focused evaluation strategy of an application security situation.

Traditional workloads use firewalls and specific routing rules to provide isolation via partitioning, traffic restrictions, and port blocking. In the container world, container runtimes and orchestrators handle this functionality through defined network security policies. One of OpenShift's strengths is the ability to comprehensively manage the wide variety of control types in logical collections such as pods and their related controls. These controls are described below.

A *NetworkPolicy* is a specification of how groups of pods are allowed to communicate with each other and other network endpoints. NetworkPolicy resources use labels to select pods and define rules that specify what traffic is allowed to the selected pods. By default, pods are not isolated, and they will accept traffic from any source.

Pods become isolated by having a NetworkPolicy that selects them. Once there is any NetworkPolicy in a namespace selecting a particular pod, that pod will reject any connections that are not allowed by any NetworkPolicy. Other pods in the namespace that are not selected by any NetworkPolicy will continue to accept all traffic.

Network policies are additive. If any policy or policies select a pod, the pod is restricted to what is allowed by the union of those policies' ingress and egress rules. Thus, order of evaluation does not affect the policy result.

Network policies allow configuration of isolation policies for individual pods. Network policies apply to pod traffic within a project, and do not require administrative privileges, which gives developers more control over their applications.

Network policies can be used to create logical zones in the network that map to the organization network zones. The benefit is that the actual pod location (which pod the node is running) is irrelevant, because network policies allow segregation of traffic regardless of where it originates.

The following example of NetworkPolicy objects demonstrate supporting different scenarios :

1. **Denying all traffic** : To make a project deny by default, add a NetworkPolicy object that matches all pods but accepts no traffic. For example:

```
kind: NetworkPolicy
apiVersion: networking.k8s.io/v1
metadata:
  name: deny-by-default
spec:
  podSelector:
  ingress: []
```

2. **Only accept connections from pods within a project** : To make pods accept connections from other pods in the same project, but reject all other connections from pods in other projects, add the following NetworkPolicy object:

```
kind: NetworkPolicy
apiVersion: networking.k8s.io/v1
metadata:
  name: allow-same-namespace
spec:
  podSelector:
  ingress:
  - from:
    - podSelector: {}
```

3 **Only allow HTTP and HTTPS traffic based on pod labels**: To enable only HTTP and HTTPS access to the pods with a specific label (`role=frontend` in following example), add a NetworkPolicy object similar to the following:

```
kind: NetworkPolicy
apiVersion: networking.k8s.io/v1
metadata:
  name: allow-http-and-https
spec:
  podSelector:
    matchLabels:
      role: frontend
  ingress:
  - ports:
    - protocol: TCP
      port: 80
    - protocol: TCP
      port: 443
```

4 **Accept connections by using both namespace and pod selectors**: To match network traffic by combining namespace and pod selectors, use a NetworkPolicy object similar to the following:

```
kind: NetworkPolicy
apiVersion: networking.k8s.io/v1
metadata:
  name: allow-pod-and-namespace-both
spec:
  podSelector:
    matchLabels:
      name: test-pods
```

```
ingress:
  - from:
    - namespaceSelector:
        matchLabels:
          project: project_name
      podSelector:
        matchLabels:
          name: test-pods
```

Since NetworkPolicy objects are additive, it is possible to combine multiple NetworkPolicy objects together to satisfy complex network requirements. For example, for the NetworkPolicy objects defined in previous examples, define both `allow-same-namespace` and `allow-http-and-https` policies within the same project. Thus, allowing the pods with the label `role=frontend` to accept any connection allowed by each policy. That is, connections on any port from pods in the same namespace, and connections on ports 80 and 443 from pods in any namespace.

A network policy does not apply to the host network namespace. Pods with host networking enabled are unaffected by NetworkPolicy object rules.

Container Network Interface

By default, Kubernetes pods are attached to a single network and have a single network interface. In Kubernetes, container networking is delegated to Software-Defined Networking (SDN) plug-ins that implement the Container Network Interface (CNI). Network plug-ins in Kubernetes adhere to the appc/CNI specification.

The CNI (Container Network Interface), a Cloud Native Computing Foundation (CNCF) project, consists of a specification and libraries for writing plug-ins to configure network interfaces in Linux containers. CNI concerns itself only with network connectivity of containers and removing allocated resources when the container is deleted. As a result of this focus, CNI has a wide range of support and the specification is simple to implement.

A CNI plug-in is responsible for allocating the network interfaces to newly created pods, and setting up the proper networking constructs to enable communications between pods as well as with external entities (ingress and egress communications). The CNI plug-in is also responsible for implementing the network policies specified by the various NetworkPolicy objects.

Ingress Traffic

To expose HTTP and HTTPS routes to Kubernetes services from clients that are outside of the cluster, use Kubernetes Ingress resources. Beyond exposing HTTP and HTTPS routes, Ingress resources allow creation of other rules that define how traffic is routed to those services.

With Ingress resources, external URLs can be set to reach services, assign name-based virtual hosts, choose TLS termination, and select to have network traffic load balanced. TLS secrets can be named in the specification, easing management of certificates.

To expose non-HTTP and HTTPS services, choose one of the following Ingress types :

- **Type=NodePort** : Using NodePort exposes ports associated with an application's service API object on every worker node on the cluster
- **Type=LoadBalancer :** Using LoadBalancer assigned an external load balancer that directs traffic to the associated service API object in the cluster

An ingress resource must be associated with an ingress controller to fulfill the ingress. The controller is usually associated with a load balancer, although it can also be associated with other front ends or the edge router. For further information on ingress, see the description of the Ingress API Object in the Kubernetes documentation.

An Ingress Controller is required to satisfy an ingress. Creating only an Ingress resource has no effect.

OpenShift Networking Features

This section describes the additional features and components provided by OpenShift to secure cloud-native deployments supplementing Kubernetes' base capabilities:

- Operators to cover the consistent deployment of Kubernetes components
- Multiple network interfaces to pods enabling traffic isolation
- OVS SDN with Network Policies enabled
- Ingress and egress traffic security enhancements
- Service Mesh to implement a zero trust network model for securing communications between container-based microservices

Network Operators

OpenShift includes a set of operators that manage the various OpenShift networking components. This ensures enforcement of best practices and minimizes human errors during initial deployment and post-installation operations.

The following operators are responsible for the management of OpenShift networking components:

- The Cluster Network Operator (CNO) deploys and manages the cluster network components on an OpenShift Container Platform cluster, including the Container Network Interface (CNI) pod network provider plug-in selected for the cluster during installation.
- The DNS Operator deploys and manages CoreDNS to provide a name resolution service to pods, enabling DNS-based Kubernetes Service discovery in OpenShift.
- The Ingress Operator implements the *ingresscontroller* API and is the component responsible for enabling external access to OpenShift Container Platform cluster services. The operator makes this possible by deploying and managing one or more HAProxy-based Ingress Controllers to handle routing. The Ingress Operator can be used to route traffic by specifying OpenShift Container Platform Route and Kubernetes Ingress resources.
- The SR-IOV Network Operator creates and manages the components of the SR-IOV stack. It manages SR-IOV network devices and network attachments to pods.

Multiple Network Interfaces

By default, Kubernetes pods are attached to a single network (the cluster-wide pod network) and have a single primary network interface. This cluster-wide pod network is configured during cluster installation and attached to every pod.

Additional networks are typically useful in situations where network isolation is needed, including data plane and control plane separation. Isolating network traffic is useful for the following performance and security reasons :

- **Performance :** Single Root I/O Virtualization (SR-IOV) network devices can be used for high performance applications. SR-IOV virtual function (VF) interfaces can be attached to pods on nodes with SR-IOV hardware.

- **Security :** Sensitive traffic can be sent onto a network plane that is managed specifically for security considerations. For example, private data that must not be shared between tenants or customers can be separated.

The Multus CNI plug-in in OpenShift allows pods to also be connected to additional networks via secondary network interfaces. The Multus CNI plug-in acts as a meta plug-in, which is to say that it can call multiple other plug-ins. This allows chaining of several other CNI plug-ins. One of these plug-ins, the primary CNI plug-in, manages the cluster-wide pod network and implements the Network Policies on that network.

Additional networks can be defined in the pod specification and will be attached to the pods by secondary CNI plug-ins.

Every pod has an *eth0* interface that is attached to the cluster-wide pod network. The additional network interfaces should be named *net1, net2, ..., netN*. Figure 6.1 shows an example of Multus CNI.

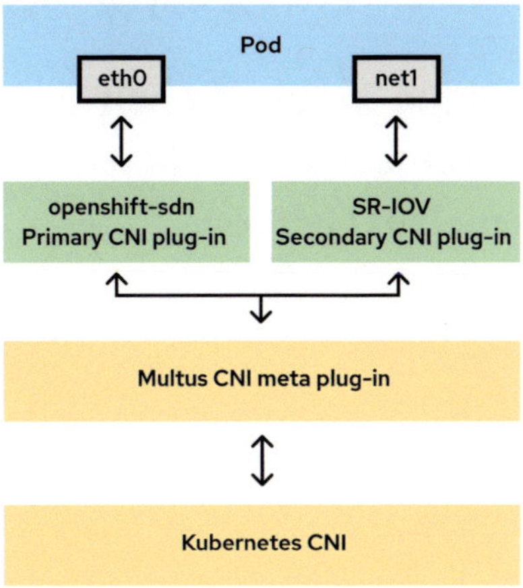

Figure 6.1: Pod with Multiple Network Interfaces

Primary CNI Plug-ins

OpenShift uses a Software-Defined Networking (SDN) approach to provide a unified cluster network that enables communication between all pods across the OpenShift cluster. This cluster-wide pod network is established and maintained by the primary CNI plug-in.

In OpenShift, Red Hat supports a number of alternatives for the primary CNI plug-in :

- **The OpenShift SDN CNI Plug-in :** Configures an overlay network using Open vSwitch (OVS). This is the default primary CNI plug-in for OpenShift.

- **The OVN CNI Plug-in** : Configures an overlay network using OVN. This plug-in first became available as a technology preview in OpenShift 4.2.
- **The OpenStack Kuryr CNI Plug-in** : Used when OpenShift is deployed on top of Red Hat OpenStack Platform, configures an overlay network using OpenStack services such as Neutron.

Only the default OpenShift SDN CNI Plug-in will be described in this book.

The OpenShift SDN CNI Plug-in

The OpenShift SDN CNI plug-in provides all Kubernetes v1 NetworkPolicy features except for egress policy types and IPBlock.

Network policies are Kubernetes resources. As such, manage them using the `oc create` and `oc delete` commands.

The OpenShift SDN plug-in configures each cluster node with an Open vSwitch bridge named *br0*. This is illustrated in Figure 6.3.

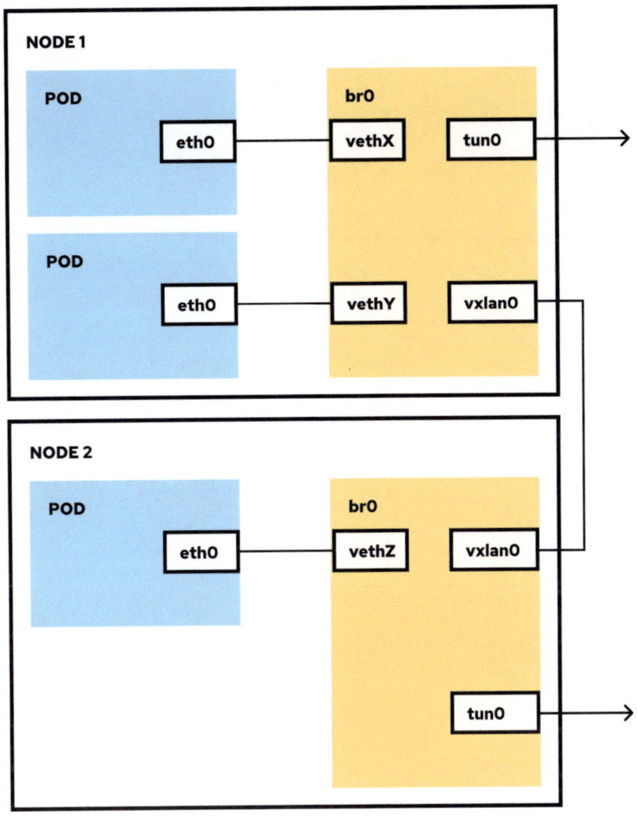

Figure 6.3: OpenShift SDN

The OpenShift SDN plug-in uses virtual Ethernet devices (*veth*) to connect pods to the br0 bridge. For each pod, the veth device is created and connects one end to the eth0 interface inside the pod and the other end to the br0 bridge.

Use the Open vSwitch `ovs-vsctl show` command on the node to display the br0 bridge and the connected ports :

```
[root@node ~]# ovs-vsctl show
1a7950b0-8dc2-4908-b682-b6dfc2b64969
Bridge "br0"
```

```
fail_mode: secure
Port "vetha4f3b73f"
Interface "vetha4f3b73f"
Port "veth47219954"
Interface "veth47219954"
Port "tun0"
Interface "tun0"
type: internal
Port "vxlan0"
Interface "vxlan0"
type: vxlan
options: {dst_port="4789", key=flow, remote_ip=flow}
Port "br0"
Interface "br0"
type: internal
ovs_version: "2.9.0"
```

The *tun0* interface on the node is an Open vSwitch port on the *br0* bridge. OpenShift uses that interface for external cluster access. OpenShift configures this external access through tun0 with a combination of network routes, Netfilter NAT rules, and entries in the br0 flow tables.

OpenShift uses the *vxlan_sys_4789* interface on the node, or vxlan0 in br0, for building the cluster overlay network between nodes. Communications between pods on different nodes go through this interface.

The OpenShift SDN plug-in implements network policies by configuring OpenvSwitch flow rules, which dictate which packets are allowed and which ones are denied.

The following excerpt shows how to allow external users to access an application with labels that match a *product-catalog* application over a TCP connection on port 8080.

```
kind: NetworkPolicy
apiVersion: extensions/v1beta1
metadata:
  name: external-access
spec:
  podSelector:
    matchLabels:
      app: product-catalog
  ingress:
  - ports:
    - protocol: TCP
      port: 8080
```

This translates to the following flow rules on the OpenvSwitch bridge on the node. The IP address 10.128.0.67 is the IP address of the pod.

```
[root@node ~]# ovs-ofctl dump-flows br0 -O OpenFlow13 --no-
stats

cookie=0x0, table=80, priority=150,tcp,reg1=0x6d285,
nw_dst=10.128.0.67, tp_dst=8080  actions=output:NXM_NX_REG2[]

cookie=0x0, table=80, priority=100,ip,reg1=0x6d285,
nw_dst=10.128.0.67 actions=drop
```

In the example above, there are a couple of things to notice :

- The first rule, which applies to table 80, allows TCP connections on port 8080.
- The second rule drops all packets that are not matched by the first rule.

OpenShift's SDN CNI options are managed by the Cluster Network Operator. This defines a central place to configure the different plug-ins and options in order to fine-tune the deployment and meet any needs.

As with many other components in OpenShift, there is a single custom resource that represents the source of truth for the operator. In this case, it is the *network.config* object, which can be inspected as follows :

```
$ oc describe network.config/cluster
apiVersion: config.openshift.io/v1
kind: Network
metadata:
  creationTimestamp: "2020-04-07T02:35:11Z"
  generation: 2
  name: cluster
  resourceVersion: "1861"
  selfLink: /apis/config.openshift.io/v1/networks/cluster
  uid: af9ebf64-89ec-4c06-bed4-25db5ddcf0b3
spec:
  clusterNetwork:
  - cidr: 10.128.0.0/14
        hostPrefix: 23
  externalIP:
        policy: {}
  networkType: OpenShiftSDN
  serviceNetwork:
  - 172.30.0.0/16
status:
  clusterNetwork:
  - cidr: 10.128.0.0/14
        hostPrefix: 23
  clusterNetworkMTU: 8951
  networkType: OpenShiftSDN
```

```
serviceNetwork:
- 172.30.0.0/16
```

Secondary CNI Plug-ins

OpenShift provides a set of CNI plug-ins for creating additional networks in the cluster. Secondary network interfaces are not controlled by Kubernetes networking constructs like Network Policies or Ingress routers. See Additional networks in OpenShift Container Platform for a list of supported CNI plug-ins.

Ingress Cluster Traffic

By default, Kubernetes services created on the OpenShift cluster are of the ClusterIP type which makes the Service exposed on a cluster only reachable from within the cluster using an internal IP address.

Services accessed via HTTP/HTTPS, and/or TLS-encrypted protocols other than HTTPS (such as TLS with the SNI header), can use Ingress Controllers along with Ingress or Route resources to allow the service to be accessible from clients located outside of the cluster.

As an alternative, services accessed through other protocols (such as UDP, TCP, or SCTP) can be exposed externally using LoadBalancer or NodePort service types

in which case the OpenShift infrastructure exposes the Service to external clients as follows :

- **LoadBalancer type :** Allows traffic to non-standard ports through an IP address assigned from a pool configured at the infrastructure level

- **NodePort type :** Exposes the service on a given port on all worker nodes of the cluster

It is also possible to allocate an external IP to a Service. The external IP address must have been provisioned at the infrastructure level and attached to a cluster node. With an external IP on the service, OpenShift sets up NAT rules to allow traffic arriving at any cluster node attached to that IP address to be sent to one of the internal pods. This is similar to the internal service IP addresses, but the external IP tells OpenShift that this service should also be exposed externally at the given IP.

The administrator must assign the IP address to a host (node) interface on one of the nodes in the cluster. Alternatively, the address can be used as a virtual IP. Virtual IPs are not managed by OpenShift and administrators are responsible for ensuring that traffic arrives at a node with this IP.

Table 6.1 Ingress Cluster Traffic provides a summary of the various methods to expose services to external clients.

Allows access to HTTP/HTTPS traffic and TLS-encrypted protocols other than HTTPS (for example, TLS with the SNI header).	Use an Ingress Controller with Ingress or Route resources.
Allows traffic to non-standard ports through an IP address assigned from a pool.	`type=LoadBalancer` in the Service specification
Expose a service on the same port on all worker nodes in the cluster.	`type=NodePort` in the Service specification
Manually assign an external IP to a service.	`externalIPs` field of the Service specification

Table 6.1: Ingress Cluster Traffic

OpenShift Routes

The need to expose services implemented on the OpenShift cluster to clients external to the cluster was addressed early on by OpenShift before Kubernetes introduced the concept of Ingress. This was addressed in OpenShift by the concept of Route resources. Red Hat is one of the top contributors to the Kubernetes community and helped shape the design principles of Route for the community which also heavily influenced the Ingress blueprint.

In OpenShift, Ingress Controllers are responsible for implementing the networking constructs described by either Route or Ingress resources.

While basic functionalities are provided by both kinds of resources, Table 6.2 *Ingress versus Route* highlights some features that are only exposed by the Route resource, in particular in the area of TLS connectivity.

Feature	Ingress	Route
Standard Kubernetes object	x	
External access to services	x	x
Persistent (sticky) sessions	x	x
Load-balancing strategies (e.g. round robin)	x	x
Rate-limit and throttling	x	x
IP whitelisting	x	x
TLS edge termination	x	x
TLS re-encryption		x
TLS passthrough		x
Multiple weighted backends (split traffic)		x
Generated pattern-based hostnames		x
Wildcard domains		x

Table 6.2: Ingress versus Route

Secured routes specify the TLS termination of the route and, optionally, provide a key and certificate(s). Secured routes can use any of the following three types of secure TLS termination:

- ***Edge Termination***
  With edge termination, TLS termination occurs at the Ingress Controller before it is sent to its destination. TLS certificates are served by the front end of the Ingress Controller, so they must be configured into the route. Otherwise, the Ingress Controller's default certificate will be used for TLS termination. As TLS is terminated at the Ingress Controller, connections from the Ingress Controller to the endpoints over the internal network are not encrypted.

- ***Passthrough Termination***
  With passthrough termination, encrypted traffic is sent straight to the destination without the Ingress Controller providing TLS termination. Therefore, no key or certificate is required. The destination pod is responsible for serving certificates for the traffic at the endpoint. This is currently the only method that can support client certificates (also known as two-way authentication).

- ***Re-encryption Termination***
  Re-encryption is a variation on edge termination where the Ingress Controller terminates TLS with a certificate, then re-encrypts its connection to the endpoint which may have a different certificate. Therefore, the full path of the connection is encrypted, even over the internal network. The Ingress Controller uses health checks to determine the authenticity of the host.

Ingress Controller and Operator

OpenShift supports the Ingress Operator which implements the ingresscontroller API and is responsible for enabling external access to OpenShift Container Platform cluster services. The OpenShift Ingress Operator can deploy and manage one or more HAProxy-based Ingress Controllers to handle routing. The Ingress Operator can be used to route traffic by specifying OpenShift Container Platform Route and Kubernetes ingress resources.

In situations where several security zones are implemented on an OpenShift Cluster, distinct Ingress Controllers are typically deployed for each security zone to enforce segregation of ingress traffic.

Egress Cluster Traffic

In an application, only selected components might need an egress path to reach external services. By default, OpenShift allows all traffic to leave the cluster with no restrictions. However, OpenShift provides means to implement fine grained filtering of egress traffic.

The traffic of a particular pod leaves the cluster with the source IP address of the node it runs on. This may not be appropriate in the following situations :

- Stateful firewalls controlling the external traffic expect the same IP addresses in both directions (ingress/egress) and might drop egress packets leaving the cluster with a worker node source IP address.

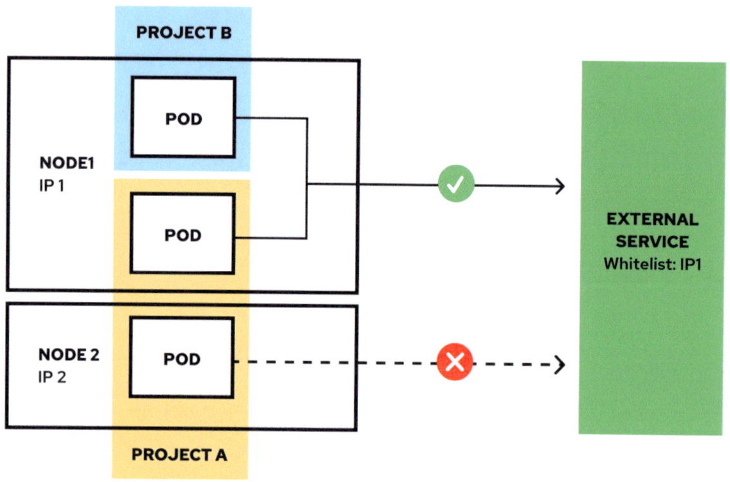

Figure 6.4: Controlling Egress Traffic

OpenShift provides several options for controlling the traffic leaving the cluster.

These options are :

- Egress firewall
- Egress routers
- Egress static IP

Egress Firewall

OpenShift allows the use of an egress firewall to limit the external hosts that some or all pods can access from within the cluster.

An egress firewall supports the following scenarios :

- A pod can only connect to internal hosts and cannot initiate connections to the public Internet
- A pod can only connect to the public Internet and cannot initiate connections to internal hosts that are outside the OpenShift Container Platform cluster
- A pod cannot reach specified internal subnets or hosts outside the OpenShift Container Platform cluster
- A pod can connect to only specific external hosts

OpenShift SDN is required to be configured to use either the network policy or multi-tenant modes to configure egress firewall policy.

Configuring the Egress Firewall

With the egress firewall, practitioners define rules to allow or deny traffic (TCP or UDP) to the outside network. Practitioners then describe these rules by creating an OpenShift EgressNetworkPolicy Custom Resource (CR) object associated with a project. This way, different projects can have different rules.

The following YAML file is an example of such an egress firewall.

```
[user@demo ~]$ cat firewall.yaml
kind: EgressNetworkPolicy
apiVersion: v1
metadata:
  name: myfirewall
spec:
```

```yaml
egress:
- type: Allow
  to:
    cidrSelector: 192.168.12.0/24
- type: Allow
  to:
    dnsName: db-srv.example.com
- type: Allow
  to:
    dnsName: analytics.example.com
- type: Deny
  to:
    cidrSelector: 0.0.0.0/0
```

This object allows the egress traffic to access the `192.168.12.0/24` network, and the `db-srv.example.com` and `analytics.example.com` systems. The last rule denies everything else. As OpenShift would allow the traffic if no rule matches, checks the rules in order, and this last rule acts as a **deny all** default. The rules only apply to the egress traffic and does not affect inter-pod communication.

To create the object and associate it with a project, use the `oc create -f file.yaml -n project` command :

```
[user@demo ~]$ oc create -f firewall.yaml -n myproject
egressnetworkpolicy.network.openshift.io/myfirewall created
```

There are several restrictions when using an egress firewall :

- No project can have more than one `EgressNetworkPolicy` object
- The `default` project cannot use egress network policy

These design choices tend to increase traffic safety of the pod boundary by requiring explicit creation and centralization of egress.

Egress Routers

When a pod establishes a network connection to an external service hosted on the network, the packets flow in the following way :

- From the pod to the br0 bridge
- From the br0 bridge to the node tun0 interface where NAT occurs
- Finally, to the external service

From that service's point of view, the connection is originating from the node IP address. The vxlan0 bridge interface is used to access other nodes. This is illustrated in Figure 6.5.

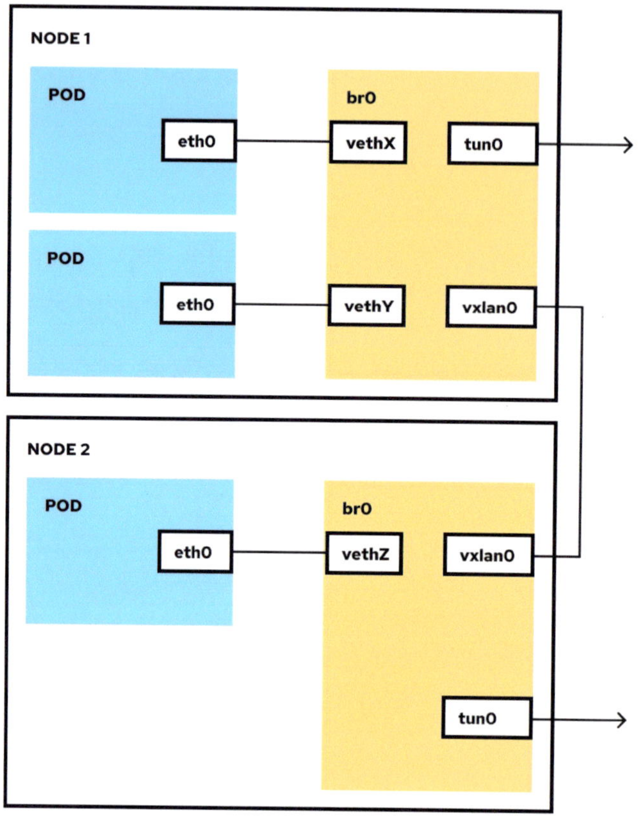

Figure 6.5: Pod to External Services (tun0) and Pod-to-Pod (vxlan0) Communications

If OpenShift relocates the pod to another node or if it replicates the pod on multiple nodes, the external service may see multiple source IP addresses. To prevent the firewall from blocking the service, all the OpenShift node IP addresses need to be authorized. If new nodes are added to the cluster, the firewall rules will need to be updated.

By using an OpenShift Egress Router, a unique identifiable source IP address is presented to the firewall and the external service.

An Egress Router is a particular pod running in the project. It acts as a proxy between the pods and the external service. Router pods have two network interfaces:

- eth0 for communication with the other cluster pods
- macvlan0 for communication with the external service

This is illustrated in Figure 6.6.

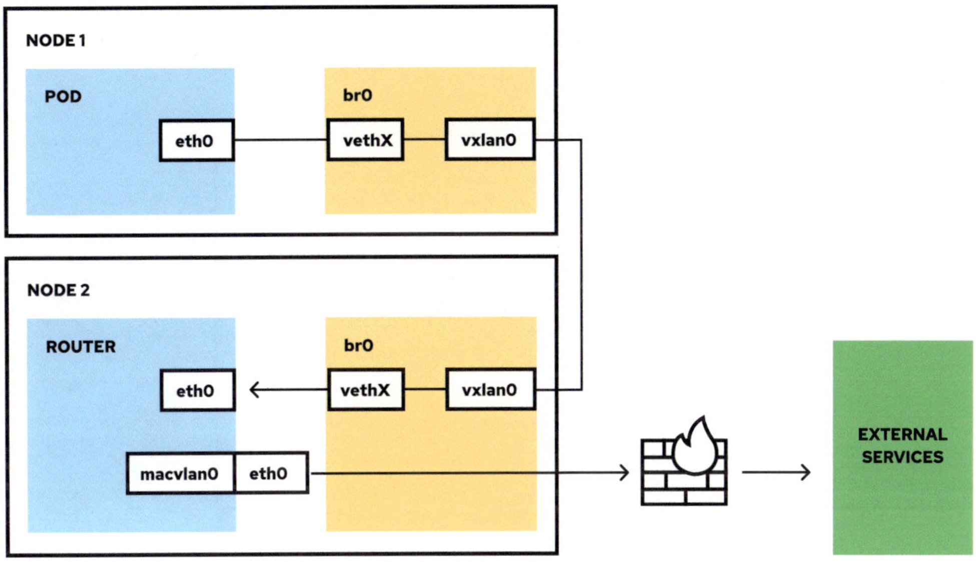

Figure 6.6: Pod Communication to External Services through the Egress Router

Macvlan interfaces are special devices that directly expose node interfaces to the container. The interface has a MAC address seen by the underlying network.

The Egress Router runs a service that redirects traffic to a specified remote server, using a private source IP address. The service allows pods to talk to servers that are setup to only allow access from whitelisted IP addresses. When deploying an Egress Router, an IP address from the host node's physical network that the host node resides is reserved by the cluster administrator to be used by the Egress Router.

Application pods access the external service using the egress service on the service's internal IP address or service name. The egress service redirects the traffic to the egress routers which in turn send the traffic to the external service with the egress IP (reserved for the host node) as the source IP. The external service accepts the traffic since the source IP (Egress Router IP) is whitelisted. This is illustrated in Figure 6.7.

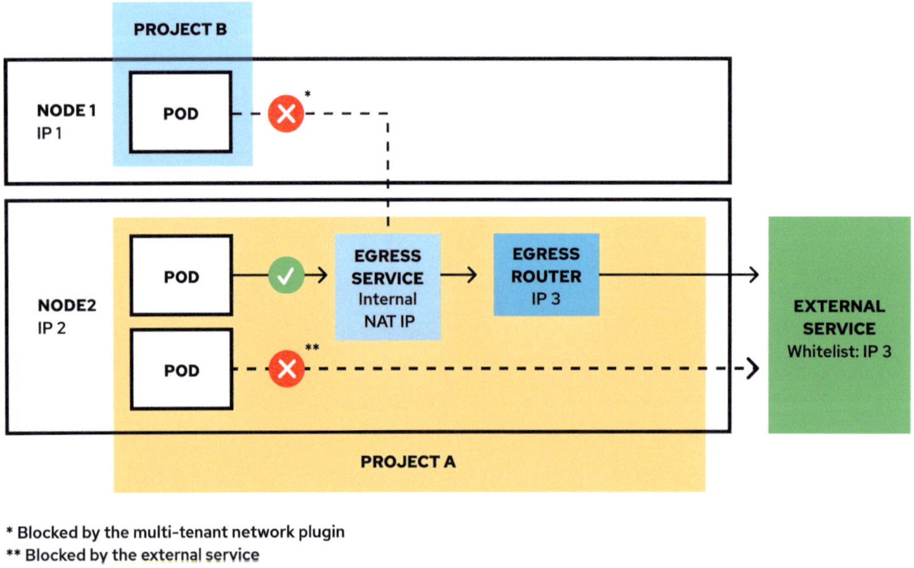

Figure 6.7: Concept of OpenShift Egress Router

Multiple egress IPs (egress pods) can be configured (one on each node) so that if a cluster detects that one egress IP has stopped working (node failure), it would fail over and use another egress IP on the other nodes that are preconfigured. This is illustrated in Figure 6.8.

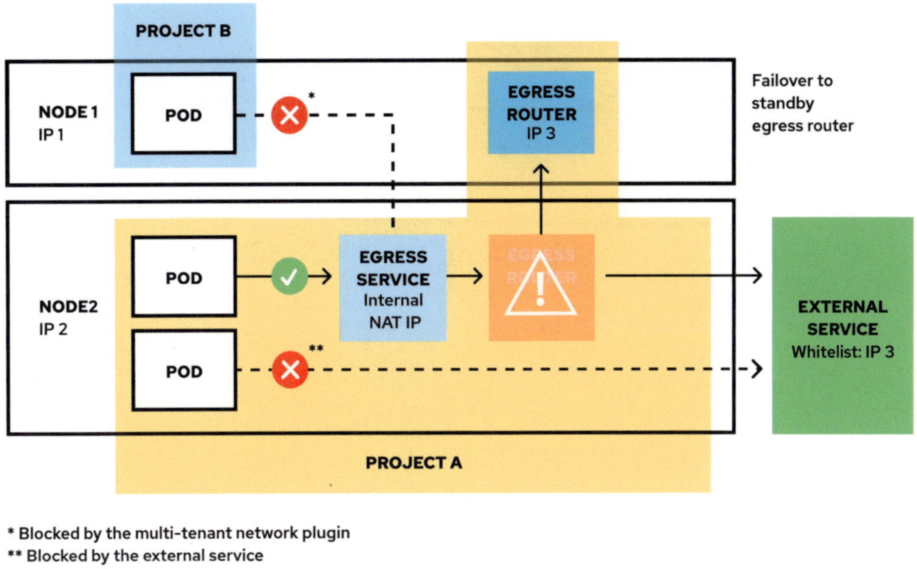

Figure 6.8: Failure to Standby Egress Router

Egress IP

Egress IP is an OpenShift feature that allows for the assignment of an IP to a namespace (the egress IP) so that all outbound traffic from that namespace appears as if it is originating from that IP address (technically it is NATed with the specified IP). This feature is useful within many enterprise environments as it allows for the establishment of firewall rules between namespaces and other services outside of the OpenShift cluster.

The Egress IP becomes the network identity of the namespace and all the applications running in it. Without egress IP, traffic from different namespaces would be indistinguishable because by default outbound traffic is NATed with the IP of the nodes, which are normally shared among projects. Then, the firewall can be configured to accept or deny requests from specific applications based on the IP address of the request. This is illustrated in Figure 6.9.

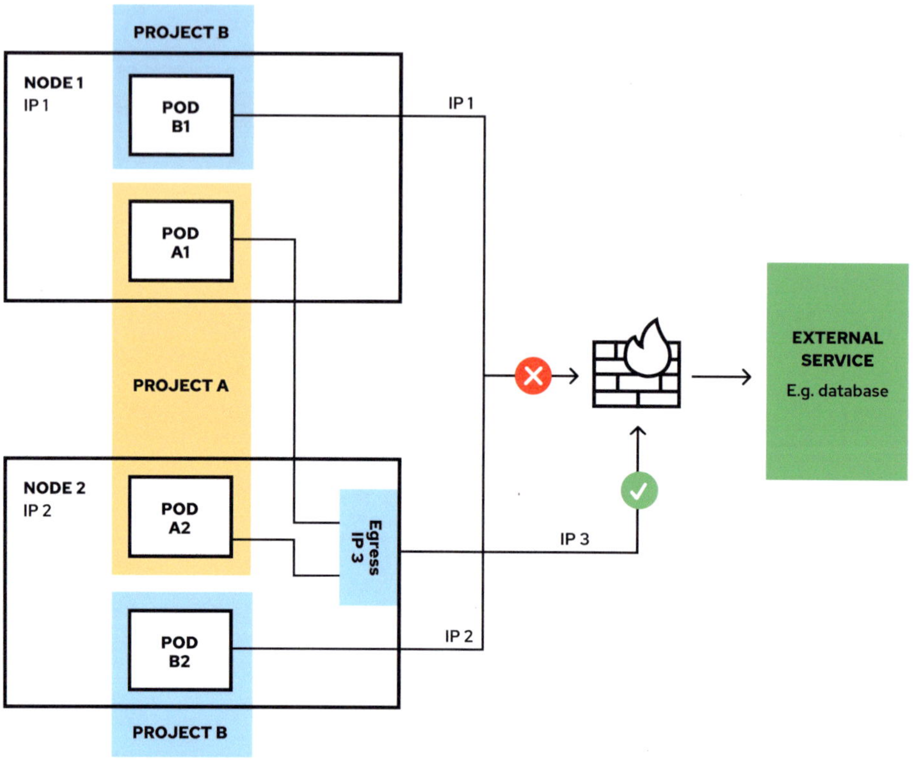

Figure 6.9: OpenShift Egress IP Concept

The concept is illustrated in the OpenShift Egress IP Concept diagram which contains two namespaces (A and B), each running two pods (A1, A2, B1, B2). Namespace A's applications can connect to a database in the company's network. B is not authorized to do so. The A namespace is configured with an egress IP so the pod's outbound connections egress with that IP. A firewall is configured to allow connections from that IP to an enterprise database. The B namespace is not configured with an egress IP so its pods egress via the node's IP. Those IPs are not allowed through the firewall to connect to the database.

Egress IPs allow for the establishment of firewall rules between namespaces and other services outside of the OpenShift cluster. The Egress IP becomes the network identity of the namespace and all the applications running in it. Without egress IP, traffic from different namespaces would be indistinguishable because, by default, outbound traffic is NATed with the IP of the nodes, which are normally shared among projects.

Egress IPs, as opposed to an Egress Router, which is deployed as a pod, are an OpenShift construct and are configured on the node via modifying the node object (). See the Configuring Egress IPs section of this chapter below

The egress IPs have nothing to do with the IPs normally assigned to the host interfaces.

Cluster admins can then assign one or multiple egress IPs (for failover) to a project, which would force all traffic from the pods in that project (regardless of which nodes they are running on) to use the primary egress IP as the source IP. Note that in this case, the OVS flows will be automatically set up to redirect any traffic from the project to the node that has the primary egress IP (Node 2 in Figure 6.10) and then sent to the destination from there.

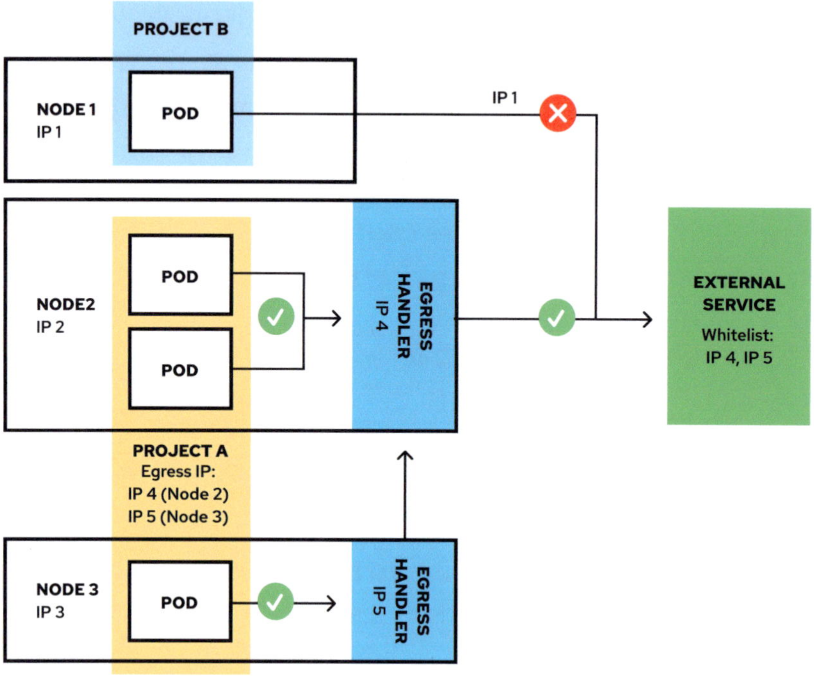

Figure 6.10: Manually Assigning Egress IPs with HA

In case of failure (such as node crashes) of the primary egress IP (IP 4), OVS will automatically configure traffic flows so that traffic from all pods in the project go through the node that owns the secondary egress IP (Node 3 on Figure 6.11) and use that egress IP (IP 5) as the source IP of all traffic.

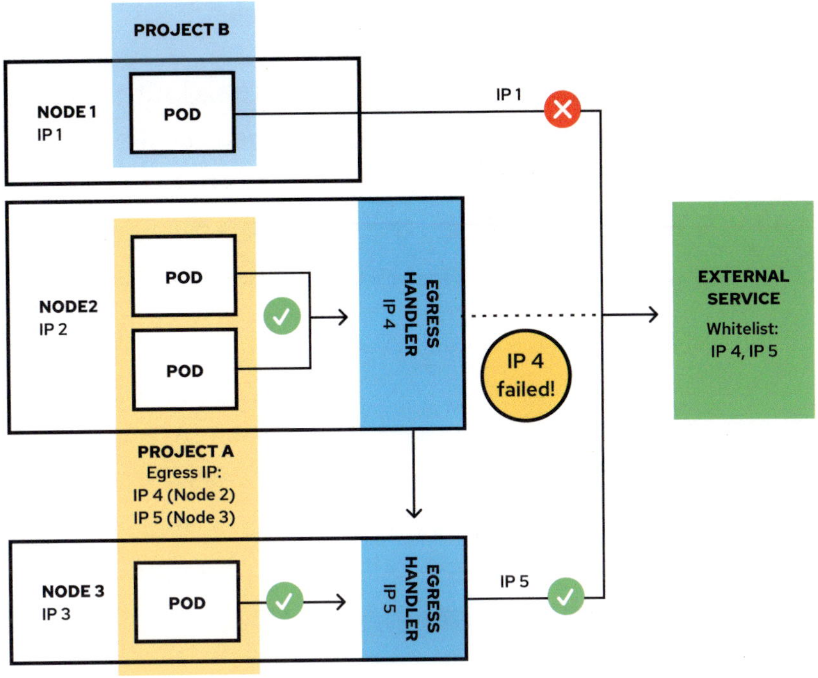

Figure 6.11: Manually Assigning Egress IPs with HA – Failover Scenario

However, enabling this feature requires that manual steps be properly configured.

Egress IPs can be automatically or manually assigned :

- **Automatically assigned** : the node HostSubnet of each node is set with a *range* of egress IPs consisting of all the addresses that can be hosted by that node. Then the project NetNamespace is patched with a *single* IP to indicate the egress IP address from that namespace.

When an egress request is made, if the first node hosting the address associated with the request is unreachable, this egress IP will automatically be assigned to another node with a HostSubnet containing an address range that includes the requests IP. This approach works best when environments are flexible with the IP addresses associated with nodes.

- **Manually assigned** : each node HostSubnet is patched with unique egress IPs (1 address, an explicit list or range can be specified) of all the addresses that can be hosted by only that node. Then, the project NetNamespace is patched to indicate the egress IPs for network traffic from that namespace. Multiple addresses can be assigned to a namespace.

When an egress request is made, if the node hosting the first address associated with the request is unreachable, the next egress IP from the NetNamespace will be attempted. This approach works best in environments such as public clouds which could have limitations on which IP addresses are associated with specific nodes.

Configuring Egress IPs

Configuration of Egress IPs for a project in OpenShift requires two steps.

The first step is to set the node HostSubnet with the egress IPs of all the addresses that can be hosted by that node.

A range can be specified :

```
$ oc patch hostsubnet <node_name> --type=merge -p \
  '{
    "egressCIDRs": [
      "<ip_address_range_1>", "<ip_address_range_2>"
    ]
  }'
```

A list or single IP address can be specified :

```
$ oc patch hostsubnet <node_name> --type=merge -p \
  '{
    "egressIPs": [
      "<ip_address_1>",
      "<ip_address_N>"
      ]
  }'
```

Note : In providers such as AWS, it will often be required to assign a secondary IP address to a node through the provider API. If the node is deleted, all assigned IPs are added back to the pool of available addresses. Therefore, it is important for nodes that are less likely to be deleted at any point to be the egress handlers. This is especially important to consider when autoscaling is utilized. If the cluster is configured with dedicated infrastructure nodes across availability zones, binding the egress IPs to those nodes is recommended to ensure cluster stability. And for HA, each project NetNamespace should be patched with at least one egress IP address from each of the infrastructure node's HostSubnet.

The second step is to patch the project's NetNamespace with egress IP addresses.

If automatic configuration is used, only one IP egress address is supported.

```
$ oc patch netnamespace <project_name> --type=merge -p \
  '{
    "egressIPs": [
      "<ip_address>"
    ]
  }'
```

But, if manual configuration is used, one or more egress IP addresses can be specified.

```
$ oc patch netnamespace <project_name> --type=merge -p \
  '{
    "egressIPs": [
      "<ip_address_1>",
      "<ip_address_N>"
      ]
  }'
```

Additional information about configuring egress IPs can be found in Configuring egress IPs for a project in the OpenShift documentation.

Service Mesh

With the transition from monolithic application to microservices, applications spread and scale differently. If microservices allow for better performance by offloading workloads to many hosts (distributed computing), they also lead to an increased network of applications or services. As such, it can become overly complex to track and monitor, in real time, all the application components. Figure 6.12 visually illustrates this complexity.

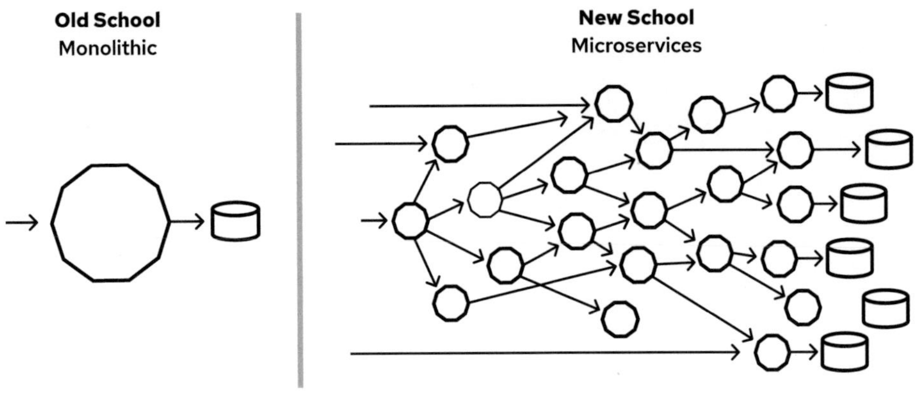

Figure 6.12: Evolution from monolithic to microservices architecture

One solution is the use of a service mesh, which is a way to control all the components that make up an application and its data. A service mesh is the network of microservices that make up applications in a distributed microservice architecture and the interactions between those microservices. It aims to reliably deliver requests through a complex topology of services. A service mesh is typically implemented as an array of lightweight and stateless network proxies that are deployed alongside application code. A service mesh is not simply a monitoring or telemetry platform decoupled from applications; rather, it is an extra layer that sits on top of running applications.

The sidecar proxy implements generic functions such as encryption, authentication, authorization, load balancing, and tracing. Application developers do not have to code these features in each microservice allowing them instead to focus on the core microservice functionality. This provides a standard hardened implementation of the generic functions enhancing the application security. This is illustrated in Figure 6.13.

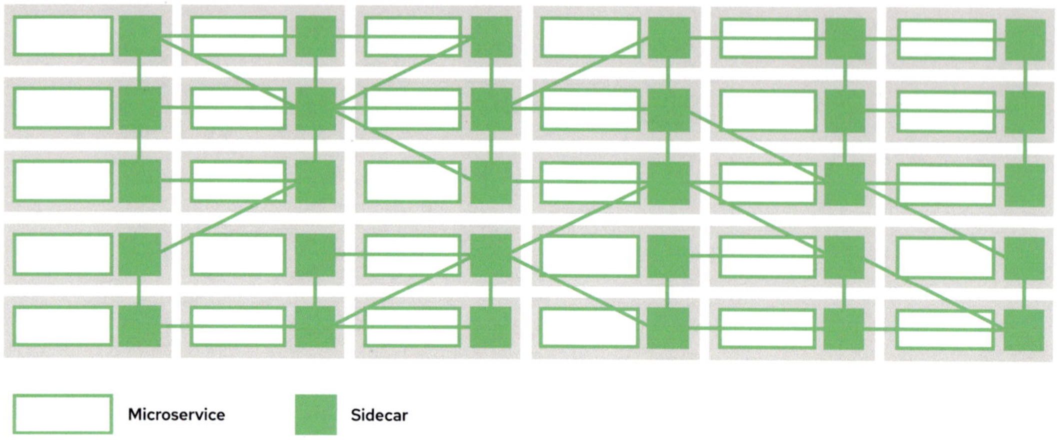

Figure 6.13: Microservices Architecture with Sidecar Proxy

Based on the open source Istio project, Red Hat OpenShift Service Mesh adds a transparent layer on existing distributed applications without requiring any change to the service. Add Red Hat OpenShift Service Mesh support to services by deploying a special sidecar proxy to relevant services in the mesh that intercepts all network communication between microservices.

Red Hat OpenShift Service Mesh offers an easy way to create a network of deployed services that provide :

- Discovery
- Load balancing
- Service-to-service authentication
- Failure recovery

- Metrics
- Monitoring

Red Hat OpenShift Service Mesh also provides more complex operational functions including :

- A/B testing
- Canary releases
- Rate limiting
- Access control
- End-to-end authentication

Red Hat OpenShift Service Mesh Architecture

Red Hat OpenShift Service Mesh is logically split into a data plane and a control plane. This is illustrated in Figure 6.14.

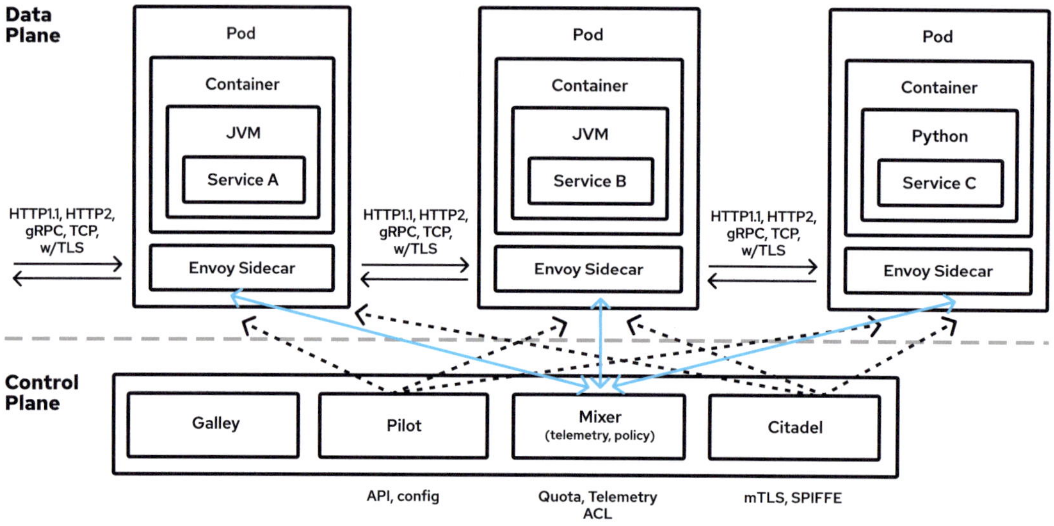

Figure 6.14: Service Mesh Data and Control Planes

The *control plane* manages and configures proxies to route traffic, and configures Mixer to enforce policies and collect telemetry.

- **Mixer** enforces access control and usage policies (such as authorization, rate limits, quotas, authentication, and request tracing) and collects telemetry data from the Envoy proxy and other services. Note : The functionality provided by Mixer is being moved into the Envoy proxies. Use of Mixer with Istio will only be supported through the 1.7 release of Istio.

- **Pilot** configures the proxies at runtime. Pilot provides service discovery for the Envoy sidecars, traffic management capabilities for intelligent routing (for example, A/B tests or canary deployments), and resiliency (timeouts, retries, and circuit breakers).

- **Citadel** issues and rotates certificates. Citadel provides strong service-to-service and end-user authentication with built-in identity and credential management. Use Citadel to upgrade unencrypted traffic in the service mesh. Operators can enforce policies based on service identity rather than on network controls using Citadel.

- **Galley** manages the service mesh configuration. Galley validates, processes, and distributes the configuration to the other service mesh components.

Red Hat OpenShift Service Mesh also uses the istio-operator to manage the installation of the control plane.

Security Aspects

The Red Hat Service Mesh adds another layer of security to OpenShift to secure the applications by implementing a zero trust network.

Control Plane

By default, Red Hat OpenShift Service Mesh installs a multi-tenant control plane. Cluster administrators should specify the projects that can access the Service Mesh and isolate the Service Mesh from other control plane instances. The main difference between a multi-tenant installation and a cluster-wide installation is the scope of privileges used by the control plane deployments, for example, Galley and Pilot.

Role-Based Access Control Features

Istio Role-Based Access Control (RBAC) provides a mechanism for use to control access to a service. It can allow administrators to identify subjects by username or by specifying a set of properties and apply access controls accordingly.

Red Hat OpenShift Service Mesh extends the ability to match request headers by using regular expressions.

The Istio Container Network Interface (CNI) Plug-in

Red Hat OpenShift Service Mesh includes CNI plug-in, which provides an alternate way to configure application pod networking. The CNI plug-in replaces the init-container network configuration eliminating the need to grant service accounts and projects access to Security Context Constraints (SCCs) with elevated privileges.

Integration with API Management

The Mixer adapter API allows the integration of a variety of infrastructure backends like metrics and logs. It is also used to integrate with API management frameworks such as Red Hat 3Scale.

The integration of Red Hat 3Scale API management with Red Hat Service Mesh adds a layer of business security to the internal microservice mesh. The 3Scale adapter communicates with the 3Scale Service Management API, authorizes requests, and reports usage.

7. Auditing

Auditing is a method of tracking security-relevant actions and events on a system. By generating and storing audit log events, a history of user or system actions can be reviewed to determine the attribution and scope of unauthorized changes. This can be used to discover and attribute events happening on the system. In turn, an information security program can identify and respond to audit events, ideally in real time, or have sufficient detail for an incident post-mortem. This improves the overall security posture when reviewed from a programmatic perspective.

Auditing goes beyond logging, or pairings of event sources and sinks. Auditing creates actionable inferences from data. These are examined by a risk management activity and possibly acted upon. Ideally, these audit inferences are phrased as automation that can alert the human elements of the information security program into action on an appropriate timescale (real-time, monthly, quarterly, annually). To illustrate an example of the difference between logging and audit : logging can record keystrokes, while auditing determines if some of those keystrokes may have done something to impact security.

In the context of OpenShift, audit functions are distributed among subsystems differently from standard Linux system processes. OpenShift provides certain available solutions and expresses default opinions regarding audit functions. This section, therefore, intends to illustrate this uniqueness, and describe strategies that allow OpenShift to fulfill a comprehensive set of audit standards which do not change regardless of the architecture at hand. Some of this fulfillment will come from augmentation and reconfiguration of the included functions.

OpenShift's Approach to Audit and Logging

OpenShift is architected in a way that leverages the utility of containerizing its own applications and subsystems. This means that many traditional Linux audit functions are architected to fit OpenShift's placement in an overall solution set.

OpenShift is designed largely with a cloud-native approach. This means that it is structured for cloud-based practices, even though it can run on bare-metal platforms. This architecture decision precipitates an impact on the responsibility boundary of what OpenShift chooses to provide by default.

This may require a bit of rethinking on role separation, since an Information Security program may need to separate the duties of the function creator (performed by an application role), and the activity review (performed by an auditor role). This is because practitioners may arrive here with a certain viewpoint regarding responsibility for conducting audits and may perceive certain practices presented herein as a change of responsibility.

As in traditional information systems, audit responsibility in OpenShift is shared between applications and the underlying platform. To meet all organizational requirements, application teams may need to understand what tools are provided by the platform to facilitate audit and logging. For example, the development team is responsible for producing audit logs for their applications, but they may be able to take advantage of logging aggregation mechanisms for collection if provided by the platform.

Non-Repudiation of Audit Data

Since audit logs contain a record of security-relevant events, it is important to ensure they are not tampered with. This involves configuring auditing services to securely collect and store audit logs, and to protect those audit logs from unauthorized access. In many cases audit logs are securely forwarded to a log storage component or Security Information and Event Management (SIEM) system that is managed by a separate operations or security team. Information systems include this type of secure forwarding configuration to maintain non-repudiation of audit data, which is often an organizational requirement.

The `auditd` service in RHEL and RHCOS meets the requirements for ensuring non-repudiation for the audit logs it processes. However, it should be noted that general log collectors such as those found in the OpenShift cluster logging stack are best-effort. OpenShift leverages its cluster logging components to aggregate audit, so the best-effort qualification is applied to audit collection and forwarding.

Auditing Capabilities

What Can Be Audited?

In the context of OpenShift Container Platform, auditing occurs at both a host operating system context and at an OpenShift API context. This chapter will address how auditing is implemented in both of these contexts.

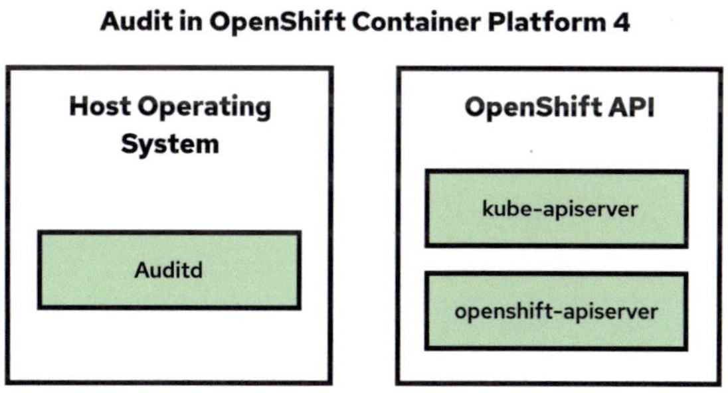

Figure 7.1: Audit in OpenShift Container Platform 4

Auditing of the host operating system consists of the standard auditing capabilities provided by the `auditd` service in Red Hat Enterprise Linux (RHEL) and Red Hat CoreOS (RHCOS). This includes recording an event--such as host authentication or attempts to access sensitive host configurations--the date and time, and the identity of the user who triggered the event. The use of the Audit system is a requirement of many organizational security policies and a number of security-related certifications. For more information, consult the auditing chapter in the RHEL 8 Security Hardening Guide.

Auditing at the OpenShift context consists of recording the HTTP requests made to the OpenShift API. The OpenShift API consists of two components : the Kubernetes API server and the OpenShift API server. Both of these components provide an audit log, each recording the events that have affected the system by individual users, administrators, or other components of the system. For more information, consult the OpenShift documentation for node audit logs and the Kubernetes Auditing documentation.

Applications deployed to OpenShift Container Platform may also be subject to auditing requirements per organizational policy. Application developers may choose to use the default cluster logging components to aggregate audit or other security-related logs. However, cluster logging is best-effort, and if application auditing requirements dictate a higher level of reliability, then developer-provided mechanisms such as writing directly to an off-cluster log store should be used instead.

Centralized Management of Audit Configuration

As discussed earlier in this book, the configuration of OpenShift Container Platform is stored and applied by the platform itself. This includes the audit configuration of the platform. This is beneficial because it ensures that security-relevant configuration such as audit is managed in a single location and applied consistently across all applicable system components.

To comply with organizational policy, an OpenShift administrator should configure the audit subsystem to capture relevant security data.

This section was written to help an OpenShift administrator learn how to configure the audit subsystem through centralized configuration management facilities. This involves identifying what events should be audited, creating rules to capture those events, and offloading audit records to a centralized facility such as a Security Operations Center (SOC).

Host Operating System Audit Configuration and Requirements

Audit is enabled by default in Red Hat Enterprise Linux CoreOS (RHCOS); however, the audit subsystem is running in a default configuration and without any audit rules. The auditd configuration (`/etc/audit/auditd.conf`) file should be modified as necessary to meet common organizational audit requirements such as retention and fault tolerance. Additionally, audit rules must be configured to record events. An example of configuring audit rules using Ignition and the OpenShift Machine Config Operator is discussed later in this section. The auditd configuration file can be updated by replacing the entire file contents using Ignition and the Machine Config Operator.

Audit retention and storage capacity planning. By default, retention of host audit is set to rotate 8MB audit log files up to a maximum of 5 files :

```
flush = INCREMENTAL_ASYNC
max_log_file = 8
num_logs = 5
```

```
max_log_file_action = ROTATE
...
```

Given the configuration above, a limited set of audit logs are retained by default. An organizational compliance profile may require changing the `max_log_file_action` from `rotate` to `keep_logs` to ensure audit is not lost. In that case, be sure to allocate at least 10 GB to store host operating system audit, and be sure to implement a forwarding or rotation mechanism that manages host disk space while preserving audit.

Audit reduction. Since auditd is only configured with the rules that are specified by the system administrator, additional reduction of host operating system audit before long-term storage is not necessary.

Audit fault tolerance. A common failure scenario for host operating system audit is running out of disk space. In the auditd configuration, several configuration keywords control system behavior when disk limits are reached :

```
...
space_left = 75
space_left_action = SYSLOG
verify_email = yes
action_mail_acct = root
admin_space_left = 50
admin_space_left_action = SUSPEND
disk_full_action = SUSPEND
disk_error_action = SUSPEND
...
```

An organizational compliance profile may require changing auditd configuration to halt the system in case the auditd process cannot create audit records. An example of this is changing the `admin_space_left_action` to `halt` to shutdown the host to ensure audit data is not lost. To prevent system outages when using this setting, be sure to allocate enough disk space on the host filesystem with proper monitoring and alerting of disk space usage.

OpenShift API Audit Configuration and Requirements

OpenShift API audit is enabled by default and is produced by both the kube-apiserver and openshift-apiserver components. The audit configuration of each is defined by a combination of default settings and corresponding custom resources named KubeAPIServer and OpenShiftAPIServer, respectively. For more information, consult the Kubernetes Auditing documentation.

Audit retention and storage capacity planning. Retention and rotation settings are set in the default settings for each API server. By default, retention is set to rotate 100MB audit log files up to a maximum of 10 files. This applies to both API server components :

```
maximumFileSizeMegabytes: 100
maximumRetainedFiles: 10
```

Given the default settings above for both API components, allow at least 2GB of storage on each master node for the OpenShift API audit. Since OpenShift API audit files are not retained for long-term review, configuring forwarding of API audit logs is recommended.

Audit reduction. For each API server component, an audit policy configuration controls which messages are logged, and at what level. This audit policy is set in the default configuration for each server component. To reduce the OpenShift API audit without modifying the default policy configuration, an external or custom component must be responsible for the reduction.

View the default audit policy configurations here :

- kube-apiserver default audit policy
- openshift-apiserver default audit policy

Audit fault tolerance. Fault tolerance settings are limited for OpenShift API audit.

OpenShift cluster logging may be used to collect and forward API audit logs. If this configuration is in place, then the Fluentd collector processes are monitored by Prometheus by default. Take care to configure Prometheus Alerting to notify an administrator of alerts, and be sure to monitor the relevant fluentd alerts as defined in the OpenShift documentation. Be aware of the limitations of using the cluster logging stack to aggregate audit logs discussed later in this chapter.

Managing Operating System Audit Configuration

In RHCOS, auditd is enabled by default but is not configured with any audit rules. Audit rules can be added to auditd by customizing the OpenShift Machine Configuration that is used to configure Red Hat CoreOS nodes.

Describing how to create an audit policy that meets specific organizational requirements is outside the scope of this book. However, the example below shows how to configure two commonly-defined settings : 1) configuring auditd to start early during boot with required kernel parameters, and 2) creating a single audit rule file to monitor authentication configuration.

1 Create an audit rules file to provide as part of the audit configuration. This will be applied to each host via a MachineConfig resource :

```
$ cat <<EOF > usergroup.rules
-w /etc/passwd -p wa -k identity
-w /etc/group -p wa -k identity
EOF
```

2 Convert the audit rules file to a URL-encoded string to use in an Ignition configuration file :

```
$ cat usergroup.rules | python3 -c \
  "import sys, urllib.parse; \
  print(urllib.parse.quote(''.join( \
  sys.stdin.readlines())))"

-w%20/etc/passwd%20-p%20wa%20-k%20identity%0A-
w%20/etc/group%20-p%20wa%20-k%20identity%0A
```

3 Create an OpenShift template capable of creating both a master and a worker MachineConfig snippet, making sure to embed the URL-encoded audit rules as file content. Also note the kernel argument `audit=1` to force auditd to start early during boot :

```
$ cat <<EOF > 50-audit-machineconfig-template.yml
apiVersion: template.openshift.io/v1
kind: Template
metadata:
 name: machine-config-audit
objects:
- apiVersion: machineconfiguration.openshift.io/v1
 kind: MachineConfig
 metadata:
```

```
      name: 50-${NODE_ROLE}-audit
      labels:
       machineconfiguration.openshift.io/role: ${NODE_ROLE}
  spec:
      config:
        ignition:
          version: 2.2.0
        storage:
          files:
          - contents:
              source: data:,-w%20/etc/passwd%20-p%20wa%20-
k%20identity%0A-w%20/etc/group%20-p%20wa%20-k%20identity%0A
            filesystem: root
            mode: 0640
            path: /etc/audit/rules.d/usergroup.rules
        systemd:
          units:
          - name: auditd.service
            enabled: true
      kernelArguments:
        - audit=1
        - audit_backlog_limit=8192
parameters:
- description: "Node role: master or worker"
  name: NODE_ROLE
  required: true
  value: worker
EOF
```

4 Create two MachineConfig resources, one for masters and one for workers. Note the different parameter values passed for NODE_ROLE:

```
$ oc process -f 50-audit-machineconfig-template.yml -p
NODE_ROLE=master | oc create -f -
machineconfig.machineconfiguration.openshift.io/50-master-audit
created

$ oc process -f 50-audit-machineconfig-template.yml -p
NODE_ROLE=worker | oc create -f -
machineconfig.machineconfiguration.openshift.io/50-worker-audit
created
```

5 Verify the MachineConfigs were created and the Machine Config Operator has applied the changes:

```
$ oc get mc
NAME
         GENERATEDBYCONTROLLER
         IGNITIONVERSION   CREATED
50-master-audit
                                             2.2.0

        9s
50-worker-audit
                                             2.2.0

        39s


...
rendered-master-1e1fd72a8847c79d34cd53d456a73d2a
         ab4d62a3bf3774b77b6f9b04a2028faec1568aca   2.2.0
          2d22h
rendered-master-e2004dfefa416c44d960ebc81cf59bdb
         ab4d62a3bf3774b77b6f9b04a2028faec1568aca   2.2.0
          9s
rendered-worker-035f057f6db110f80437cee11ce8a314
```

```
         ab4d62a3bf3774b77b6f9b04a2028faec1568aca   2.2.0
          2d22h
rendered-worker-3cc6346f1fe8fdc179c36892f0e6b35a
         ab4d62a3bf3774b77b6f9b04a2028faec1568aca   2.2.0
          39s

$ oc get node
NAME                                   STATUS
        ROLES        AGE         VERSION
ip-10-0-143-57.ec2.internal        Ready,SchedulingDisabled
worker   29h         v1.16.2
...

$ oc describe node ip-10-0-143-57.ec2.internal
Name:                       ip-10-0-143-57.ec2.internal
Roles:                      worker
...
Annotations:                machine.openshift.io/machine:
openshift-machine-api/aws009-6qh5c-worker-us-east-1a-wtvqm

        machineconfiguration.openshift.io/currentConfig:
rendered-worker-035f057f6db110f80437cee11ce8a314

        machineconfiguration.openshift.io/desiredConfig:
rendered-worker-3cc6346f1fe8fdc179c36892f0e6b35a

...
```

6 Obtain a debug session to an updated node and verify the auditd rules:

```
$ oc debug node/ip-10-0-143-57.ec2.internal
Starting pod/ip-10-0-143-57ec2internal-debug ...
To use host binaries, run `chroot /host`
Pod IP: 10.0.143.57
```

```
If you don't see a command prompt, try pressing enter.
sh-4.2# chroot /host
sh-4.4# cat /etc/audit/rules.d/usergroup.rules
-w /etc/passwd -p wa -k identity
-w /etc/group -p wa -k identity
sh-4.4# cat /etc/audit/audit.rules
## This file is automatically generated from /etc/audit/rules.d

-w /etc/passwd -p wa -k identity
-w /etc/group -p wa -k identity

sh-4.4# auditctl -l
-w /etc/passwd -p wa -k identity
-w /etc/group -p wa -k identity

sh-4.4# exit
exit
sh-4.2#
sh-4.2# exit
Removing debug pod ...
```

Managing OpenShift API Audit Configuration

OpenShift API audit logs are produced by both the kube-apiserver and openshift-apiserver components. The audit configuration of each is defined by a combination of default settings and corresponding custom resources named KubeAPIServer and OpenShiftAPIServer, respectively.

The openshift-kube-apiserver-operator manages the kube-apiserver component, including its audit configuration. The KubeAPIServer cluster-scoped custom resource partially defines kube-apiserver audit configuration, combined with other default values.

```
$ oc describe kubeapiserver/cluster
```

The openshift-apiserver-operator manages the openshift-apiserver component, including its audit configuration. The OpenShiftAPIServer cluster-scoped custom resource partially defines openshift-apiserver audit configuration, combined with other default values.

```
$ oc describe openshiftapiserver/cluster
```

See the Kubernetes Auditing documentation for more information about the API audit log configuration, but be sure to coordinate any desired changes with Red Hat Support to ensure those changes can be supported.

OpenShift Components that Facilitate Audit Generation and Collection

By default, any audit logs generated by auditd on the host operating system or the OpenShift API server components will be rotated in place. OpenShift provides log collection tools to assist with aggregating log files.

OpenShift Cluster Logging

The OpenShift Container Platform includes a suite of cluster logging components to facilitate aggregating logs from cluster nodes, including node system logs and application container logs. By default, audit logs are not collected by cluster logging.

To use cluster logging to collect and forward audit logs, configure log forwarding for audit logs, which is discussed later in this chapter.

Limitations of Using Cluster Logging for Application Audit Logs

When using cluster logging to collect and store audit logs generated by hosted applications, be aware of how cluster logging components associate a log to the container that produced it.

The container runtimes provide minimal information to identify the source of log messages : project, pod name, and container id. This combination of attributes is not sufficient to uniquely identify the source of the logs. For example, if a pod with a given name and project is deleted before the log collector begins processing its logs, information from the API server, such as labels and annotations, might not be available. In this case, there might not be a way to distinguish the log messages from a similarly named pod and project or trace the logs to their source. This limitation means log collection and normalization is considered **best effort.**

If hosted applications leverage the cluster logging services to collect application audit logs, also be aware of default log retention settings for the log store. By default, the logging-curator will run periodically, and prune all log records after a configurable time. Consider increasing the retention time for the desired index (such as the `.operations` index for event router output) as described in the OpenShift documentation.

OpenShift Event Router

OpenShift Container Platform events are records of important life-cycle information in a namespace and are useful for monitoring and troubleshooting resource scheduling, creation, and deletion. When reviewing cluster activity, it can be useful to also include the OpenShift events to provide more context for cluster behavior. The Event Router component listens to all OpenShift events across all namespaces, and copies them to `STDOUT` to allow reading by the logging collector.

OpenShift events can be viewed in Kibana by searching for fields with `kubernetes.event.*` in the `.operations.*` index.

The Event Router must be deployed manually by a cluster administrator. See more information in the OpenShift documentation.

Configuring Audit Log Forwarding with Cluster Logging

Since audit log retention on each host is limited, audit records should be aggregated and forwarded to a secure log store or Security Information and Event Management (SIEM) system.

Systems that store audit logs must be compliant with applicable organizational and governmental regulations and must be properly secured. The internal OpenShift Container Platform Elasticsearch instance that is part of the OpenShift logging stack does not meet the requirements for secure storage of audit logs. Instead, log forwarding to a secure destination should be configured for both host and OpenShift audit logs.

There are two methods for configuring log forwarding for OpenShift Container Platform : 1) using the Fluentd `out_forward` plug-in; or 2) using the Technology Preview Log Forwarding feature of cluster logging.

Forwarding Cluster Logs Using the 'out_forward' Fluentd Plug-in

The Fluentd `out_forward` plug-in can send a copy of the logs to an external log aggregator, instead of the default Elasticsearch. Optional TLS support ensures that logs can be sent using secure communication as required by the organization.

Consult the OpenShift documentation for details on configuring log forwarding using the Fluentd `out_forward` plug-in.

Make sure to include the following :

- A secure-forward `ConfigMap` in the openshift-logging namespace that contains a `secure-forward.conf` file. The `secure-forward.conf` file must specify :
    - TLS settings, including the CA certificate of the log receiver
    - Hostname and port of the log receiver
- A secret containing the CA certificate of the log receiver

Also, make sure to configure the log receiver appropriately. For more information on configuring the Fluentd `in_forward` plug-in, see the Fluentd documentation.

Forwarding Cluster Logs Using Log Forwarding (Technology Preview)

Log Forwarding is a Technology Preview feature only. Technology Preview features are not supported with Red Hat production service level agreements (SLAs) and might not be functionally complete. Red Hat does not recommend using them in production. These preview opportunities provide early access to upcoming product features, enabling customers to test functionality and provide feedback during the development process.

For more information about the support scope of Red Hat Technology Preview features, see https://access.redhat.com/support/offerings/techpreview/

Log Forwarding provides an easier way to forward logs to specific endpoints outside the OpenShift Container Platform cluster than configuring the Fluentd plug-ins directly. The ability to send different types of logs to different systems allows control of who in the organization can access each type of log. Optional TLS support ensures that logs can be sent using secure communication as required by the organization.

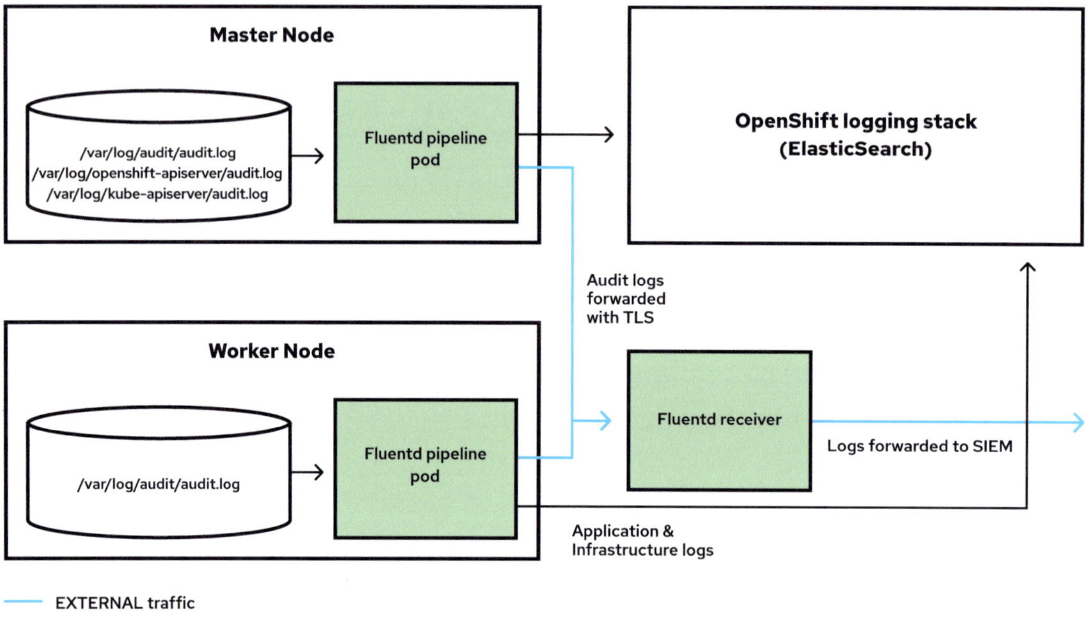

Figure 7.2: Forwarding audit logs to an off-cluster SIEM

Consult the OpenShift documentation for details on configuring log forwarding using the Log Forwarding feature of the cluster logging stack.

Make sure to include the following :

- Configure the `logs.audit` parameter to forward to a secure log store
- Consider configuring `logs.infra` parameter to forward to a secure log store. If the Event Router is deployed, then this will include forwarding of all the OpenShift events, which can sometimes be helpful during an audit review

- Configure TLS by specifying a secret containing a key, certificate, and certificate authority
- Configure a forwarding pipeline for each log source : logs.app, logs.infra, and logs.audit

Reviewing Audit Logs

Accessing Audit Logs

OpenShift provides a tool to view node log files with the `oc adm node-logs` command. Using the `--path` argument, this command can list and display the contents of any log file stored in `/var/log/`, including auditd and OpenShift API audit log files.

Host operating system audit logs for each node are written to `/var/log/audit/audit.log`. To list the available auditd log files and then display the contents of a specific file, do the following :

```
$ oc adm node-logs <node-name> --path=audit/
audit.log

$ oc adm node-logs <node-name> audit.log --path=audit/audit.log
[output omitted]
```

Similarly, the audit logs for the OpenShift API can be viewed in the respective folder for each component :

```
$ oc adm node-logs <node-name> audit.log --path=kube-
apiserver/audit.log
$ oc adm node-logs <node-name> audit.log --path=openshift-
apiserver/audit.log
```

Since OpenShift API services run in a highly available mode across three master nodes, API audit records should be reviewed from all sources in aggregate. If forwarding audit logs to a SIEM, it is preferred to view them from that system instead of from each node individually. Alternatively, the `oc adm must-gather` CLI command can aggregate a snapshot of OpenShift API audit for review on-demand. For more information, see the OpenShift documentation.

Only OpenShift cluster administrators and users with the `system:node-admins` role can execute the `oc adm node-logs` command.

See the OpenShift documentation for more examples of viewing API audit log files. More information on the `oc adm node-logs` command can be found with `oc adm node-logs -h`. The RHEL 8 Security Hardening Guide contains more information about auditd and host operating system audit.

Interpreting OpenShift API Audit

OpenShift API audit logs each completed request executed by the API. Each audit log record is formatted as JSON. Below is a partial example of an API audit record :

```
{
        "kind": "Event",
        "apiVersion": "audit.k8s.io/v1",
        "level": "Metadata",
        "auditID": "ad209ce1-fec7-4130-8192-c4cc63f1d8cd",
        "stage": "ResponseComplete",
        "requestURI":
"/api/v1/namespaces/openshift-kube-controller-
manager/configmaps/cert-recovery-controller-lock?timeout=35s",
        "verb": "update",
        "user": {
                "username":
"system:serviceaccount:openshift-kube-controller-
```

```
manager:localhost-recovery-client",
            "uid": "dd4997e3-d565-4e37-80f8-7fc122ccd785",
            "groups": [ ... ]
        },
        ...
        "objectRef": {
            "resource": "configmaps",
            "namespace": "openshift-kube-controller-manager",
            "name": "cert-recovery-controller-lock",
            ...
        },
        "responseStatus": {
            "metadata": {},
            "code": 200
        },
        "requestReceivedTimestamp": "2020-04-
02T08:27:20.200962Z",
        ...
}
```

Notable information from the sample above includes:

1. `auditID`: A unique audit ID, generated for each request.
2. `requestURI`: The request URI as sent by the client to a server.
3. `verb`: The Kubernetes verb associated with the request. For non-resource requests, this is the lowercase HTTP method.
4. `user`: The authenticated user information.
5. `objectRef`: Optional. The object reference this request is targeted at. This does not apply for List-type requests, or non-resource requests.

6 `responseStatus` : Optional. The response status, populated even when the ResponseObject is not a Status type. For successful responses, this will only include the Code. For non-status type error responses, this will be auto-populated with the error Message.

7 `requestReceivedTimestamp` : The time that the request reached the API server.

For more information about OpenShift API audit, consult the OpenShift documentation for API audit and the Kubernetes Auditing documentation.

Performing an Event-driven Audit Review

An event-driven audit is the manual performance of ad-hoc audit functions that use and go beyond the automated audit functions. These manual actions serve to resolve the event that precipitated the need for an audit. Examples of these triggering situations include :

- manual audit actions to respond to security team findings and requests,
- manual audit actions to understand and resolve emergent system availability conditions such as resource exhaustion symptoms,
- manual audit actions to respond to a reported security incident, including creation of data for outside support staff or confirmation of a suspected intrusion, and
- manual audit actions to characterize available events to be created by developers for future automated logging.

Ideally, these will be presented in a way that facilitates correlation between various data sources. The strategy here is also based, as much as possible, on the presentation of CLI-based actions to facilitate incorporation of successful and automatable recipes into ongoing event generation, recording, and alerting.

The `oc adm must-gather` command can aggregate a snapshot of OpenShift API audit for review on-demand. For more information, see the OpenShift documentation.

8. Encryption, Secret Management, and Data Protection

Encryption is a key capability for protecting sensitive data. Many regulatory and compliance frameworks require the use of strong and *validated* encryption to secure data at rest and in motion. Secrets management is equally important. The term *secret* is a general way to refer to sensitive data, such as passwords, OAuth tokens, and SSH keys. In Kubernetes, a secret is an object that is used to store sensitive information.

Secrets can be created by the user and by the system. Restricting access to secrets is one mechanism for protecting them. However, encryption provides an even more compelling solution. In addition to secrets, OpenShift leverages core encryption technologies including certificates, disk encryption, and secure network transport mechanisms.

Encryption

Encryption provides protection for both data in motion and data at rest. Many encryption functions are necessarily convolved with related verification functions, and these functions are frequently treated together as a totality of a security control. Therefore, encryption and signing may be collectively referred to here as *encryption*. Encryption, and related cryptographic message authentication functions that decryption implies, can :

- Encode the content of a message (encryption)
- Authenticate the origin of a message (message digest creation and PKI signing)
- Decode the content back into readability (decryption)
- Ensure that the content of the message has not changed since it was sent (message digest verification)
- Prevent senders from denying they sent the encrypted message (nonrepudiation via signature validation).

These encryption functions require three components that specify and fully secure a transaction supporting all of the functions above :

- The date (establishment of shelf life, session key expiry, and partial non-repudiation)
- High quality entropy

- The encryption engine (primitive, algorithm, scheme)
- Encryption key management (forward secrecy, escrow, PKI vs shared secret).

OpenShift promotes phrasing application interactions largely as socketed IP services, and most commonly as HTTP and HTTPS. Since developers frequently implement IP transport encryption by leveraging TLS functions and related certification, much of the discussion here will address this. This is likely because IPSec was traditionally less under control of a developer in a production environment, and outside consumer client sessions could not be depended on to negotiate any deeper than TLS during a session.

Encrypted Transport Layer Security (TLS) provides end-to-end encryption for data sent between applications over the Internet. TLS does not secure data at rest. HTTPS enables encrypted communication with websites via the TLS protocol. Network level encryption applies cryptography at the network layer. OpenShift control plane components enforce industry standards including HTTP/2 defaults and TLS 1.2 or TLS 1.3. Certificate key sizes are not configurable (RSA certificates are 2048, ECDSA for kubelet certificates). Older TLS versions should not be used as US public sector deployments may mandate versions higher than TLS 1.1 for cloud service providers.

FIPS

To use FIPS validated modules with OpenShift Container Platform, the RHEL or RHEL CoreOS nodes must be configured for FIPS mode at installation time. FIPS requires that all key material is generated on a host that is in FIPS mode. This ensures that all self-tests are executed prior to key generation. For more information on FIPS, see the chapter on Risk

Management and Regulatory Readiness. For more information on configuring FIPS mode, see the chapter on RHEL CoreOS Security.

Network Time and Date for Encryption

OpenShift systems employing common encryption and related authentication schemes can only assert validity when given accurate and synchronous system time. Poor timekeeping has practical impact : Good clocks provide protection against ill-timed session expiration. High resolution synchrony offers correlation between system events during a forensics-related investigation. Regarding encryption, the time accuracy and synchrony of encryption systems establish a shelf life for encryption certificates, assist in estimation of forward secrecy for intercepted traffic, and provide a bit of temporal context when determining message authenticity.

The matter of time synchrony is serious enough that a FedRAMP authorization will not go forward without a key – authenticated NIST– or DoD-derived clock tree in place within all elements of the cloud infrastructure. Some regulatory requirements regarding time are quite specific. For example, the DoD mandates use of the network time protocol (NTP) by name. For OpenShift, this requires replacement of the default chronyd service with ntpd in an implementation, or maintenance of a Plan of Actions and Milestones (PoAM). Security practitioners should satisfy their program management that the time service in use by OpenShift and its applications is sufficient for the required precision and accuracy that the program specifies.

Information Security Program policy creators should analyze and determine a required level of clock quality and methodology of validation. Then, they should promulgate and validate this. To assist in this policy creation, clock quality can largely be grouped by what security objective it can meet :

Security objective	Minimum time accuracy
All time-dependent cryptographic functions are able to function and be verifiable	OpenShift and applications derive time from a scheme that must use a universal time base or correctly interpolate time zone, savings time, civil time declarations, and leap information. A national standards-derived source or otherwise justified ensemble should be specified.
TLS certificate validity and renewal is valid for clients	OpenShift and applications should derive time within a minute (due to timed release of announcement embargo on web-distributed information, the certificates that secure these releases should be maintained as timely)
TLS session expiry, cryptographic user session authentication and expiry, and system availability vigilance are valid	OpenShift and applications should derive time within a second
Forensic correlation of activities between systems (encrypted and unencrypted) is possible, traceable, and useful	OpenShift, applications, and related event generation should derive time within hundreds of milliseconds or less from a standards-derived clock tree or ensemble
System availability performance analysis and improvement (especially TLS standup and load balancing) is possible and useful	OpenShift, applications, and related event generation should derive time within tens of milliseconds or less
System availability performance analysis and improvement (esp. full stack response) is possible and useful	OpenShift, applications, and related event generation should derive time within milliseconds or less

The information security program should specify all required quality elements from the above that are determined to be necessary, hopefully in a manner traceable to a related risk analysis.

Actual time server selection and settings for OpenShift-provided RHCOS systems may be made via a MachineConfig, as described in Chapter 2 : Red Hat Enterprise Linux CoreOS Security..

Entropy

Like the neglect of time synchrony, entropy service is frequently presumed to be *just there* in Linux. This can leave the issue dangling until a security validation exercise prompts further establishment of truth. At that point, remediation of the discovered status into a compliant state can precipitate a production impact.

More advanced entropy requirements should specify validation runs of the `rngtest` command on the underlying RHCOS system, as required.

Information security programs may need to establish random number quality, source selection, and validity. A truly random number is hard (and slow) to find, therefore practically acceptable standards for cryptographically secure pseudo-random number generators (CSPRNGs) exist. This effort is a bit confounded by the endlessly swirling random information on the Internet regarding the need for "true" randomness and drama regarding purposefully weakened RNGs. The subject is shrouded in folklore and leads to intuitive but wrong conclusions, such as whether adding randomness to a weak random source makes the result more usefully random or not.

Regardless, the decision for acceptable entropy remains in the discretion and responsibility of the Information Security Program. Linux can offer multiple source types, "true" random (slow) and pseudorandom (fast and non-blocking) numbers, of varying statistical quality. A risk analysis is generally performed, and use cases are phrased. Sources could include :

- /dev/random - can block
- /dev/urandom - a nonblocking PRNG where reads may fail
- /dev/srandom - a fast, good, user-installable PRNG kernel module
- getrandom() - comes from urandom
- rngd - daemon for feeding random data to the kernel's random number entropy pool
- virtio-rng - a guest kernel module and
- RDRAND - a controversial source of hardware randomness

The actual suitability of the source depends on the use case at hand. Designers of an OpenShift application built to generate a Root CA would want extremely high quality of randomness, possibly directly derived from an exotic and specialized hardware source. Meanwhile, an OpenShift web application generating a disposable web session navigation cookie may be able to tolerate less randomness and a lower burden of proof for validators. Sessions that seem ephemeral are subject to later traffic analysis.

Due to the hundreds of upstream repositories that compose OpenShift and its dependency projects, and any possible future changes, this guide cannot provide a blanket assurance that only this or that RNG source is truly in use.

However, a more rapid validation strategy leans on assurances provided by OpenShift itself. OpenShift indicates an ability to use randomness that is improved by rngd. Use of `rngtest` against that will use actual statistical measurement of the system at hand to establish a base quality level of at least FIPS 140-2. Practitioners of serious information security programs are urged to perform this test in-situ, as many typical (and normally trustworthy) Linux default distribution installations on metal do *fail* this test, albeit at a small rate aboard each afflicted distro instance. For example, the following shows what can happen when an Information Security program calls for better randomness than that provided by the state of the (otherwise-approved trustworthy) OS on which OpenShift is installed :

```
root@OCP4metal:~ # cat /etc/os-release | grep PRETTY
PRETTY_NAME="Red Hat Enterprise Linux 8.0 (Ootpa)"
root@OCP4metal:~ # cat /proc/cpuinfo | grep -o rand | uniq
rand
root@OCP4metal:~ # ps ax | grep rng
 1251 ?        Ssl    0:40 /sbin/rngd -f
31694 pts/0    S+     0:00 grep --color=auto rng
root@OCP4metal:~ # cat /dev/random | rngtest -c 1000
rngtest 6.6
Copyright (c) 2004 by Henrique de Moraes Holschuh
This is free software; see the source for copying conditions.
 There is NO warranty; not even for MERCHANTABILITY or FITNESS
FOR A PARTICULAR PURPOSE.

rngtest: starting FIPS tests...
rngtest: bits received from input: 20000032
rngtest: FIPS 140-2 successes: 998
rngtest: FIPS 140-2 failures: 2
rngtest: FIPS 140-2(2001-10-10) Monobit: 0
rngtest: FIPS 140-2(2001-10-10) Poker: 0
```

```
rngtest: FIPS 140-2(2001-10-10) Runs: 0
rngtest: FIPS 140-2(2001-10-10) Long run: 2
rngtest: FIPS 140-2(2001-10-10) Continuous run: 0
rngtest: input channel speed: (min=235.945; avg=794.893;
max=8861.729)Kibits/s
rngtest: FIPS tests speed: (min=21.099; avg=83.878;
max=87.493)Mibits/s
rngtest: Program run time: 24799317 microseconds
```

The entropy quality establishment effort is a bit more involved when OpenShift runs aboard a public cloud. Designers of OpenShift Deployments and applications should obtain assurance of entropy quality from their cloud provider or provide their own randomness as a service to the application. This can lead Information Security Programs to look at a larger risk picture that leads to a hybrid solution. Entropy sources and high-level certificate generation could occur aboard extreme-security in-house cloud enclaves. Web applications and other crucial certificates and keys are sent to cloud-deployed OpenShift applications, along with an on-demand entropy stream. Finally, in-cloud entropy sources can be allowed to remain for minor cryptographic functions.

Such hybridization strategies prompt thinking regarding the security of certificate material as well, which is now discussed below.

Public Key Certificates

Strong certificate use within the platform is critical to modern application security. The only way for public key infrastructure (PKI) to scale for a container orchestration platform is by increasing the use and reach of automation. OpenShift provides integrated management of X.509 certificates for internal cluster components. Containerized applications are responsible for managing their own certificates signed by organizational CAs or may make use of the OpenShift Service CA if they wish.

The platform includes multiple certificate authorities (CAs) providing independent chains of trust, increasing the security posture of the cluster. These internal self-signing CAs enable automation because the key is known to the cluster. The certificates generated by each CA are used to identify a particular OpenShift platform component to another OpenShift platform component. CA bundles are used when more than one communication path needs to be authenticated.

- Communication between the API server, and the kubelet is secured by the kubelet serving CA.
- Communication with etcd is secured by the etcd serving CA.
- Authentication to the kubeconfig is managed by the admin-kubeconfig-client CA.

The OpenShift CAs are managed by the cluster and are only used within the cluster. This means that :

- Each cluster CA can only issue certificates for its own purpose within its own cluster.
- CAs for one OpenShift cluster cannot be used for a different OpenShift cluster, thus avoiding cross-cluster interference.
- Cluster CAs cannot be used by an external CA that the cluster does not control.

Like all secrets, long-term certificates are a point of vulnerability. OpenShift automatically manages rotation of certificates generated by the internal CAs.

With OpenShift 4, it is not possible to replace certificates for internal platform components with certificates from a different CA. Generating certificates with the right properties is complex and error prone. Furthermore, orchestrating a roll-out of externally provided certificates introduces the risk of cluster downtime due to mistakes in certificates or delays in installing or updating certificates. Similarly, providing the ability to use an external CA adds complexity. The cluster would require access to the CA's private key so that it could automatically provision certificates for various cluster components. The presence of the CA's private key on the cluster also introduces the risk that an individual or service with access to the private key on the cluster could mint certificates for the company's other services and reduces the value of key rotation. A platform compromise would then put the company's entire infrastructure at risk. Use of an external CA also would remove the benefit that the individual independent chains of trust provide today, adding the risk that a certificate might be used for the wrong purpose.

To increase security for external access points, custom certificates from an external CA can and should be installed for the public host names of the OpenShift Container Platform API and web console. This confines the use of the internal CA to the cluster components. See :

- Replacing the default ingress certificate
- API server certificates
- Securing the registry

Organizational Policies Regarding Self-Signed Certificates

Many organizations have policies restricting the use of self-signed certificates. The reason for this is simple : self-signed certificates cannot guarantee a valid identity, since a trusted third-party (certificate authority) did not verify (sign) the certificate. For this reason, self-signed certificates should not be used to secure applications meant to be consumed by external clients, such as clients not under the control by the same organization.

However, systems and ecosystems that can establish trust, such as by exchanging a common certificate authority (CA), can provide verification of identity for certificates signed by an organization- or system-controlled CA. OpenShift Container Platform creates an ecosystem where certificates signed by an internal CA are trusted by all components of the platform. This allows all of these internal components to communicate securely. The internal OpenShift CAs are not officially exposed or supported for certificate creation or trust outside of the cluster.

There are valid use cases where self-signed certificates are found in practice. For example, all root CAs are self-signed. Web-of-trust PKI offerings such as VeriSign use Intermediate CAs for issuing certificates, but ultimately validate down to a self-signed root CA that they manage. In OpenShift, a local, self-signed CA in the infrastructure provides a root trust anchor just the same.

OpenShift platform components use a *trust anchor pinning* strategy for internal TLS connections. This effectively creates different trust domains between CAs and limits the reach of TLS clients by way of an explicit CA trust. An example of this strategy is :

- A TLS client is provided the OpenShift CA as a trust anchor, completely excluding public or other system CA bundles
- A TLS server is provided with a server certificate signed by the OpenShift CA

- ***Success scenario***
  The TLS client tries to connect to the TLS server, and properly validates the server certificate with the loaded CA.

- ***Failure scenario***
  The same TLS client tries (maliciously) to connect to a server that has a server certificate from a different CA, such as the etcd CA. The TLS client cannot validate the certificate as it does not have the etcd CA as a trust anchor. This is the stage in the connection where a CA exception prompt would normally be seen in a web browser. However, since the internal TLS clients are non-interactive, the connection can only fail.

In both the success and failure scenarios described above, the trust anchor pinning strategy guarantees secure connections for both client and server applications.

Configuring Organizational Certificate Authorities

An Organizational CA or certificate should be used to expose externally-facing OpenShift components. For example, the applications running on OpenShift, the OpenShift Console & API, along with any sort of externally facing OpenShift Operators should be signed by a CA that their respective clients will trust.

If an organization does not maintain its own Root CA, then signed certificates must be obtained from trusted third parties such as Verisign. These certificates would be the ones that should be applied in these cases as external clients are likely to also trust the third-party CA.

When a user is interacting with a system, they require a level of trust that only a signed and third-party validated certificate can provide. For organizations that may issue their own certificates, it is important to note that a trusted CA bundle will need to be shared amongst the end-user systems to ensure that trust is validated. For example, use a named certificate for Console or API access, but use a Trusted CA bundle for operator access to outside resources. For more information, see :

- Replacing the default ingress certificate
- API server certificates
- Securing the registry
- Configuring a custom PKI

Certificate Management for Applications

Applications deployed into OpenShift do not have their certificates managed by default. Application developers can provide a certificate for their application manually by creating a secret object that contains the key and certificate files, and then mounting that secret in their deployment. If the application will serve clients that are external to the OpenShift cluster, creation and signing of application certificates are done outside of the OpenShift context, such as by the organization's security team.

Alternatively, the self-signed application wildcard certificate can be replaced with a wildcard certificate provided by the organization. Typically, this is done in non-production environments so that development can proceed quickly, without the need to manually provision organizational certificates for every deployed application. Production application deployments are more carefully planned; therefore, it is less of a burden to provision those certificates without the use of a wildcard.

Certificates with Secure Ingress and Routes

Application developers have the ability to secure HTTP traffic with either Kubernetes Ingress or OpenShift route objects. OpenShift Route objects support four different TLS termination methods :

- None (for HTTP routes)
- Edge
- Passthrough
- Re-encrypt

Ingress objects support TLS edge termination. In addition, edge terminated or re-encrypted routes can be configured to use HTTP Strict Transport Security (HSTS) if required.

When creating an edge-terminated or re-encrypt route, the application certificate that should be presented to clients is included in the route definition. Passthrough routes provide HTTPS ingress to the backing application without any termination, so a certificate must be presented by that application.

For more information on these options, see :

- Creating a re-encrypt route
- Creating an edge route
- Enabling HTTP strict transport security
- OpenShift Blog - Kubernetes Ingress vs OpenShift Route

Service Serving Certificates

If an application in OpenShift will only serve clients running in the same OpenShift cluster, then a developer may choose to delegate management of application certificates to the platform by using service serving certificates. For applications load-balanced by a service object, the service serving certificates feature of OpenShift automatically generates a server certificate that is valid for the network name of the service. The application backing the service can load this certificate and serve HTTPS traffic within the cluster. Clients of such an application need only trust the service CA that is managed by OpenShift. For more information, see Securing service traffic using service serving certificates.

Length of Key Considerations

The subject of key length choices rapidly becomes complex. This is due to the varied effectiveness of key length for various algorithms available. Many of these are automatically negotiable at session time. Other than use of MachineConfigs to lock out certain algorithm types, the most effective strategy is to simply enable FIPS mode in RHEL or RHCOS. FIPS mode enforces good minimum key length usage and will even return a failure when an algorithm is given a weak-sized key later.

Secrets Management

Secrets should be protected in-transit and at-rest. In OpenShift, platform secrets are managed by the cluster, including certificates as described above. For applications, there are three ways to pass secrets to containers :

- build secrets into the image
- use environment variables
- and by mounting a volume into a container that contains a file with the secrets

Kubernetes secrets support environment variables and mounted volumes. Secrets should never be built into container images, as anyone who has access to the image can view the secrets. Updating the secret would also involve rebuilding and redeploying the image. Environment variables are safer. However, information from environment variables can be leaked. For these reasons, it is recommended to use secret data volumes.

Secret Data Volumes

Secrets are mounted into containers using a volume plug-in. Secret data volumes are backed by temporary file-storage facilities (tmpfs) and never come to rest on a node. For more information on mounting secret volumes, refer to Providing sensitive data to Pods.

Etcd Datastore Encryption

Etcd is a distributed key-value datastore used by Kubernetes to store configuration data. Etcd is only available to OpenShift administrators. The data in etcd represents the entire state of the Kubernetes cluster. The datastore is continually monitored for changes which are then applied to the running state of the system. By default, secret objects are stored in etcd and retrieved as needed via the API. In OpenShift, all traffic between the API server and the worker nodes is encrypted, ensuring that secrets stored in etcd and transmitted to pods are encrypted in-transit.

The default configuration of etcd stores secret objects with base64 encoding. While this means the secret is not easily read, base64 does not provide the same level of protection as encryption. Additional protection for secrets at-rest can be provided by encrypting the etcd datastore. Once enabled, encryption cannot be disabled. The AES-CBC cipher is used to encrypt the datastore. Keys are created and automatically rotated by a Kubernetes Operator and stored on the master node's file system. Keys are available as a secret via the kube API to a cluster administrator.

Once encryption is enabled in a healthy cluster, all relevant items in etcd will be encrypted within a day. It is critical that the etcd data store be backed up separately from the file system with the key. A backup of both the encrypted etcd data and encryption keys must be available. For more information, see Encrypting etcd data.

External Vaults

External vaults can be deployed to OpenShift for application secret management. For example, the Vault Operator can be used to create and manage the open source version of Hashicorp Vault on OpenShift. Red Hat partners also offer commercially supported integrations in the Red Hat Ecosystem catalog. A number of these solutions integrate with hardware security modules (HSMs) for even more secure key management.

Protecting Cluster Data on Disk

Organizational policies may require system configuration data or other operational data to be encrypted at rest. When installing OpenShift Container Platform in a public cloud environment, there may be provider-specific services that encrypt block devices that are used by server instances. Alternatively, protection of data at rest can be achieved by enabling full-disk encryption that is managed by utilities on the operating system.

Leveraging Disk Encryption from Public Cloud Providers

By default, the OpenShift Installer will automatically configure disk encryption at the provider level when available. Currently this is available for Amazon Web Services (AWS) and Google Cloud Platform (GCP). For AWS, disk encryption is provided by enabling encrypted Elastic Block Store (EBS) volumes. Google Cloud Platform uses encryption at rest by default. Alternatively, RHEL CoreOS can take advantage of the virtual trusted platform module (vTPM) provided by Google Shielded VMs for instance-level encryption of the root filesystem.

If the OpenShift cluster is installed with user-provisioned infrastructure, configuring a disk encryption service from a cloud provider must be included when the infrastructure is created, before the OpenShift Installer begins installation.

RHEL CoreOS Full-Disk Encryption

RHEL CoreOS supports full-disk encryption for both Network Bound Disk and TPM2 backed encryption modes. Please see the full disk encryption section of the RHEL CoreOS Security chapter for more details.

Currently, RHEL CoreOS does not support key-cycling for full-disk encryption. Full disk encryption is implemented through LUKS which uses passphrases to unlock the actual key. The passphrase for unlocking the key is discerned by Clevis through meta-data in the LUKS header and the backend (either a TPM2 or a Tang server). If the passphrase needs to be cycled, administrators must do a rolling-replacement of nodes using the updated configuration. Future versions of RHEL CoreOS are expected to have key-cycling support.

During the initial boot, the master key and the unlock passphrase are randomly generated, after which Clevis binds to the disk to allow unattended unlocking of the disk. RHEL CoreOS does not support third-party Key Escrow or *bring-your-own keys* at the time of this writing.

OpenShift Service Mesh

OpenShift Service Mesh, based on the open source Istio project, is an optional component that can be used to encrypt traffic between services (east-west traffic) on an OpenShift cluster. OpenShift Service Mesh builds with RHEL 8 OpenSSL for encryption. OpenShift Service Mesh can be deployed on a per-project basis. More information on OpenShift Service Mesh is available in Chapter 6: Network Security.

9. Securing CI/CD

Continuous Integration and Continuous Delivery (CI/CD) has become a ubiquitous process for automated production and quality control of software applications. It's natural for these processes to leverage the speed and added security afforded by adopting container technologies such as OpenShift. The question becomes, what changes or additions are necessary to ensure conventional pipeline processes accommodate containers and their security?

Best Practices for an Application CI/CD pipeline

Consider the following baseline application CI/CD pipeline as shown in Figure 9.1. The basic steps that are typical of most pipelines in a traditional, non-containerized environment are shown below. In this example, a Java-based application is being built using a technology such as Spring Boot, and the deployment will be to a virtual machine or bare-metal server.

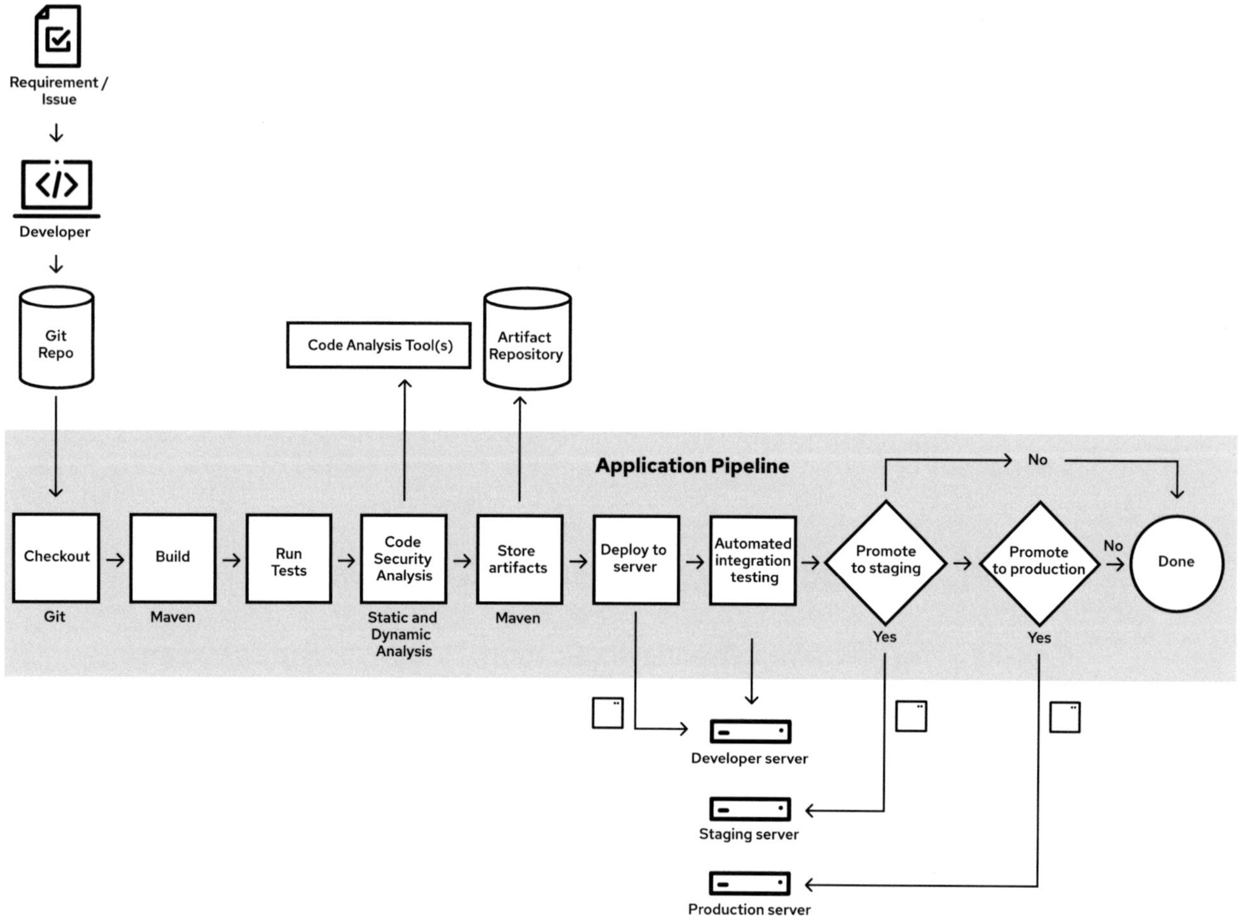

Figure 9.1: Traditional CI/CD Pipeline with a Deployment to a Non-Containerized Environment

New features and bug fixes are represented as individual issues in an issue management system such as GitHub, GitLab, Jira, etc. They are then ultimately assigned to a developer who clones code from a git repository via a fork or by creating a new repository. After implementing a fix, the code is pushed back into the repository, resulting in the application pipeline being started. The exact details of this initial flow are out of the scope of this book, but at a high level, this is the set of steps that results in a new instance of an application CI/CD pipeline being created.

Continuous Integration

There are several tools that can be used to implement this pipeline, including Jenkins, GitLab CI, Tekton, and Bamboo. The examples in this chapter will focus on Jenkins. Once the code has been pushed, the pipeline will perform a `git clone` (checkout stage of the pipeline) and build the application code. In the case of this Java application, Maven will then be used to build the application. The output will be a Java Archive (JAR) file which, in the case of Spring Boot, is a deployable unit that can be run by a Java Virtual Machine (JVM).

The application is built to avoid performing any analysis of code that may prevent a successful build. This serves as the initial check provided to the developer in terms of the viability of the committed code. Once the code has been successfully built, all unit tests for the code can then be executed. Some typical tools used for Java unit testing include Junit, Mockito, TestNG, and Cucumber.

The amount of code coverage (lines of code executed by the unit tests) required to continue with the pipeline is set by the software development organization. Values typically range from 70% to 100%. The failure of any unit test will result in pipeline failure. The primary goal for unit testing is to avoid brittle code. Brittle code is also the source for application security vulnerabilities and potential exploits by malicious actors.

Once the unit test phase has been completed, static code analysis is then performed. SonarQube is an example of an open source static code analysis tool. It can analyze most popular programming languages including Java, Java Script, Python, Go, and C++. SonarQube focuses on programming best practices. However, it does provide some basic security-related rules, such as checking for potentially hard-coded passwords. There are other third-party source code analysis tools, such as HP Fortify, that are specifically designed to detect security-related coding issues. After the scans are complete, the JAR file can be stored for posterity in an artifact repository, such as Sonatype Nexus or JFrog Artifactory.

Continuous Delivery

The previous stages make up the CI portion of the CI/CD pipeline. The automated delivery of the JAR file to the development server is the CD portion of the pipeline. Once the application has been successfully (and automatically) installed in the development server, automated integration and QA testing can then take place. These tests verify the functionality of the running application. They can be as simple as smoke tests or an extensive exercise of most capabilities of the running application. Selenium and Robot are example frameworks that can be used to perform automated integration tests on web-based applications.

In this pipeline, there are manual gates for deploying the application into additional environments. Members from the testing organization may have the appropriate authority to promote the application to the staging environment. While promotion to the production environment may require higher levels of authorization, automatic deployment into a production environment is possible in some of the most mature organizations – this is known as continuous deployment. If any of the pipeline steps fail, the entire pipeline is marked as failed, and everyone (developers, testers, management, security, etc.) is notified. The results are analyzed, the solution is iterated, corrections are submitted, and a new instance of the pipeline is executed.

The previous example has demonstrated a CI/CD pipeline with basic levels of security, deploying a more traditional, non-containerized environment. In this traditional paradigm, the security and deployment of the platform is unfortunately decoupled from the deployment of the application. This presents a block to automation and reinforces silos between development and operations organizations. The advent of DevOps coupled with container technology enables a holistic, systems view of software, and the platforms they run on.

Container-based CI/CD Pipeline

The pipeline in Figure 9.2 expands on the previous example, incorporating container-based deployment and security steps.

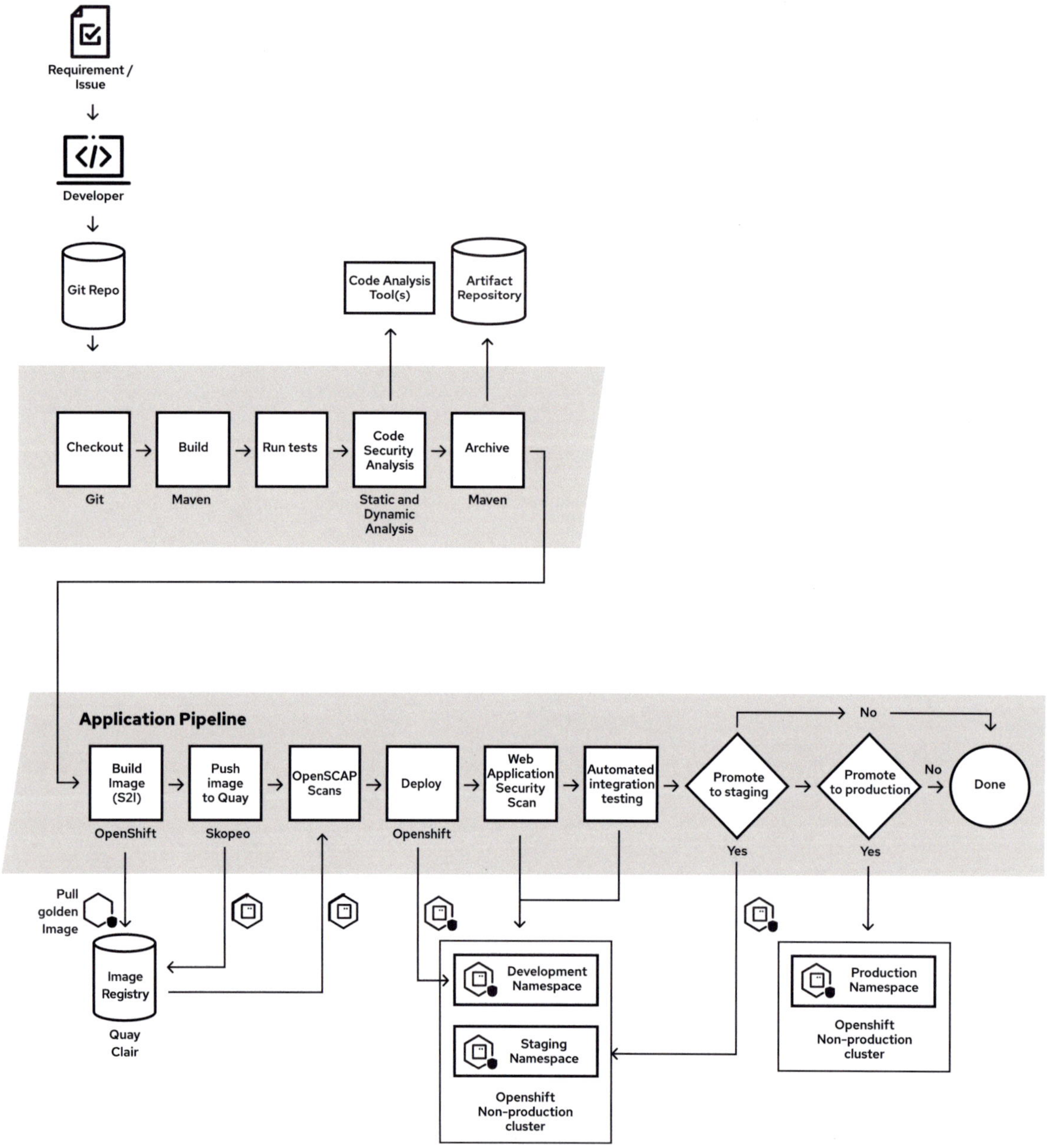

Figure 9.2: Application CI/CD Pipeline with a Deployment to a Containerized Environment

Example source code for the pipeline shown in Figure 9.2, including the Jenkinsfile, can be found in Sample SpringBoot / Angular application on

Github.

The initial CI stages start from a developer working on an issue continuing through archival development of the JAR file to Nexus via Maven, all of which are identical. The next step is to merge the JAR artifact into a container image that can run the JAR – in this case an image that has OpenJDK installed on it. The golden base image is retrieved from an enterprise image registry.

In this case we are using Red Hat Quay, which has some additional security features built into it – most notably Clair, which will perform image scans for potential operating system vulnerabilities. Note that this golden image is considered secure by the time it is pulled by the application pipeline. The base image is created from a Red Hat Universal Base Image (UBI), which is derived from currently supported versions of Red Hat Enterprise Linux (RHEL), such as RHEL 7 and RHEL 8. Creation and management of this secure base image is discussed later.

Source-to-Image (s2i) build strategy is used to take the JAR file and place it in a location of the base image's file system. The base image is configured to run the JAR file from this location. Once this process is complete, a new application image will be created and stored in the internal OpenShift registry by default. This image will only be available within the namespace where the build was completed and will not be generally available. Other techniques for building the application image (other than s2i) can be explored in the OpenShift documentation on Build Strategies. Once the image has been created, it is pushed into the enterprise registry as a candidate image.

Skopeo

Skopeo is an open source utility that allows images to be copied between different image storage mediums (registries, TAR files, etc.). It is used by the pipeline to copy the candidate image from the internal OpenShift registry into the enterprise registry.

Container Registry and Image Scanning

The enterprise registry is the official source-of-truth for images. At this point in the pipeline, compliance and vulnerability scans are performed using the Security Content Automation Protocol (SCAP). Projects that must adhere to the Defense Information Systems Agency (DISA) Security Technical Implementation Guides (STIGs) can use OpenSCAP. An open source SCAP interpreter, included in Red Hat Enterprise Linux, evaluates for compliance during this step. OpenSCAP is also able to check whether any of the latest known vulnerabilities are present within the image.

For simplicity, the security gates that are checked are not depicted in this pipeline. They are shown and discussed in the container hardening pipeline section which follows. In addition to OpenSCAP there are several third-party tools that can be used to perform additional security scans or examine images that are not based on RHEL. Some examples include Twistlock, Anchore, BlackDuck, and Sysdig.

Multiple Environments

Once the scans have been performed and passed, the secure container image is deployed into a development environment. Multiple environments can be present in a single OpenShift cluster. These include environments for individual developers and teams of developers, amongst others. For the purposes of this example, there is a development environment and staging environment depicted within the non-production OpenShift cluster.

Once the image has been deployed into a namespace, additional scans and tests are executed. The Open Web Application Security Project (OWASP) Zed Attack Proxy (ZAP) tool can be used to perform additional security scanning of the actual application. A baseline scan is performed by point OWASP ZAP to the web entry point of the deployed web application. This is another technique for increasing application level security. OWASP ZAP will crawl the application looking for potential vulnerabilities in HTML, JavaScript, to name a few. The results can be manually inspected by the security team in addition to setting up automatic pipeline gates.

Automated Testing

The next step is to perform automated testing against the deployed containerized application, just as was performed in the previous non-containerized pipeline. Once those tests pass, the pipeline is poised to deploy the application into the next environment. The production namespace is shown in a separate OpenShift cluster – this is a recommended best practice. It gives greater flexibility by decoupling infrastructure requirements, organizational ownership and other concerns between production and non-production deployments.

One thing to note, is that once a secured container image has been created for the application, the same immutable container image is used for deploying the container into the different OpenShift Deployment environments for that application. OpenShift provides several mechanisms for configuring the dynamic aspects of the containerized application :

- Persistent volumes can be used for storing file system data that must be saved between restarts of the application
- Configuration maps can be used to store configuration data that is required by the application
- Secrets are used to store sensitive data used by the application, such as certificates, keys, and passwords

Supply Chain Security

The foundation of CI/CD supply chain security is using trusted components that include the pipeline software, image scanners, and the base images on which the application container images are built. These items must not only come from trusted sources but must be refreshed on an on-going basis to remain secure.

Trusted Supply Chain

When developers first start experimenting with container images, they often obtain an image from a publicly available image registry. Many of these registries will allow anyone to push images and usually do not provide a security posture for these images. In some cases, the registries will not make the image specification files available. While this is fine for experimentation and non-critical application workloads, it is not a viable solution for the enterprise.

Trusted supply chains attempt to resolve this issue by enforcing more stringent requirements in terms of how images are created, and through a tighter security stance. The concept is that the image comes from a trusted source and every time that image is extended, the supply chain keeps track of how it was done and scans for potential vulnerabilities or non-compliance. The previous pipeline example demonstrated this concept; however, the origin of the golden base image had not yet been discussed. This golden image was produced from a container hardening pipeline, which is the starting point of the trusted supply chain.

Image Hardening Pipeline

An image hardening pipeline is used to create the trusted golden images upon which containerized applications will be built.

The container image specification files for each of the base images are stored in version control, no different than application source code. The pipeline is automatically started whenever the source changes. Scripts used by the container image specification file are stored alongside the specification file in source control. In this example, all applicable DISA STIG controls will be applied to the hardened image.

The hardening process can be performed by bash scripts stored in the git repository. These scripts are derived from the ones generated by the OpenSCAP tool using the ComplianceAsCode/SCAP Security Guide content delivered natively in Red Hat Enterprise Linux. Just like in the other pipelines, the first step is to clone the source code from the git repository. The next step is to build the image, which will also apply any of the hardening scripts. The question becomes what images will be used as the base of the new image? The Universal Base Images (UBI) provided by Red Hat will serve this purpose.

Using a Secure Container Base Image

A base image is one of the simplest types of images. Sometimes users will refer to corporate standard build, or even an application image as the "base image." Technically this is not a base image. These are intermediate images. An intermediate image is any container image that relies on a base image. Typically, core builds, middleware, and language runtimes are built as layers on top of a base image. These images are not used on their own, they are typically used as a building block to build a standalone image.

A base image is an image that has no parent layer. Typically, a base image contains a fresh copy of an operating system. Base images normally include tools (such as yum, rpm, apt-get, dnf, microdnf) necessary to install packages and make updates to the image over time. While base images can be "hand crafted," in practice they are typically produced and published by open source projects (such as Debian, Fedora, or CentOS) and vendors (such as Red Hat). The provenance of base images is critical for security. In short, the sole purpose of a base image is to provide a starting place for creating derivative images.

What is the Red Hat Universal Base Image (UBI)?

Since provenance is a concern when using container base images, just pulling the latest upstream code does not guarantee security, since regressions and new CVEs are often introduced without notice. A trusted image must be downloaded from a trusted source.

The objective of the Red Hat Universal Base image is to provide the highest quality and most flexible base container image available. UBI images are created so container images can be built on a foundation of official Red Hat software that can be freely shared and deployed.

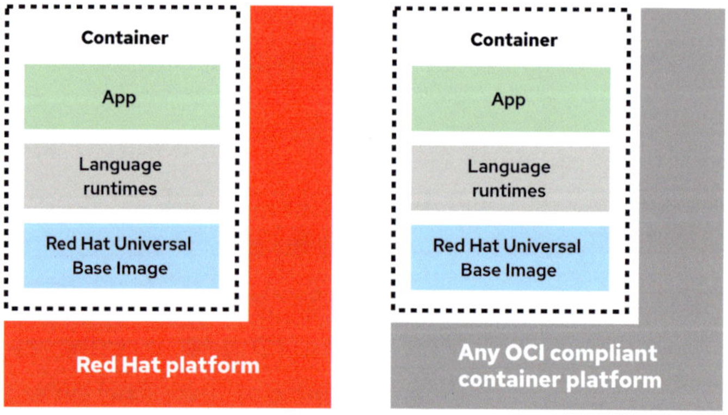

Figure 9.3: UBI Image in Relation to the Platform

The types of UBI image that can be used to build applications on include the following :

- **Base Images** – Derived from RHEL, a Red Hat Universal Base image release offers three main types of base images :
    - **ubi :** A standard base image built on enterprise grade packages from RHEL. Good for 80% of users' needs
    - **ubi-minimal :** When users are sensitive to size, this is the image to use. Built on microdnf, it provides the smallest on-disk size
    - **ubi-init :** This image allows users to easily run multiple services (mysql, httpd) in a single container. It allows a user to leverage the knowledge built into systemd unit files without having to figure out how to start the service
- **Language Runtime Images** – These are ready-to-run container images, where a user only needs to add their application code. A set of language runtime images is provided for UBI 7 and UBI 8. These include :
    - UBI 7 – php-72, nodejs-8, ruby-25, python-27, python-36
    - UBI 8 – dotnet-21-runtime, perl-526, php-72, nodejs-10, ruby-25, python-27, python-36

All UBI images are configured to access dedicated YUM repositories that offer RHEL RPM packages. These repositories include the latest versions of a set of freely available RPMs that users can access to rebuild container images anytime they want. These repositories, and broader usage of the UBI images, do not require a Red Hat subscription. Attributes of these repositories include :

- By default, only the latest RPM for each package are provided
- If users need access to historic RPMs, they will need to synchronize them themselves

Advantages of the Red Hat UBI

The Red Hat UBI content follows the Red Hat Enterprise Linux schedule. New versions of the Red Hat Universal Base Image are released whenever there is a new release of RHEL. Building on UBI is a safe choice because updates will be received for the life cycle of the underlying RHEL content.

New container images built are governed by the Red Hat Image Updates Policy. This includes images built for critical CVE's and during releases. Also, a YUM repository is provided with the latest set of RPMs for any given release. This will allow users to update container images during rebuilds, ensuring that the latest Errata (Security, Bug Fixes, Enhancements) is picked up and applied.

UBI Images come from a known, trusted source – the Red Hat Image Registry. While git repositories are used to store source code, image registries store the binary files that comprise a container image. The registry is fronted by a publicly facing web interface that provides detailed information on the security posture of the image, including a simple health index (letter grade) for quick reference. Figure 9.4 is a screenshot from the Red Hat container registry showing the tag history of the UBI 7 image.

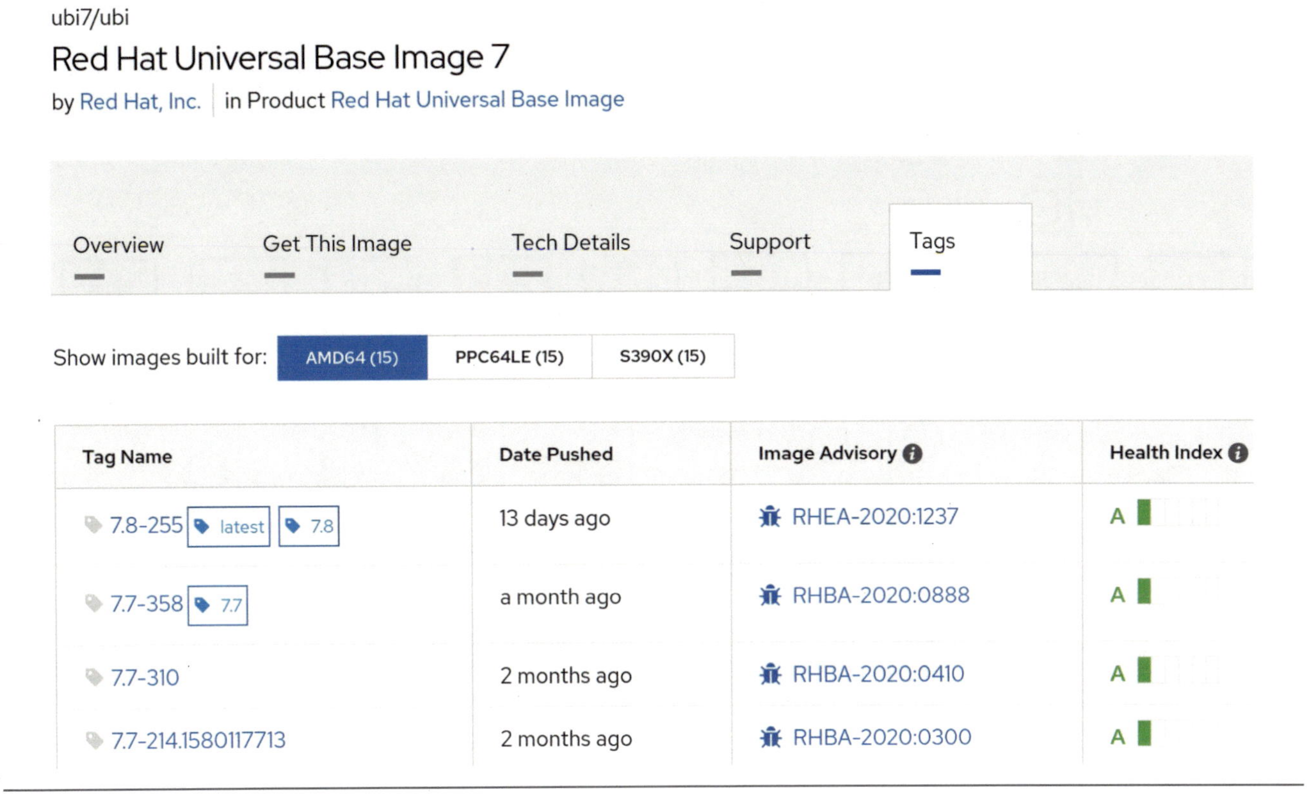

Figure 9.4: UBI Image on the Red Hat Container Registry

Hardening Pipeline Flow

Just as in the application pipeline, hardening images against a known compliance baseline can be built using OpenShift mechanisms (s2i, Docker build) or other open source tools such as Podman and buildah.

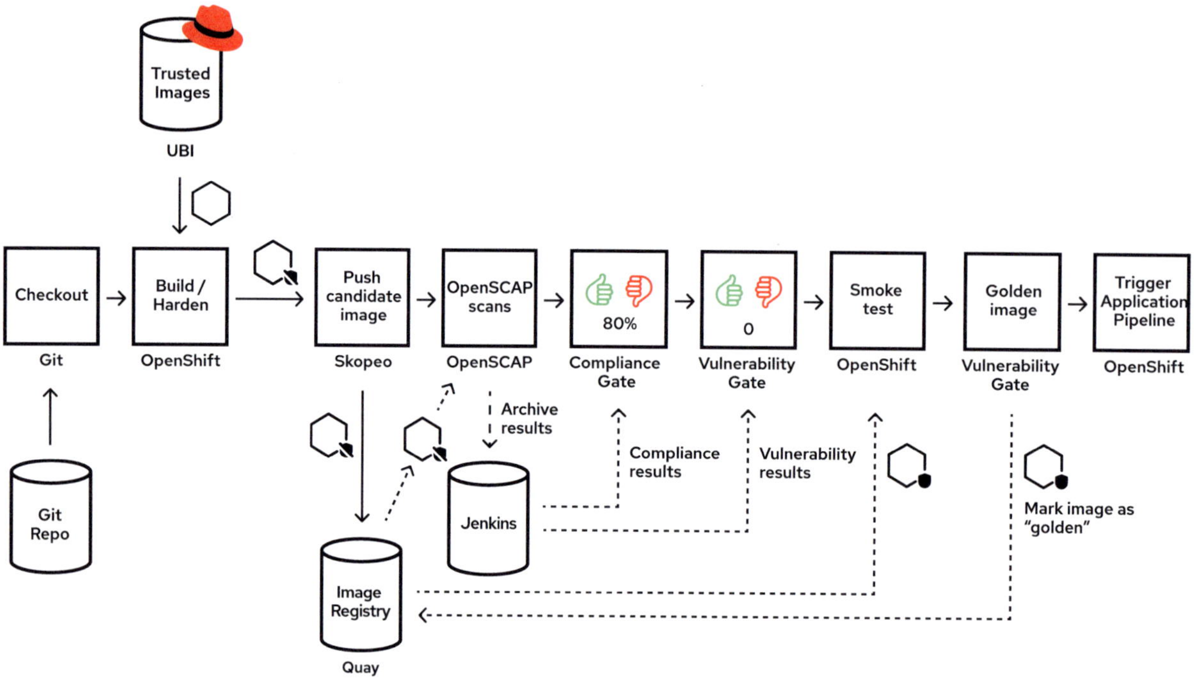

Figure 9.5: CI/CD Base Image Hardening Pipeline Using UBI

After the candidate image has been created, it is pushed into the enterprise image registry. Hardening has been applied; however, the image is not yet considered secure until it passes the upcoming scans.
OpenSCAP compliance and vulnerability scans are run against the image, just as they were in the application CI/CD pipeline. The scans can be performed from a bastion host or run by a custom container as an agent within Jenkins.

In this pipeline diagram the compliance and vulnerability gates are explicitly depicted. The acceptable compliance level is a program level standard; in this example we are setting the threshold to require 80% of all checks to pass. In addition to simply failing the pipeline, the gate stage can be implemented such that the pipeline is paused and the appropriate people are notified to look at the results and determine whether the pipeline should continue or be terminated.

The following is an example using the *oscap-docker* command line to run a RHEL 7 STIG compliance scan against an image based upon the Red Hat UBI 7 base image:

```
$ sudo oscap-docker image \
   ${ENTERPRISE_REGISTRY}/${NAMESPACE}/ubi-openjdk:latest \
   xccdf eval --profile \
   xccdf_org.ssgproject.content_profile_stig-rhel7-disa \
   --report report.html \
   /usr/share/xml/scap/ssg/content/ssg-rhel7-ds.xml
```

There are many profiles available, such as the RHEL 8 STIG, PCI-DSS, and HIPAA, along with a UBI8 base image. The vulnerability gate in this example is configured to fail the pipeline if there are any vulnerabilities detected, regardless of severity. This could similarly be updated to pause the pipeline until the results are examined by a security professional. Any third-party security tools can be run with similar gates in place for evaluating their results.

At this point in the pipeline, the image is considered secured, however additional tests can be run to verify that basic functionality of the image is still intact. The smoke test phase verifies that the image comes up and functions as expected. Since this pipeline is building a base image for OpenJDK, the smoke test simply calls `java -version` to verify the java executable is accessible from the path. Once the smoke test passes, the image is ready for general consumption by marking it as a golden image. This is done by updating the tag of the image within the enterprise image registry.

The hardening pipeline can be started by events other than changes to the image source code. Consider the situation where a new vulnerability is discovered and is fixed by the latest UBI image in the Red Hat container registry. In this situation, the pipeline can be manually started (or started via a hook) in order to incorporate the latest UBI image and incorporate the fix into the hardened base image.

Many third-party container security tools such as Twistlock also perform continuous scans of images running within an OpenShift or Kubernetes cluster. If these tools detect a potential problem, this can also be used as a hook to initiate the hardening pipeline or log a trouble ticket that can be resolved by a developer and start the pipeline.

List of Acronyms

Acronym/ Term	Explanation of acronym / definition	Chapter #
3PAO	Third-Party Assessment Organization	1 (Risk)
AC	Access Control	1 (Risk)
ACL	Access Control List	6 (NetSec)
ACME	Automatic Certificate Management Environment	8 (ESM)
ACSC	Australian Cyber Security Centre	1 (Risk)
AES	Advanced Encryption Standard	2 (CoreOs)
ANSSI	Agence Nationale de la Sécurité des Systèmes d'Information National Cybersecurity Agency of France	1 (Risk)
API	Application Programming Interface	2 (CoreOs)
AT	Awareness and Training	1 (Risk)
ATO	Authority To Operate	1 (Risk)
AU	Audit and Accountability	1 (Risk)
AWS	Amazon Web Services	2 (CoreOS)
AZ	Availability Zone	6 (NetSec)
CA	Certificate Authority	4 (Kube)
CAC	Common Access Card	5 (IAM)
CBC	Cipher Block Chaining	2 (CoreOS)
CC	Common Criteria	1 (Risk)
CD	Continuous Deployment	0 (Intro)
Ceph RBD	Ceph Rados Block Device	3 (Cont)
cgroup	Control Group	3 (Cont)
CI	Continuous Integration	0 (Intro)
CLI	Command Line Interface	0 (Intro)
CM	Configuration Management	1 (Risk)
CMVP	NIST Cryptographic Module Validation Program	1 (Risk)
CNCF	Cloud Native Computing Foundation	6 (NetSec)
CNI	Container Networking Interface	6 (NetSec)
CNO	Cluster Network Operator	0 (Intro)
COBIT	Control Objectives for Information and Related Technologies	1 (Risk)
CP	Contingency Planning	1 (Risk)

CPU	Central Processing Unit	2 (CoreOS)
CSPRNG	Cryptographically Secure Pseudo-Random Number Generator	8 (Encryption)
CVO	Cluster Version Operator	0 (Intro)
COTS	Commercial Off-the-Shelf	1 (Risk)
CR	Custom Resource	6 (NetSec)
CRI-O	Container Runtime Interface for Open Container Initiative	2 (CoreOs)
CRC	Code Ready Containers	0 (Intro)
CVE	Common Vulnerability and Exposures	3 (Cont)
DISA	Defense Information Systems Agency	1 (Risk)
DoS	Denial of Service	6 (NetSec)
DDoS	Distributed Denial of Service	6 (NetSec)
DHCP	Dynamic Host Configuration Protocol	2 (CoreOs)
DN	Domain Name	5 (IAM)
DNS	Domain Name Server	2 (CoreOS)
DoD	(United States) Department of Defense	8 (ESM)
DTLS	Datagram Transport Layer Security	1 (Risk)
EBS	Elastic Block Storage	2 (CoreOS)
ECDSA	Elliptic Curve Digital Signature Algorithm	8 (ESM)
EFK	ElasticSearch, Fluentd and Kibana	4 (Kube)
ELS	Extended Life Cycle	1 (Risk)
EUS	Extended Update Support	1 (Risk)
fapolicyd	File Access Policy Daemon	2 (CoreOs)
FDE	Full Disk Encryption	2 (CoreOs)
FedRAMP	Federal Risk and Authorization Management Program	1 (Risk)
FIPS	Federal Information Processing Standards	2 (CoreOs)
FISMA	Federal Information Systems Management Act	1 (Risk)
GCP	Google Cloud Platform	2 (CoreOs)
GID	Group ID	3 (Cont)
gRPC	gRPC Remote Procedure Call (*recursive acronym*)	6 (NetSec)
HA	High Availability	6 (NetSec)
HIPAA	Health Insurance Portability and Accountability Act	1 (Risk)

HMAC	Keyed-hash Message Authentication Code	5 (IAM)
HSM	Hardware Security Module	8 (ESM)
HSTS	HTTP Strict Transport Security	8 (ESM)
HTML	Hypertext Markup Language	9 (CI/CD)
HTTP	Hypertext Transfer Protocol	6 (NetSec)
HTTPS	Hypertext Transfer Protocol Secure	6 (NetSec)
IA (NIST)	Identification and Authentication	1 (Risk)
IA	Information Assurance	1 (Risk)
IAM	Identity and Access Management	5 (IAM)
ID	Identity	3 (Cont)
IdP	Identity Provider	5 (IAM)
IP	Internet Protocol	1 (Risk)
IPv6	Internet Protocol version 6	1 (Risk)
iSCSI	Internet Small Computer System Interface	3 (Cont)
ISM	Information Security Manual	1 (Risk)
ISSA	Information Systems Security Association	1 (Risk)
IDE	Integrated Development Environment	0 (Intro)
IdM	Identity Management	5 (IAM)
IdP	Identity Provider	5 (IAM)
IEC	Commission électrotechnique internationale	1 (Risk)
ISO	International Organization for Standardization	1 (Risk)
I/O	Input / Output	2 (CoreOS)
IP	Internet Protocol	6 (NetSec)
IPC	Inter-Process Communication	3 (Cont)
IPSec	IP Security	8 (ESM)
IR	Incident Response	1 (Risk)
ISSA	Information Systems Security Association	1 (Risk)
ISV	Independent Software Vendor	0 (Intro)
IUT	Implementation Under Test	1 (Risk)
JAB	Joint Authorization Board	1 (Risk)
JAR	Java Archive	9 (CI/CD)

JSON	JavaScript Object Notation	2 (CoreOS)
JVM	Java Virtual Machine	6 (NetSec)
JWT	JSON Web Token	5 (IAM)
KASLR	Kernel Address Space Layout Randomization	2 (CoreOS)
KMS	Key Management Service	8 (ESM)
LDAP	Lightweight Directory Access Protocol	5 (IAM)
LTS	Long-Term Support	9 (CI/CD)
LUKS	Linux Unified Key Setup	2 (CoreOS)
MAC	Media Access Control	6 (NetSec)
MAC	Mandatory Access Control	3 (Cont)
MA	Maintenance	1 (Risk)
MCO	Machine Config Operator	0 (Intro)
MIP	Modules in Process	1 (Risk)
MP	Media Protection	1 (Risk)
MITM	Man-In-The-Middle	6 (NetSec)
mTLS	Mutual TLS	6 (NetSec)
MCS	Multi-Categories Security	3 (Cont)
NAT	Network Address Translation	6 (NetSec)
NBDE	Network-Bound Disk Encryption	2 (CoreOS)
NCCoE	National Cybersecurity Center of Excellence	1 (Risk)
NIST	National Institute of Standards and Technology	0 (Intro)
NSA	National Security Agency	3 (Cont)
NSS	Network Security Services	1 (Risk)
NTP	Network Time Protocol	8 (ESM)
OAuth	Open Standard for Authorization	5 (IAM)
OCI	Open Container Initiative	2 (CoreOs)
OCP	OpenShift Container Platform	0 (Intro)
OES	Operators of Essential Services	1 (Risk)
OIDC	OpenID Connect	5 (IAM)
OLM	Operator Lifecycle Manager	0 (Intro)
OpenSSH	Open Secure SHell (tool)	1 (Risk)

OpenSSL	Open Secure Sockets Layer (library)	1 (Risk)
OpenSCAP	Open Security Content Automation Protocol	0 (Intro)
OS	Operating System	2 (CoreOS)
OTA	Over-the-Air	6 (NetSec)
OTP	One-Time Password	5 (IAM)
OVAL	Open Vulnerability Assessment Language	1 (Risk)
OVN	Open Virtual Network	6 (NetSec)
OVS	OpenVSwitch	6 (NetSec)
OWASP	Open Web Application Security Project	9 (CI/CD)
PCI-DSS	Payment Card Industry Data Security Standard	1 (Risk)
PE	Physical and Environmental Protection	1 (Risk)
PKCS	public-key cryptography standards	1 (Risk)
PKI	Public Key Infrastructure	8 (ESM)
PL	Planning	1 (Risk)
PID	Process Identifier	3 (Cont)
PIV	Personal Identity Verification	5 (IAM)
PoAM	Plan of Action and Milestones	8 (ESM)
PRNG	Pseudo-Random Number Generator	8 (ESM)
PS	Personnel Security	1 (Risk)
PSP	Pod Security Policies	4 (Kube)
QA	Quality Assurance	9 (CI/CD)
RA	Risk Assessment	1 (Risk)
RBAC	Role-Based Access Control	4 (Kube)
RHCOS	Red Hat Enterprise Linux CoreOS	2 (CoreOS)
RHEL	Red Hat Enterprise Linux	2 (CoreOS)
RMF	Risk Management Framework	1 (Risk)
RNG	Random Number Generator	8 (ESM)
RPM	RPM Package Manager (*a recursive backronym*)	
RSA	Rivest–Shamir–Adleman	8 (ESM)
S2I	Service to Image	9 (CI/CD)
SA	Service Account	4 (Kube)

SA	System and Services Acquisition	1 (Risk)
SAML	Security Assertion Markup Language	5 (IAM)
SC	System and Communications Protection	1 (Risk)
SCAP	Security Content Automation Protocol	1 (Risk)
SCC	Security Context Constraints	3 (Cont)
SCTP	Stream Control Transmission Protocol	6 (NetSec)
SDN	Software Defined Network	6 (NetSec)
seccomp	Secure Computing mode	3 (Cont)
SELinux	Security Enhanced Linux	3 (Cont)
SHA	Secure Hash Algorithm	5 (IAM)
SI	System and Information Integrity	1 (Risk)
SIEM	Security Information and Event Management	4 (Kube)
SLA	Service Level Agreement	7 (Audit)
SLO	Single LogOut	4 (Kube)
SNI	Server Name Indication	4 (Kube)
SOC	Security Operations Center	7 (Audit)
SP 800	Special Publication 800-series	1 (Risk)
SPIFFE	Secure Production Identity Framework for Everyone	6 (NetSec)
SRTM	Security Requirements Traceability Matrix	1 (Risk)
SR-IOV	Single Root I/O Virtualization	6 (NetSec)
SSH	Secure SHell	1 (Risk)
SSL	Secure Socket Library	1 (Risk)
SSPI	Security Support Provider Interface	1 (Risk)
SSSD	System Security Services Daemon	5 (Ident)
STIG	Security Technical Implementation Guides	1 (Risk)
TAR	Tape ARchiver (compression tool)	9 (CI/CD)
TCP	Transmission Control Protocol	6 (NetSec)
TLS	Transport Layer Security	2 (CoreOS)
TMPFS	Temporary File System	8 (ESM)
TPM	Trusted Platform Module	3 (CoreOS)
UBI	Universal Base Images	0 (Intro)

UID	User Identity	3 (Cont)
UDP	User Datagram Protocol	6 (NetSec)
URI	Uniform Resource Identifier	7 (Audit)
URL	Uniform Resource Locator	2 (CoreOS)
USGv6	United States Government acquisition standards for IPv6 equipment	1 (Risk)
UTS	UNIX Time Sharing	3(Cont)
VS Code	Visual Studio Code	0 (Intro)
VIP	Virtual IP	6 (NetSec)
VF	Virtual Function (in scope of SR-IOV)	6 (NetSec)
VM	Virtual Machine	3 (Cont)
vTPM	Virtual Trusted Platform Module	8 (Encrypt)
WWW	World Wide Web	5 (IAM)
X.509	standard defining the format of public key certificates	1 (Risk)
XCCDF	eXtensible Configuration Checklist Description Format	1 (Risk)
YAML	Yet Another Markup Language	9 (CI/CD)
YUM	Yellowdog Updater, Modified	9 (CI/CD)
ZAP	Zed Attack Proxy	9 (CI/CD)

Links

Introduction

https://prometheus.io/

https://grafana.com/

1. Risk Management and Regulatory Readiness

https://csrc.nist.gov/Projects/cryptographic-module-validation-program/Certificate/3571

https://csrc.nist.gov/Projects/cryptographic-module-validation-program/Certificate/3565

https://csrc.nist.gov/Projects/cryptographic-module-validation-program/Certificate/3563

https://csrc.nist.gov/Projects/cryptographic-module-validation-program/Certificate/3538

https://csrc.nist.gov/Projects/cryptographic-module-validation-program/Certificate/3270

https://csrc.nist.gov/Projects/cryptographic-module-validation-program/Certificate/3067

https://csrc.nist.gov/Projects/cryptographic-module-validation-program/Certificate/3063

https://csrc.nist.gov/Projects/cryptographic-module-validation-program/Modules-In-Process/IUT-List

https://csrc.nist.gov/Projects/cryptographic-module-validation-program/Modules-In-Process/Modules-In-Process-List

https://www.iso.org/standard/50341.html

https://www.cnss.gov/CNSS/issuances/Policies.cfm

https://www.niap-ccevs.org/Profile/PP.cfm

https://www.nist.gov/cyberframework/online-learning/informative-references

https://cloudsecurityalliance.org/research/working-groups/cloud-controls-matrix

https://www.cyber.gov.au/ism

https://www.cyber.gov.au/publications/essential-eight-explained

https://mojo.redhat.com/external-link.jspa?url%3Dhttp%253A%252F%252Fwww-x.antd.nist.gov%252Fusgv6%252Findex.html

https://access.redhat.com/articles/2918071%23usgv6-tested-product-list-7

https://www.nccoe.nist.gov/

https://nvd.nist.gov/ncp/repository

https://nvlpubs.nist.gov/nistpubs/SpecialPublications/NIST.SP.800-70r4.pdf

https://csrc.nist.gov/Projects/scap-validation-program/validated-products-and-modules

https://nvd.nist.gov/ncp/repository?authority%3DRed%2BHat%26startIndex%3D0

2. Red Hat Enterprise Linux CoreOS Security

https://github.com/coreos/ignition

https://kubernetes.io/docs/concepts/workloads/controllers/daemonset/

https://kubernetes.io/docs/concepts/configuration/assign-pod-node/

https://docs.openshift.com/container-platform/4.3/operators/operator_sdk/osdk-getting-started.html

https://github.com/openshift/machine-config-operator/blob/master/docs/custom-pools.md

https://access.redhat.com/documentation/en-us/red_hat_enterprise_linux/8/html/security_hardening/configuring-automated-unlocking-of-encrypted-volumes-using-policy-based-decryption_security-hardening

https://docs.openshift.com/container-platform/4.3/architecture/architecture-rhcos.html

https://access.redhat.com/solutions/4073041

https://access.redhat.com/solutions/4057081

3. Container Security

https://github.com/kubernetes/cri-api

https://katacontainers.io/

https://github.com/containers/libpod/tree/master/cmd/podman

https://github.com/kubernetes-sigs/cri-tools/blob/master/docs/crictl.md

https://www.openshift.com/blog/crictl-vs-podman

http://man7.org/linux/man-pages/man7/capabilities.7.html

https://docs.openshift.com/container-platform/4.3/authentication/managing-security-context-constraints.html%23security-context-constraints-about_configuring-internal-oauth

https://github.com/openshift/machine-config-operator/tree/master/docs%23applying-configuration-changes-to-the-cluster

https://media.ccc.de/v/ASG2019-140-generating-seccomp-profiles-for-containers-using-podman-and-ebpf

https://nvd.nist.gov/vuln/detail/CVE-2015-3627

https://nvd.nist.gov/vuln/detail/CVE-2015-3630

https://nvd.nist.gov/vuln/detail/CVE-2015-3631

https://nvd.nist.gov/vuln/detail/CVE-2016-9962

https://nvd.nist.gov/vuln/detail/CVE-2019-5736

https://github.com/openshift/machine-config-operator/tree/master/docs%23applying-configuration-changes-to-the-cluster

https://github.com/containers/image/blob/master/docs/containers-policy.json.5.md

4. Kubernetes Security

https://docs.openshift.com/container-platform/4.3/machine_management/deploying-machine-health-checks.html

https://prometheus.io/

https://grafana.com/

http://www.fluentd.org/architecture

https://www.elastic.co/products/elasticsearch

https://www.elastic.co/guide/en/kibana/current/introduction.html

https://docs.openshift.com/container-platform/4.3/logging/cluster-logging.html%23cluster-logging

https://docs.openshift.com/container-platform/4.3/nodes/clusters/nodes-containers-events.html%23nodes-containers-events-list_nodes-containers-events

https://docs.openshift.com/container-platform/4.3/support/remote_health_monitoring/about-remote-health-monitoring.html

https://docs.openshift.com/container-platform/4.3/authentication/certificates/replacing-default-ingress-certificate.html%23replacing-default-ingress_replacing-default-ingress

https://docs.openshift.com/container-platform/4.3/web_console/configuring-web-console.html

https://docs.openshift.com/container-platform/4.3/web_console/disabling-web-console.html

https://docs.openshift.com/container-platform/4.3/applications/projects/working-with-projects.html

https://docs.openshift.com/container-platform/4.3/applications/quotas/quotas-setting-per-project.html

https://docs.openshift.com/container-platform/4.3/applications/quotas/quotas-setting-across-multiple-projects.html

https://docs.openshift.com/container-platform/4.3/authentication/managing-security-context-constraints.html%23security-context-constraints-about_configuring-internal-oauth

https://kubernetes.io/docs/concepts/policy/pod-security-policy/%23policy-order

https://docs.openshift.com/container-platform/4.3/authentication/managing-security-context-constraints.html%23scc-prioritization_configuring-internal-oauth

https://docs.openshift.com/container-platform/4.3/authentication/managing-security-context-constraints.html%23security-context-constraints-creating_configuring-internal-oauth

https://docs.openshift.com/container-platform/4.3/authentication/managing-security-context-constraints.html%23security-context-constraints-pre-allocated-values_configuring-internal-oauth

https://kubernetes.io/blog/2020/04/06/kubernetes-1-18-feature-api-priority-and-fairness-alpha/

5. Identity and Access Management Security

https://docs.openshift.com/container-platform/4.3/authentication/understanding-authentication.html

https://docs.openshift.com/container-platform/4.3/authentication/configuring-internal-oauth.html%23oauth-token-request-flows_configuring-internal-oauth

https://docs.openshift.com/container-platform/4.3/authentication/configuring-internal-oauth.html%23oauth-configuring-internal-oauth_configuring-internal-oauth

https://docs.openshift.com/container-platform/4.3/authentication/tokens-scoping.html

https://docs.openshift.com/container-platform/4.3/authentication/understanding-identity-provider.html%23supported-identity-providers

https://docs.openshift.com/container-platform/4.3/authentication/identity_providers/configuring-request-header-identity-provider.html

https://docs.openshift.com/container-platform/4.3/authentication/using-rbac.html

6. Network Security

https://kubernetes.io/docs/concepts/services-networking/ingress/

https://docs.openshift.com/container-platform/4.3/networking/multiple_networks/understanding-multiple-networks.html%23additional-networks-provided https://docs.openshift.com/container-platform/4.3/networking/openshift_sdn/assigning-egress-ips.html

7. Auditing

https://access.redhat.com/documentation/en-us/red_hat_enterprise_linux/8/html/security_hardening/auditing-the-system_security-hardening

https://docs.openshift.com/container-platform/4.3/nodes/nodes/nodes-nodes-audit-log.html%23nodes-pods-audit-log-basic_nodes-nodes-audit-log

https://kubernetes.io/docs/tasks/debug-application-cluster/audit/

https://kubernetes.io/docs/tasks/debug-application-cluster/audit/

https://github.com/openshift/cluster-kube-apiserver-operator/blob/release-4.3/bindata/v4.1.0/kube-apiserver/defaultconfig.yaml%23L42

https://github.com/openshift/cluster-openshift-apiserver-operator/blob/release-4.3/bindata/v3.11.0/openshift-apiserver/defaultconfig.yaml%23L9

https://github.com/openshift/cluster-openshift-apiserver-operator/blob/release-4.3/bindata/v3.11.0/openshift-apiserver/defaultconfig.yaml%23L9

https://docs.openshift.com/container-platform/4.3/logging/config/cluster-logging-collector.html%23cluster-logging-collector-alerts_cluster-logging-collector

https://github.com/openshift/cluster-kube-apiserver-operator

https://github.com/openshift/cluster-openshift-apiserver-operator

https://kubernetes.io/docs/tasks/debug-application-cluster/audit/

https://docs.openshift.com/container-platform/4.3/logging/config/cluster-logging-curator.html%23cluster-logging-curator-yaml_cluster-logging-curator

https://docs.openshift.com/container-platform/4.3/logging/cluster-logging-eventrouter.html

https://docs.openshift.com/container-platform/4.3/logging/config/cluster-logging-external.html%23cluster-logging-collector-fluentd_cluster-logging-external

https://docs.fluentd.org/v1.0/articles/in_forward

https://access.redhat.com/support/offerings/techpreview/

https://access.redhat.com/support/offerings/techpreview/

https://docs.openshift.com/container-platform/4.3/logging/config/cluster-logging-external.html%23cluster-logging-external

https://docs.openshift.com/container-platform/4.3/logging/config/cluster-logging-external.html%23cluster-logging-external

https://docs.openshift.com/container-platform/4.3/logging/config/cluster-logging-log-forwarding.html%23cluster-logging-log-forwarding-about_cluster-logging-log-forwarding

https://docs.openshift.com/container-platform/4.3/support/gathering-cluster-data.html%23about-must-gather_gathering-cluster-data

https://docs.openshift.com/container-platform/4.3/nodes/nodes/nodes-nodes-audit-log.html%23nodes-nodes-audit-log-basic-viewing_nodes-nodes-audit-log

https://access.redhat.com/documentation/en-us/red_hat_enterprise_linux/8/html/security_hardening/auditing-the-system_security-hardening

https://docs.openshift.com/container-platform/4.3/nodes/nodes/nodes-nodes-audit-log.html%23nodes-pods-audit-log-basic_nodes-nodes-audit-log

https://kubernetes.io/docs/tasks/debug-application-cluster/audit/

https://docs.openshift.com/container-platform/4.3/support/gathering-cluster-data.html%23about-must-gather_gathering-cluster-data

8. Encryption, Secret

https://www.fedramp.gov/assets/resources/documents/CSP_TLS_Requirements.pdf

https://docs.openshift.com/container-platform/4.3/authentication/certificates/replacing-default-ingress-certificate.html

https://docs.openshift.com/container-platform/4.3/authentication/certificates/api-server.html

https://docs.openshift.com/container-platform/4.3/registry/securing-exposing-registry.html

https://docs.openshift.com/container-platform/4.3/authentication/certificates/replacing-default-ingress-certificate.html

https://docs.openshift.com/container-platform/4.3/authentication/certificates/api-server.html

https://docs.openshift.com/container-platform/4.3/registry/securing-exposing-registry.html

https://docs.openshift.com/container-platform/4.3/networking/configuring-a-custom-pki.html

https://docs.openshift.com/container-platform/4.3/networking/routes/secured-routes.html%23nw-ingress-creating-a-reencrypt-route-with-a-custom-certificate_secured-routes

https://docs.openshift.com/container-platform/4.3/networking/routes/secured-routes.html%23nw-ingress-creating-an-edge-route-with-a-custom-certificate_secured-routes

ttps://docs.openshift.com/container-platform/4.3/networking/routes/route-configuration.html%23nw-enabling-hsts_route-configuration

https://www.openshift.com/blog/kubernetes-ingress-vs-openshift-route

https://docs.openshift.com/container-platform/4.3/authentication/certificates/service-serving-certificate.html

https://kubernetes.io/docs/concepts/configuration/secret/

https://docs.openshift.com/container-platform/4.3/nodes/pods/nodes-pods-secrets.html

https://docs.openshift.com/container-platform/4.3/authentication/encrypting-etcd.html

https://operatorhub.io/operator/vault

https://catalog.redhat.com/software/containers/explore

https://docs.aws.amazon.com/AWSEC2/latest/UserGuide/EBSEncryption.html

https://cloud.google.com/security/encryption-at-rest

https://github.com/istio/istio

9. Securing CI/CD

https://github.com/RedHatDemos/SecurityDemos/tree/master/2020Labs/OpenShiftSecurity/spring-boot-angular-ecommerce

https://docs.openshift.com/container-platform/4.3/builds/build-strategies.html

https://access.redhat.com/containers/?tab%3Dtags%23/registry.access.redhat.com/ubi7/ubi

Contributors

Gabriel Alford

Gabriel is a Senior Solutions Specialist Architect in the Office of the Chief Technologist at Red Hat's North America Public Sector where he focuses on developing and implementing security technologies and standards. He is one of many at Red Hat who are working to enable Government Readiness in Red Hat's products. Before Red Hat, he spent 10 years as a Systems Administrator, IT Infrastructure Engineer, and security implementer in the aerospace industry.

Keith Basil

Basil is a Senior Principal Product Manager focused on leading the product management, positioning, and business strategy for security within the Red Hat Cloud Platform Business Unit. He is personally passionate about enabling the evolution of next generation edge and decentralized computing models. As a project team lead, the OpenShift Security Guide represents his second publication using the Book Sprint process – the OpenStack Security Guide was his first. Outside of work, you may catch a glimpse of him riding a dirt bike through wooded and rough terrain in some remote part of the world.

Bruce Benson

Bruce designs and builds secure enterprise-scale open source clouds, with the help of teammates at Red Hat NAPS, for clients everywhere. He recently delivered Red Hat's lead consultancy on the team that created and defended the first all-open source FedRAMP cloud. Bruce's designs have rendered movies, studied particle physics, chased bad guys, hacked into banks, and inconspicuously transformed the lives of traders, sailors, doctors, and pilots. He keeps an interest in EE hardware design, where he once created the first commercially-available Linux HPC product, and a variety of other unusual embedded life-critical real-time Linux designs. The chance to more directly help the people who depend on open source led him to leverage the engineering discipline into a fulfilling consultancy role.

Erica von Buelow

Full-stack software engineer, perpetual math lover, amateur artist. Erica was a core developer on the Operator Lifecycle Manager project from inception to 1.0 release, and is currently the technical lead for the OpenShift Auth Team. Previous roles include being a software engineer for the Quay Container Registry and quay.io products.

François Duthilleul

François is a Senior Solutions Architect in the Red Hat's Telco Technology Office and collaborates with telecom service providers and partners across EMEA. Passionate about security, François leads the NFV security domain and is the Red Hat's technical interface to the National Cybersecurity Agency of France (ANSSI). Before Red Hat, he spent more than 15 years contributing to network evolution especially towards cloud platforms. Outside of work, you may come across him at a rock concert, on a road bike, playing badminton with friends, or hiking abroad with his family.

Christopher Grimm

Chris is a Solutions Architect as part of Red Hat's North American Public Sector team with over 15 years of experience in Information Systems Architecture, Engineering and Security. An advocate of implementing security during the design phase, he has been driving IT systems toward innovative and upcoming technology in an effort to migrate away from ailing legacy systems. Chris is an active member of the information security community regularly participating in events such as B-Sides Charleston where he helped develop the CTF (Capture the Flag) event and is also a Red Team member of the Palmetto Cyber Defense Competition.

Frédéric Herrmann

Frédéric Herrmann is a Principal Solution Architect with the Red Hat EMEA Telco Technology Office (TTO). In this role, he works closely with the telecom service providers in the region on their NFV initiatives. He is also involved in the security aspects of NFV and in the evolution of the network to cloud-native network functions.

Ben Howard

A dedicated open source and Linux engineer with progressive experience in Linux, engineering, and development, Ben currently develops the tools used to build core components of Red Hat and Fedora CoreOS. Prior roles include reworking Kubernetes deployment tooling, and creating a Layer 7 pre-processor for Istio traffic routing.

Jakub Hrozek

Jakub has been with Red Hat for 14 years, currently working on OpenShift security technologies such as the OpenShift Compliance Operator. Previous roles have included being the SSSD maintainer, working on identity management, and developing operating system installation hardening tools.

Nathan Kinder

Nathan is a Senior Manager in Engineering at Red Hat, focused on a broad range of security technologies in Red Hat OpenShift Container Platform, Red Hat OpenStack Platform, and Red Hat Enterprise Linux. He has 20+ years of experience developing applications related to identity and access management, and has been a significant contributor to numerous open source projects. Prior to Red Hat, Nathan worked on the development of LDAP technologies at Netscape Communications Corp.

Khary Mendez

Khary is a Senior Principal Consultant with Red Hat North America Public Sector with more than 20 years of experience in developing software solutions and driving organizational change. He also has extensive experience teaching, mentoring, and rapidly getting individuals and organizations up to speed on newer technologies and methodologies.

Pierre-André Morey

With 10+ years of experience in the cloud industry, Pierre-André supports telecommunication customers as a cloud Senior Technical Account Manager within EMEA Telco and NFV team. His daily work is to ensure that product features and cloud configurations match the requirements from the National Cybersecurity Agencies such as ANSSI, to handle complex operational issues, as well as to provide in-depth technical root cause analysis while ensuring a smooth communication path between engineering, support, and end-customers.

Christopher Negus

Chris authored the Red Hat Linux Bible, Linux Bible, Linux Toolbox series, Linux Toys, and many other books on Linux. He joined Red Hat as an RHCE instructor and examiner, at which time he achieved an RHCA certification. He is currently a Principal Technical Writer on OpenShift and container tools docs. Many years ago, Chris worked at AT&T Bell Labs with the UNIX development team.

Kirsten Newcomer

Kirsten is a Senior Principal Product Manager for Red Hat's Cloud Platforms, focused on Security. Kirsten works closely with Red Hat's many security professionals across the Red Hat portfolio of enterprise-ready open source offerings. Kirsten is a diversified software management professional with 15+ years of experience in

Kevin O'Donnell

Kevin is a Managing Architect for Red Hat in the North America Public Sector division and has been in the field for more than 20 years. He leads multiple Red Hat teams across high profile and strategic customers across the Department of Defense. Kevin has a proven track record of analyzing, architecting, budgeting, proposing, deploying, accrediting, staffing, and managing IT solutions to meet and exceed the customers' requirements and expectations. Dedicated team leader with experience supporting mission critical operational systems, services, and applications.

Juan Antonio Osorio

Juan Antonio "Oz" Osorio Robles is a Mexican living in Finland, open source advocate, metalhead, and craft beer enthusiast. He's also a software engineer working for Red Hat on cloud security (OpenShift/Kubernetes, Red Hat CoreOS, and OpenStack).

Bryan Parry

Bryan is a Principal Consultant with Red Hat. He enjoys helping clients across industries accelerate delivery of business value and apply security policies consistently with OpenShift and other Red Hat technologies.

Matt Rogers

Having been involved in projects such as MIT krb5, Libreswan, freeIPA, and Samba, Matt Rogers currently works on the OpenShift Security Engineering team. Focused on projects such as the OpenShift Compliance Operator, Matt helps ensure regulatory readiness of OpenShift and creates security automation technologies.

Ava Shulman

Ava is an OCP Infrastructure Consultant with Red Hat North America. As a Red Hat Certified Specialist in OpenShift Administration she primarily works with clients in the delivery of OpenShift among other Red Hat technologies. She is passionate about all things security and volunteers at several conferences including BSides and DEFCON. Ava is also a PADI certified diver and can be found exploring aquatic life, reefs, and wrecks whenever she is near warmer waters!

Shawn Wells

Shawn is the Chief Security Strategist of Red Hat's North America Public Sector organization, where he is the senior-most leader accountable for information assurance of all Red Hat technologies, products, and U.S. Government programs. Recent projects include collaborating with the Department of Defense and U.S. Intelligence Community to establish national guidance and security policies on operating systems, hypervisors, and container platforms; co-authoring Linux container security guidance with NIST; and co-developing the United States National Checklist for OpenShift.

Colophon

This book was written using the Book Sprints (www.booksprints.net) method, a strongly facilitated process for collaborative authorship of books.

Book Sprints project manager: Barbara Rühling

Facilitation: Barbara Rühling and Karina Piersig

Copy editing: Raewyn Whyte and Christine Davis

HTML book design: Manuel Vazquez

Illustrations and cover design: Henrik Van Leeuwen and Lennart Wolfert

Fonts: *Red Hat Diplay* and *Red Hat Text* designed by Jeremy Mickel, *Overpass* designed by Delve Fonts

ISBN 978-1-952790-00-3

Made in the USA
Las Vegas, NV
03 November 2026

57425087R00193